A Baby's Cry

Also by Cathy Glass

Damaged
Hidden
Cut
The Saddest Girl in the World
Happy Kids
The Girl in the Mirror
I Miss Mummy
Mummy Told Me Not to Tell
Run, Mummy, Run
My Dad's a Policeman (a Quick Reads novel)
The Night the Angels Came
Happy Adults

Cathy Glass

SUNDAY TIMES BESTSELLING AUTHOR

A Baby's Cry

The heartbreaking
true story of a
mother torn between
fear and love for her
newborn child

HarperElement
An Imprint of HarperCollins*Publishers*
77–85 Fulham Palace Road,
Hammersmith, London W6 8JB

www.harpercollins.co.uk

and HarperElement are trademarks of
HarperCollins*Publishers* Ltd

First published by HarperElement 2012

3

A catalogue record of this book
is available from the British Library

ISBN 978-0-00-744263-8

Printed and bound in Great Britain by
Clays Ltd, St Ives plc

MIX
Paper from
responsible sources
FSC™ C007454

FSC™ is a non-profit international organisation established to promote
the responsible management of the world's forests. Products carrying the
FSC label are independently certified to assure consumers that they come
from forests that are managed to meet the social, economic and
ecological needs of present and future generations,
and other controlled sources.

Find out more about HarperCollins and the environment at
www.harpercollins.co.uk/green

To Dad with love

Acknowledgements

Many thanks to my editor, Anne; my literary agent, Andrew; Carole, Simon, Vicky and all the team at HarperCollins.

Prologue

Children can come into foster care at any age and it is always sad, but most heartbreaking of all is when a newborn baby, sometimes only a few hours old, is taken from their mother and brought into care.

Certain details in this story, including names, places, and dates, have been changed to protect the family's privacy.

A Baby's Cry

Chapter One

Secretive

'Could you look after a baby?' Jill asked.

'A baby!' I said, astonished.

'Yes, you know. You feed one end and change the other and they keep you up all night.'

'Very funny, Jill,' I said. Jill was my support social worker from Homefinders, the agency I fostered for. We enjoyed a good working relationship.

'Actually, it's not funny, Cathy,' she said, her voice growing serious. 'As we speak a baby is being born in the City Hospital. The social services have known for months that it would be coming into care but they haven't anyone to look after it.'

'But Jill,' I exclaimed, 'it's years since I've looked after a baby, let alone a newborn. Not since Paula was a baby, and she's five now. I think I might have my pram and cot in the loft but I haven't any bottles, baby clothes or cot bedding.'

'You could buy what you need and we'll reimburse you. Cathy, I know you don't normally look after babies – we save you for the more challenging children – and I wouldn't have asked you, but all our baby carers are full. The social worker is desperate.'

I paused and thought. 'How soon will the baby be leaving hospital?' I asked, my heart aching at the thought of the mother and baby who were about to be separated.

A Baby's Cry

'Tomorrow.'

'Tomorrow!'

'Yes. Assuming it's a normal birth, the social worker wants the baby collected as soon as the doctor has given it the OK.'

I paused and thought some more. I knew my children, Paula (five) and Adrian (nine), would love to foster a baby, but I felt a wave of panic. Babies are very tiny and fragile, and it seemed so long since I'd held a baby, let alone looked after one. Would I instinctively remember what to do: how to hold the baby, sterilize bottles, make up feeds, wind and bath it, etc.?

'It's not rocket science,' Jill said, as though reading my thoughts. 'Just read the label on the packet.'

'Babies don't come with labels, do they?'

Jill laughed. 'No, I meant on the packet of formula.'

'Why is the baby coming into care?' I asked after a moment.

'I don't know. I'll find out more from Cheryl, the social worker, when I call her back to say you can take the baby. Can I do that? Please, Cathy – pretty please if necessary.'

'All right. But Jill, I'm going to need a lot of advice and …'

'Thanks. Terrific. I'll phone Cheryl now and then get back to you. Thanks, Cathy. Speak to you soon.'

And so I found myself standing in my sitting room with the phone in my hand expecting a baby in twenty-four hours.

Panic took hold. What should I do first? I had to go into the loft, find the cot and pram and whatever other baby equipment might be up there, and then make a list of what I needed to buy and go shopping. It was 10.30 a.m. Adrian and Paula were at school. There's plenty of time to get organized and go shopping, I told myself, so calm down.

First, I went to the cupboard under the stairs and took out the pole to open the loft hatch; then I went upstairs and on to the landing. Extending the pole, I released the loft hatch and slowly lowered the loft ladders. I don't like going into the loft

2

because I hate spiders and I was sure the loft was a breeding ground for them. I gingerly climbed to the top of the ladders and then tentatively reached in and switched on the light. I scanned the loft for spiders before going in completely.

I spotted the cot and pram straightaway. They were both collapsed and covered with polythene sheeting to protect them from dust; I intended to sell them one day. I also spotted a bouncing cradle. All of these Adrian and Paula had used as babies. Carefully stepping around the other stored items in the loft and ducking to avoid the overhead beams, I kept a watchful eye out for any scurrying in the shadows and crossed to the baby equipment. Removing the polythene I saw they were in good condition and I carried them in their sections to the loft hatch opening and down the ladders; then I stacked them on the landing, to be assembled later. I returned up the ladders and switched off the loft light, and then closed the hatch and took the pole downstairs, where I returned it to the cupboard.

Perching on a breakfast stool in the kitchen I took a pen and paper and began making a list of the essential items I'd need to buy: cot mattress, cot and pram bedding, baby bath, changing mat, bottles and formula milk, first-size clothes, nappies, nappy wipes, baby bath cream, etc. As my list grew, so too did my anticipation and I began to feel a little surge of excitement at the thought of looking after a baby – although I was acutely aware that my gain would be another woman's loss, as it meant that a mother would shortly be parted from her baby, which is always very very sad.

When the shopping list of baby equipment appeared to be complete and I couldn't think of anything else, I tucked the list into my handbag, locked the back door and, slipping on my sandals, left the house to drive into town. It was a lovely summer's day and as I drove my thoughts returned to the mother who was now in labour and whose baby I would shortly be looking after. I knew that taking her baby straight into care from hospital wasn't a decision the social services would have taken lightly, as families are kept together wherever possible. The social services, therefore, must have had serious concerns for the baby's safety. Possibly the mother had a history of abuse or neglect towards other children she'd had; maybe she was drink and or drug dependent; possibly she had mental health problems; or maybe she was a teenage mother who was unable to care for her infant. Whatever the reason, I hoped, as I always did with the children I fostered, that the mother would eventually recover and be able to look after her child, or if she was a teenage mother that the necessary support could be put in place to allow mother and child to be reunited.

When you think of the months of planning and the preparation that parents make when they find out they are expecting a baby, it was incredible that an hour after entering Mothercare I was pushing the trolley towards the checkout with all the essential items I would need, plus a few extras: I couldn't resist the cuddly soft-toy elephant from the 'baby's first toys' display, nor the bibs embroidered with Disney characters and the days of the week, nor the Froggy rattle set. I'd pay for these from my own money while the agency had said they would fund the essentials.

It was 1.15 as I paid at the till and then wheeled the trolley from the store and to the lift in the multistorey car park. I was expecting Jill to phone any time with more details and I had my mobile in my handbag with the volume on loud. Sure enough, as I closed the car boot and was about to get into the car my phone went off. Jill's office number flashed up and when I answered she said, 'It's a boy. He's called Harrison, and he's healthy.'

'Excellent,' I said. 'And his mother is well too?'

'I believe so. Cheryl didn't say much other than you should be ready to collect him tomorrow afternoon. She will telephone again tomorrow morning with the exact time to collect him.'

Secretive

'All right, Jill. I'll be ready. I've just been shopping and I think I've got everything.'

'Good. And Cathy, just to confirm the baby is healthy. There are no issues of him suffering withdrawal from drink or drugs. His mother is not an addict.'

'Thank goodness,' I said. 'That's a relief.' For I was aware of the dreadful suffering endured by babies who are born addicted to their mother's drugs. Once the umbilical cord is cut and the drug is no longer filtering into the baby's blood they go 'cold turkey', just like adults withdrawing from a drug. Only it's worse for babies because they don't understand what's happening to them. They scream in pain from agonizing cramps for hours and can't be comforted by their carer. They shiver, shake, vomit and even fit, just as an adult addict does. It's frightening and pitiful to watch, and it often takes many months before the baby is free from withdrawal. 'Thank goodness,' I said again.

'And, Cathy,' Jill said, her voice growing serious, 'you need to prepare yourself for the possibility that you might meet Harrison's mother at the hospital tomorrow. A nurse will be with you, but I thought I should warn you.'

'Oh, yes, thank you. I hadn't thought of that. That will be upsetting – poor woman. Do you know anything more about her?'

'No. I asked Cheryl but she seemed a bit evasive. Secretive almost. I'll be speaking to her again tomorrow to clarify arrangements for collecting the baby, so I hope I'll find out more then.'

And that was the first indication of just how unusual this case would be. Jill was right when she said the social worker was being secretive, but it was not for any reason she or I could have possibly guessed.

Chapter Two
Helping

When I arrived home I unloaded all the bags of baby equipment from the boot of the car and then took them upstairs, where I stacked them in the spare bedroom. This was the bedroom I used for fostering and it was rarely empty, for there was always a child to be looked after. However, I'd already decided that baby Harrison wouldn't be using this bedroom for the first few months but would be sleeping in the cot in my room, as Adrian and Paula had done when they were babies. This was a precautionary measure so that I could check on him and answer his cries immediately. And again my thoughts went sadly to Harrison's mother, who wouldn't have the opportunity to hear her baby cry at night or see him chuckle with delight during the day.

Having unloaded the car, I left all my purchases in their bags and wrappers in the bedroom and had just enough time for a cold drink before I had to leave to collect Adrian and Paula from school. They attended a local primary school about a five-minute drive away. They didn't know yet that we were going to foster a baby and as I drove I pictured the looks on their faces when I told them. They would be so excited. Some of their friends had baby brothers and sisters and Paula, in particular, loved playing babies with her dolls: feeding them with a toy bottle, changing their nappies and sitting them on the potty.

Sometimes Adrian joined in and more than once I'd been very moved by overhearing them tenderly nursing their 'little darling' and discussing their baby's progress. Now we were going to do it for real, and I should make sure Adrian and Paula fully appreciated that a baby could not be treated as a toy and mustn't be picked up unless I was in the room, which I'm sure they knew.

'A baby!' Paula squealed in delight as I met her in the playground and told her. 'What, a real one?'

I smiled. 'Yes, a real baby. I'm bringing him home from the hospital tomorrow.'

'I can't wait to tell my teacher!' Paula exclaimed.

A minute later Adrian bounded over from his classroom exit, which was further along the building.

'A baby!' he exclaimed in surprise when I told him.

'Yes, he was born today in the City Hospital,' I said. 'I'm going to collect him tomorrow afternoon.'

'How was he born?' Paula asked innocently as we began across the school playground.

'Same as those rabbits you saw last year,' Adrian said quickly, glancing over his shoulder to make sure his friends hadn't heard Paula's question.

'Yuck!' Paula said, screwing up her face. 'That's horrid.'

The previous summer we'd gone with friends to a working farm which had open days, and by chance in a fenced-off area of a barn we'd seen a rabbit giving birth. All the children watching had been enthralled and a little repulsed at this sight of nature in the raw, but as the man standing behind me had remarked: 'At least we won't have to explain the birds and bees to the kids now!'

'What's the baby's name?' Adrian now asked, changing the subject.

'Harrison,' I said.

'Harrison,' Paula repeated. 'That's a long name. I think I'll call him Harry.'

'Yes, that's fine,' I agreed. 'Baby Harry sounds good.' And I briefly wondered why his mother had chosen the name Harrison, which was an unusual name in England and more popular in America.

When we arrived home Adrian and Paula ran upstairs to the spare bedroom to see all the baby things I'd told them I'd bought. 'It's like Christmas!' Paula called, for rarely were there so many store bags and packages in the house.

After dinner the children didn't want to play in the garden, as they had been doing recently in the nice weather, but wanted to help me prepare Harrison's bedroom. I thought it was a good idea for them to be involved, so that they wouldn't feel excluded when Harrison arrived and I was having to devote a lot of my time to him.

The three of us went upstairs and I gave Paula the job of starting to unwind the polythene from the new cot mattress, while Adrian helped me carry the sections of the cot into my bedroom. He also helped me assemble it and once the frame was bolted into place he and Paula carried in the new mattress. I lowered in the mattress and then fetched the new bedding from the spare room. Taking the blankets and sheets out of their wrappers, we made up the cot. I felt a pang of nostalgia as I remembered first Adrian and then Paula sleeping in the cot as tiny babies.

'It's not very big,' Adrian remarked. 'Did I fit in there?'

'Yes. You were a lot, lot smaller then,' I said, smiling. Adrian was going to be tall like his father, who unfortunately no longer lived with us.

'Can I climb in?' Adrian said, making a move to lift a leg over the lowered side.

Helping

'No, you'll break it,' I said. 'And don't be tempted to try and get in when I'm not here, will you?'

Adrian shook his head.

'What about me?' Paula asked. 'I'm smaller than Adrian. Can I get in?'

'No. You're too heavy too. It's only made for a baby's weight. And just a reminder: you both know you mustn't ever pick up Harrison when I'm not in the room?' Both children nodded. 'I want you to help me, but we have to do it together, OK?'

'OK,' Adrian said quickly, clearly feeling this was obvious, while Paula said: 'Ellen in my class has a baby sister and her mother told her babies don't bounce. That seems a silly thing to say because of course babies don't bounce. They're not balls.'

'It's a saying,' I said. 'To try and explain that babies are fragile and need to be treated very gently.'

'I'll tell Ellen,' Paula said. 'She didn't understand either.'

'Well, she's daft,' Adrian said, unable to resist a dig at his sister.

'No she's not,' Paula retaliated. 'She's my friend. You're daft.' Whereupon Adrian stuck out his tongue at Paula.

'Enough,' I said. 'Are you helping me or not?' I'd found since Paula had started school that the gap between their ages seemed to have narrowed and sometimes Adrian delighted in winding up his sister – just as many siblings do.

'Helping,' they chorused.

'Good.'

With the cot made up and in place a little way from my bed we returned to the spare bedroom, where I left Adrian and Paula, now friends again, to finish unpacking the bags and packages while I took the three-in-one pram downstairs, a section at a time. It was a pram, pushchair and car seat all in one. I set up the pram in the hall and another wave of nostalgia washed over me as I remembered how proud I'd felt pushing

9

Adrian and Paula in the pram to the local shops and park. The pram base unclipped to allow the pushchair, which was also the car seat, to be fitted, and I guessed I'd be using the car seat first when I collected Harrison from the hospital. I returned upstairs, where Adrian and Paula had finished unpacking all the items.

'Well done,' I said. 'That's a big help.'

They watched as I stood the baby bath to one side – I'd take it into the bathroom when needed – and then I set the changing mat on the bed and arranged disposable nappies, lotions, creams and nappy bags on the bedside cabinet. Now I was organized I was starting to feel more confident that I would remember what to do. As Jill had said: you simply feed one end and change the other – repeatedly, as I remembered.

Once we'd finished unpacking, the children played outside while I cleared up the discarded packaging and then, downstairs, distributed it between the various recycling boxes and the dustbin. I hadn't heard from Jill since her phone call earlier and I wasn't really expecting to until the following day, when she'd said she'd phone once she'd spoken to Cheryl, the social worker, with the arrangements for collecting Harrison and I hoped some more background information. Apart from knowing Harrison's first name, that I was to collect him tomorrow afternoon and that his mother wasn't drink or drug dependent, I knew nothing at all about Harrison. Although it wasn't unusual for there to be a lack of information if a foster child arrived as an emergency, this placement wasn't an emergency. Jill had said that the social services had known about the mother for months, so I really couldn't understand why arrangements had been left until the last minute and no information was available. Usually when a placement is planned (as this one should have been) before the child arrives I receive essential information on the child, which includes relevant medical and social history; the background to the case; and the child's routine – although, as

Helping

Harrison was a newborn baby it would be largely up to me to establish his routine. I assumed Jill would bring the necessary forms with her when she visited the following day.

That night Paula was very excited at the prospect of Harrison's arrival, and after I'd read her a bedtime story she told me all the things she was going to do for him: help feed him; change and wind him; play with him; push the pram when we took him to the park to feed the ducks and so on. Clearly Harrison was going to be very well looked after and also very busy; I knew I would be busy too – especially with contact. When a young baby is brought into foster care there is usually a high level of contact initially, when the parents see their baby with a supervisor present, usually for a couple of hours each day, six or even seven days a week. This is to allow the parents to bond with their baby and vice versa, and also so that a parenting assessment can be completed as part of the legal process that will be running in the background. But a high level of contact has its down side, for if the court decides not to return the baby to live with its parents and instead places the child for adoption, then clearly the bond that has been created between the parents and the baby has to be (painfully) broken. However, the alternative – if there is no contact – is that a baby could be returned to parents without an attachment, which can have a huge negative impact on their future together and particularly for the child. I was, therefore, anticipating taking Harrison to and from supervised contact at the family centre every day.

So that when Jill phoned the following morning and said there wouldn't be any contact at all I was shocked and confused.

Chapter Three
Alone in the World

'What, none?' I asked in amazement. 'No contact at all?'

'No,' Jill confirmed, but she didn't give a reason.

'What about Harrison's father? Grandparents? Aunts? Uncles? There must be someone who wants to see him, surely?'

'Not as far as I know,' Jill said; then, after a pause: 'Look, Cathy, I've just spoken to Cheryl and she's given me a little background information but it is highly confidential, and of a very delicate nature. I think it would be better if I saw you in person to tell you what I know.'

'All right,' I agreed reluctantly, for I was now intrigued and would have preferred to know straightaway.

'But I'm afraid it won't be today,' Jill continued. 'An emergency has arisen with a new carer – their child's gone missing – and I need to talk to the police. Can I come tomorrow morning, say ten-thirty?'

'Yes, I'll be here.'

'Good. Now to the arrangements for this afternoon. Cheryl has asked that you collect Harrison at one o'clock from the maternity ward at the City Hospital. The nurses will be expecting you, so go straight up to the ward. And don't forget your ID; they'll ask for it.' Jill was referring to my fostering ID card, which carers are expected to carry with them when on fostering business.

'I'll remember,' I confirmed.

'If you need me, phone my mobile – I'll leave it on silent – but I'm not expecting a problem.'

'Will I be meeting Harrison's mother at the hospital?' I asked. This was now starting to worry me.

'I think you might,' Jill said. 'She will be discharged at the same time as her baby. But Cheryl has assured me that Harrison's mother is very pleasant and won't give you any trouble. And it will be reassuring for her to meet you – to see who is looking after Harrison.'

'Yes, I can see that,' I said, confused, for this didn't sound like an abusive or negligent mother. 'And Harrison's mother doesn't want any contact with her baby after today?' I queried again.

'No. I'll explain tomorrow. Oh, yes, and Cathy, Harrison has dual heritage. Mum is British Asian, I'm not sure about Dad, but there are no cultural or religious needs, so just look after Harrison as you would any baby.'

'Yes, Jill. All right.'

It was now 10.30 a.m. and my nervous anticipation was starting to build. I would leave the house in two hours – at 12.30 p.m. – to arrive at the hospital for 1.00. I went upstairs to the spare bedroom and double-checked I had everything I needed. I decided to make up a bag of essential items to take with me to the hospital. Although the hospital was only a twenty-minute drive away I wouldn't know when Harrison had last been fed or changed, so it made sense to be prepared. Taking a couple of nappies, nappy bags and a packet of baby wipes I went downstairs and found a small holdall in the cupboard under the stairs. Tucking these items into the holdall I went through to the kitchen and took a carton of ready-made formula from the cupboard – I'd bought a few cartons for emergency use, as they could be used at room temperature anywhere. The powder formula was in the cupboard and the bottles I'd sterilized that morning were in the sterilizing unit, ready. I remembered I'd fed Adrian and Paula more or less 'on demand' rather than following a strict feeding routine, and I anticipated doing the same with Harry, although of course it would be formula not breast milk.

I placed the carton of milk and a sterilized bottle into a clean plastic bag and put them in the holdall. I then went into the hall and placed the holdall on top of the carry car seat, which I'd previously detached from the pram. I'd no idea what Harry had in the way of clothes; I assumed not much. Children coming into care usually come from impoverished backgrounds, so when I'd been shopping the day before I'd bought some first-size sleepsuits and also a pram blanket. Although it was summer and Harry would be nestled in the 'cosy' in the car seat, he would be leaving a very warm hospital ward, so I put the blanket in the holdall.

Having checked that I had everything I needed for Harry's journey home, I busied myself with housework, while keeping a watchful eye on the time. My thoughts repeatedly flashed to Harrison and his mother, and I wondered what she was doing now. Feeding or changing Harrison? Sitting by his crib gazing at her baby as he slept, as I had done with Adrian and Paula? Or perhaps she was holding Harrison and making the most of their time together before she had to say goodbye? What she could be thinking as she prepared to part from her baby I couldn't begin to imagine.

Shortly after twelve noon I brought in the washing from the line, put out our cat, Toscha, for a run and locked the back door. With my pulse quickening from anticipation and anxiety I went down the hall, picked up my handbag, the holdall and the baby seat, and went out the front door. Having placed the bags and car seat in the rear of the car, I climbed into the car and started the engine. I pulled off the drive, steeling myself for what I was about to do.

In the ten years I'd been fostering I'd met many parents of children in care but never a mother whose baby I was about to take away. Usually an optimist and able to find something positive in any situation I was now struggling as I visualized going on to the hospital ward. What was I going to say to the mother, whose name I didn't even know? The congratulations we normally give to new parents – *What a beautiful baby, you must be very proud* – certainly wouldn't be appropriate. Nor could I rely on the reassurance I usually offer the distraught parents of children who've just been taken into care – that they will see their children again soon at contact – for there was no contact and Harrison's mother wouldn't be seeing her son again soon. And supposing Harrison's father was there? Jill hadn't mentioned that possibility and I hadn't thought to ask her. Supposing Harrison's father was there and was upset and angry? I hoped there wouldn't be an ugly scene. There were so many unknowns in this case it was very worrying, and without doubt taking baby Harrison from his parents was the most upsetting thing I'd ever been asked to do.

It was 12.50 as I parked in the hospital car park, and then fed the meter. I placed the ticket on my dashboard and leaving the holdall on the back seat I took out my handbag and the carry car seat and crossed the car park. It was a lovely summer's day in early July, a day that would normally lighten my spirits whatever mood I was in, but not now. As I entered the main doors of the hospital I felt my stomach churn. I just wanted to get this awful deed over and done with and go home and look after Harrison.

Inside the hospital I followed the signs to the maternity ward – up a flight of stairs and along a corridor, where I turned right.

I now stood outside the security-locked doors to the ward. Taking a deep breath to steady my nerves I delved in my handbag for my ID card and then pressed the security buzzer. My heart was beating fast and I felt hot as my fingers clenched around the handle of the baby seat I was carrying.

Presently a voice came through the intercom grid: 'Maternity.'

'Hello,' I said, speaking into the grid. 'It's Cathy Glass. I'm a foster carer. I've come to collect Harrison.'

It went quiet for a moment and I thought she'd gone away. Then as I was about to press the button again her voice said: 'Come through,' and the door clicked open.

I went in and then down a short corridor, which opened on to the ward. It was a long traditional-style ward with a row of beds either side, each one separated by a curtain and bedside cabinet. Beside each bed was a hospital crib with a baby. I glanced anxiously around and then a nurse came over.

'Mrs Glass?'

'Yes.' I showed her my ID card.

She nodded. 'You've come for Harrison.'

'Yes.'

'This way.'

My mouth went dry as I followed the nurse down the centre of the ward. Other mothers were resting on their beds or standing by the cribs tending to their babies; some glanced up as we passed. The ward was very warm and surprisingly quiet, with only one baby crying. There was a joyous atmosphere, with baby congratulation cards strung over bed heads, although I imagined this was in contrast to how Harrison's mother must be feeling.

'He's over here, so we can keep an eye on him,' the nurse said, leading me to the last bed on the right, which was closest to the nurses' station.

The curtain was pulled back and my eyes went first to the crib containing Harrison and then to the empty bed beside it. 'Is Harrison's mother here?' I asked.

'No. She left half an hour ago, as soon as she was discharged.'

A mixture of relief and disappointment flooded through me. Relief that what could have been a very awkward and upsetting meeting had been avoided, but disappointment that I hadn't had the opportunity to reassure her I would take good care of her baby. And I guess I'd been curious too, for I knew so little about Harrison's mother or background.

'He's a lovely little chap,' the nurse said, standing by the crib and gazing down at him. 'Feeding and sleeping just as a baby should.'

My heart melted as I joined the nurse beside the crib and looked down at Harrison. He was swaddled in a white blanket with just his little face visible from beneath a small white hat. His tiny features were perfect and his light brown skin was flawless. His eyes were closed but one little fist was pressed to his chin as though he was deep in thought.

'He's a beautiful baby,' I said. 'Absolutely beautiful. He looks very healthy. How much does he weigh?'

'He was seven pounds two ounces at birth,' the nurse said. 'That's three thousand two hundred and thirty-one grams. The social worker phoned and said to tell you she will bring the paperwork when she visits you later in the week.' I nodded and gazed down again at Harrison as the nurse continued: 'And the health visitor will see you in the next few days and bring Harrison's red book.' (The red book is a record of the baby's health and development and is known as the red book simply because the book is bound in red.)

'Thank you,' I said.

'Oh yes, and Mum has left some things for Harrison,' the nurse said, pointing to a grey trolley case standing on the floor by the bed. 'Rihanna wasn't sure what you would need.'

'Rihanna is Harrison's mother's name?' I asked.

'Yes, she's a lovely lady. Why isn't she keeping her baby?' The nurse looked at me as though she thought I would know, while I was surprised she didn't know.

'I've no idea,' I said. 'I haven't any details. I don't even know Harrison's surname.'

'It's Smith,' the nurse said. 'Which I understand is his father's surname.'

'Was the father here?'

'Oh no,' the nurse said, again surprised I didn't know. 'Rihanna wouldn't allow any visitors.'

I looked at her, even more puzzled and intrigued, as a woman in a bed behind us called 'Nurse!' The nurse turned and said, 'I'll be with you in a minute, Mrs Wilson.' Then to me: 'Well, good luck. Do you need any help getting to the car?'

'No. I'll be fine.'

The nurse watched me as I set the carry car seat and my handbag on the floor and turned to the crib. 'When was he last fed?' I asked as I leant forward, ready to pick up Harrison.

'Rihanna fed and changed him before she left, so he'll be fine for a couple of hours.'

'Thanks,' I said. I gently tucked my hands under Harrison's tiny form and picked him up. 'Is this blanket his?' I asked, for it was similar to those the other babies had on their cots.

'Yes. Mum brought it in, and the clothes he's wearing.' I saw Harrison was dressed in a light blue sleepsuit similar to the ones I'd bought from Mothercare.

I lowered Harrison carefully into the carry car seat as the nurse left to attend to the other mother. His little face puckered at being moved but he didn't wake or cry. He was so cute, my heart melted. I gently fastened the safety harness and then tucked the blanket loosely over him. His little fist came up to his chin but he obligingly stayed asleep.

Straightening, I looped my handbag over my shoulder, took the handle of the trolley case in one hand and the carry car seat in the other, and began slowly down the ward towards the exit. A few mothers looked up as I passed; it must have seemed strange for them to see me arrive alone and then leave with a baby. I wondered if Rihanna had spoken to any of the other mothers on the ward; I'd made lasting friendships when I'd been in hospital having Adrian and Paula, but somehow I didn't think that would be so for Rihanna. The nurse had said Rihanna had refused to allow visitors, and the secrecy surrounding her and Harrison led me to believe that for whatever reason Rihanna was very alone in the world, as indeed was her son.

I left the building and carefully made my way across the hospital car park, all the while glancing at Harrison, whose little eyes were screwed shut against the light.

'We'll be home soon,' I whispered as we arrived at the car.

I unlocked the car, and then leaning into the back carefully placed the carry car seat into position. I strapped it securely into place with the seatbelt. Harrison's bottom lip gave a little sucking motion as babies often do but he stayed asleep. I checked that all the straps were secure and then stood for a moment looking at Harrison, completely overawed. The responsibility hit me. Here I was solely in charge of this tiny newborn baby, who would be relying on me – a stranger – for everything he needed: for life itself. The responsibility of any parent is enormous but as a foster carer it seemed even greater – being responsible for someone else's child – and I hoped I was capable of the task.

Quietly closing the car door so I wouldn't wake him, I stowed the trolley case and my handbag in the boot, then went round and climbed into the driver's seat. That was the worst part over with, I told myself, the bit I'd been dreading. I was pleased I'd collected Harrison and there'd been no upsetting scene; and shortly I would be home and looking after him. What I didn't know then was that in collecting Harrison I had begun a very upsetting and traumatic journey that would often reduce me to tears. For now I was simply one very proud foster mother of a darling little baby boy.

Chapter Four

Bonding

Harrison slept peacefully during the car ride home and didn't wake until I pulled on to the drive and cut the engine. When the soporific motion of the car stopped he gave one little whimper and then his brow furrowed as though he was trying to make sense of what was going on around him.

'It's OK, love,' I soothed gently, as I got out and then opened the rear door. 'We're home now.'

Releasing the belt that held his car seat in place I carefully lifted out the seat and closed the door. I held the handle of the seat with one hand while I opened the boot with the other. I took out the bags and trolley case and then pressed the fob to lock the car. In the porch I stood the trolley case to one side while I opened the front door, now remembering that two hands are not enough when you have a baby. Harrison gave another little cry, louder this time, so I guessed he was starting to feel hungry. Leaving the bags in the hall I carried him in the seat through to the kitchen and stood it safely on the floor to one side. I knew it wasn't recommended to leave a baby asleep for long periods in one of these seats – they're bad for the baby's spine, as they are curled slightly forward and not flat – so once I'd fed Harrison I would tuck him into his pram, where he could lie flat.

A Baby's Cry

I took one of the sterilized bottles from the sterilizing unit and, using water I'd previously boiled and following the instructions on the packet of formula (which I'd also read earlier), I carefully made up the milk. Although I'd breastfed both my children I'd also used formula milk for Adrian, as he'd been a big baby who'd been constantly hungry. It occurred to me how different this homecoming was from when I'd arrived home with Adrian and Paula: John, my husband, had collected me from hospital and my parents had been waiting at home to welcome me and help with their new grandchild. Now there was just Harrison and me, and that seemed to highlight how alone Harrison was in the world.

Feeling rather clever that I'd made up the bottle of formula without any mishaps I carefully lifted Harrison from the car seat and carried him through to the sitting room to feed him. I sat on the sofa and gently laid him in the crook of my left arm and then put the teat of the bottle to his lips. Obligingly, he immediately opened his mouth, latched on to the teat and began sucking hungrily. I relaxed back a little on the sofa and looked at him in my arms as he fed. I'd forgotten how all-consuming feeding is for a newborn baby – it occupies and takes over their whole body. Harrison's eyes were closed in concentration, and as he gulped down the warm milk little muscles in his face twitched with delight, while his fists and feet flexed open and closed in contentment. For a baby feeding is what matters most in the whole wide world and their life revolves around it.

As Harrison fed I could feel the warmth of his little body pressed against mine; likewise he would be able to feel the comfort of my body. The close bodily contact between a mother and baby, especially during feeding, is vital to the bonding process. I wondered how Harrison's mother had felt when she'd fed Harrison for the last time before she'd left the hospital; when she'd gazed down at her son knowing that once she'd fed and changed him and returned him to the crib she would never touch or feel him again. It was so very, very sad and I found it impossible to imagine.

Harrison gulped down half the milk in the bottle and then suddenly stopped, pulled a face and spat out the teat. I wondered if he might need winding before he took the rest of the bottle, so I gently raised him into a sitting position and, supporting his chin with my right hand, I began gently rubbing his back with the palm of my left hand. His little white hat had slipped to one side and I took it off; it was warm in the house. Harrison had beautiful hair – a fine dark down covered most of his head, which made him look older than a newborn. After a moment of being winded he burped and a small rivulet of milk trickled from the corner of his mouth and on to his sleep-suit. I now realized I'd forgotten to bring in a bib with me. I carefully stood and carried Harrison into the kitchen, where I took one of the bibs I'd bought from the drawer, and then tore off a strip of kitchen towel and wiped the milk from his mouth and the sleepsuit. Returning to the sofa I lay Harrison in my left arm again and, tucking the bib under his chin, gave him the rest of the bottle.

Toscha, our cat, sauntered in, clearly curious, having let herself in through the cat flap. She miaowed, as she always did when she first saw either the children or me, and then rubbed herself around my legs. 'Good girl,' I said. 'This is Harrison.' But I would make sure Toscha was kept well away from Harrison, for much as we loved her I knew it was dangerous and unhygienic to allow animals near young babies. Toscha gave another little miaow and wandered off, her curiosity satisfied.

Now the bottle of milk was finished I wondered if Harrison might need a change of nappy, so I stood to go upstairs, where the changing mat, nappies and creams were – in the spare bedroom. But before I got to the sitting-room door the phone rang. I returned to the sofa and picked up the handset from the corner unit.

'Hello?'

'How's the little man doing?' Jill asked. She was phoning from her mobile; I could hear traffic in the background.

'Great,' I said. 'He's in my arms now. I've fed him; he's taken all the bottle, and now I'm going to change him.'

'There! I told you you'd remember what do to,' she said. 'It's like riding a bicycle: you don't forget once you've done it. Have you got everything you need?'

'Yes, I think so. The hospital said the health visitor would visit in the next few days, so I'll be able to ask her, if there's anything I don't know.'

'Good. I'll see you tomorrow then at ten-thirty and Cheryl would like to visit you and Harrison on Friday morning. She said it would be between eleven and twelve o'clock. Is that OK with you?'

'Yes. Fine.'

'She'll bring the paperwork. Do you want me to come then as well?'

'Not unless you want to. I know what to do.'

'Great. See you both tomorrow.'

As I put the phone down Harrison went very still and frowned. A smell rose from his nappy.

'I think it's time for a nappy change, little fellow,' I said, kissing the tip of his nose. He looked into my eyes and seemed to smile at me. I felt an overwhelming surge of love and protectiveness towards him, just as any mother would.

Upstairs, I went into the spare bedroom, which contained all the baby equipment apart from the cot, which was in my bedroom. I lay Harrison on the changing mat on the bed and began unbuttoning his sleepsuit. He watched me as I worked and then he waved his little fists in the air. I took off the nappy, cleaned him with the baby wipes, and then put him in a clean nappy. He was so good throughout the whole process, as if he sensed I was new to this and was helping me. I placed the soiled nappy and wipes in a nappy bag, which I knotted, ready to throw in the bin. It was only then I remembered that as a foster carer I was supposed to use disposable gloves when changing a baby's nappy, just as I was supposed to use them when clearing up bodily fluids from any foster child. This was part of our 'safer caring policy', designed to keep the whole family safe from the transmission of infectious diseases. HIV, Hepatitis B and C (for example) can be spread through bodily fluids – blood, saliva, faeces, etc. – and whereas a birth mother usually knows she hasn't any of these diseases and therefore hasn't transmitted them to her baby through the umbilical cord, I as the foster carer usually did not know (unless I was told), so we practised safer caring. And while Jill had said Harrison's mother wasn't a drug addict – so the chances of Harrison carrying a virus were slim – I obviously couldn't be certain. Having placed Harrison safely in the bouncing cradle, I went through to the bathroom and thoroughly washed my hands in hot soapy water. I then returned to the bedroom and took the packet of disposable gloves I'd bought the day before from the drawer and placed them beside the changing mat so that I would remember to use a pair next time.

It was now 2.30 and at three o'clock I would need to leave the house to collect Adrian and Paula from school. I carried Harrison and the bouncing cradle downstairs and sat him in the cradle in the sitting room while I went into the kitchen and poured myself a glass of water. I hadn't had time for lunch; I'd make up for it at dinner, but I was thirsty. I drank the water and then returned to the sitting room. I wanted to quickly telephone my parents. I hadn't told them Harrison was coming; it had all happened so quickly, and also I'd wanted to save them from worrying. Harrison, now fed and changed, was clearly feeling very comfortable and starting to doze so, perching on the sofa, I quietly picked up the phone and dialled my parents' number. Mum's voice answered with their number.

'Hi, Mum, it's Cathy,' I whispered so that I didn't disturb Harrison. 'I have a baby boy.'

'Pardon?' she said. 'I can't hear you properly. It's a bad line. I thought you said you'd had a baby?'

'I have,' I said slightly louder, smiling to myself. 'We're fostering a baby. He's only two days old.'

'A baby. Two days old!' Mum repeated, surprised, and confirming she'd heard right.

'Yes. I collected him from the hospital a couple of hours ago. He's called Harrison and he's lovely.'

'Good gracious me!' Mum exclaimed. 'How are you managing with a baby?'

'All right so far. I've fed and changed him and he didn't complain. Soon I'll take him in the car to meet Adrian and Paula from school. Come and visit as soon as you like.'

'We will,' Mum said excitedly. 'I'll speak to your father as soon as he arrives home from work and we'll arrange to come over. How long do you think you'll have him for?'

'I don't know yet. I'm seeing Jill tomorrow, so I should know more then.'

'You'll get very attached to him,' Mum warned. 'I know you do with all the children you look after, but a baby ... Well, how will you ever be able to give him up?'

'I'll worry about that when the time comes,' I said, lightly dismissive. 'He's only just arrived.' Yet as I finished talking to Mum and we said goodbye I knew she was right. It was going to be heartbreaking when we eventually had to say goodbye to Harrison, and not only for Adrian, Paula and me but also for Harrison.

* * *

Bonding

At 2.50, allowing plenty of time to collect Adrian and Paula from school, I carefully lifted Harrison, still asleep, from the bouncing cradle and tucked him into the carry car seat. The trolley bag from Harrison's mother was still in the hall and I now took it upstairs and put it in Harrison's room, where it would be out of the way. I'd unpack it later when I had the time. Downstairs again, I picked up the pram chassis (which the baby seat fitted into) and, opening the front door, took it out to the car, where I stowed it in the boot. I returned to the hall and carried Harrison in the seat to the car and strapped him under the rear belt, carefully checking all the straps. While all this took time and conscious thought I knew that very soon it would become an easy routine which I would follow automatically on leaving the house, just as I had with Adrian and Paula.

I felt self-conscious and also excited as I entered the play-ground pushing the pram that afternoon. Although Adrian and Paula knew I would be collecting Harrison from the hospital, it had all happened so quickly that none of my friends and moth-ers to whom I chatted in the playground knew I would be arriv-ing with a baby. I was right in thinking it would cause some interest and comments, for within a minute of entering the play-ground Harrison was the centre of attention. 'Oh, what a darling baby!' ... 'Isn't he cute!' ... 'That was quick work, Cathy!' ... 'He's not very old' ... 'You're a sly one – who's the lucky guy?' ... 'I'm broody' ... and so on.

When the bell rang, signalling the end of school, I pushed the pram towards the door Paula would come out of. Those mothers with children in the same class came with me, still chatting and asking questions about Harrison, while others went off to collect children from different exits. While I was able to answer questions about Harrison's name, weight and when he was born, to most of the other questions I replied a polite 'Sorry I don't know.' And even if I had known details of

Harrison's background, confidentiality forbade me from sharing these with anyone apart from the other professionals
involved in his case.

As soon as Paula came out she grinned and rushed over. 'Can
I see him?' she said, edging her way in between two mothers
who were still leaning over the pram.

'Hi, Harry,' Paula said, and gave a little wave.

Harry replied by opening his mouth wide and giving a big
yawn.

An affectionate chorus of 'Aaahhh' went up from the two
mothers before they went off to collect their own children.

'Can I push the pram?' Paula asked, passing me her reading
folder to carry and taking hold of the handlebar.

Adrian appeared with Josh, a boy from his class. 'That's him,'
Adrian said to Josh, pointing at the pram.

'I've got one at home,' Josh said, pulling a face. 'They're very
smelly. Poo!' he said, holding his nose for emphasis. Both boys
dissolved into laughter.

'Sshh, you'll wake him,' Paula cautioned, assuming a maternal role.

'Mine cries and poos all day and night,' Josh said happily,
pulling another face, before running over to his mother, who
was also pushing a pram.

'Have you had a good day at school?' I finally got to ask.

'Yes. I got ten out of ten in the spelling test,' Adrian said.
'And Andrew's asked me to his football party. Can I go?'

'I'm sure you can. When is it?'

'He's giving out the invitations tomorrow. An ex-Liverpool
player's going to coach us.'

'Sounds good,' I said.

We began across the playground, with Adrian still chatting
excitedly about the forthcoming football party, and Paula
proudly pushing the pram and shushing Adrian not to disturb

Bonding

Harrison, while Harrison was trying to open his eyes and see what all the fuss was about. I wondered if Harrison's mother had fully appreciated the joy of being with children when she'd made the decision not to see her son; or perhaps she had and, unable to keep Harrison, had decided that no contact would be less painful than seeing him and having to say goodbye.

I was nearer the truth than I realized.

Chapter Five

The Case

Normally when we arrive home from school we fall into an easy routine. The children play while I make dinner; then after dinner Adrian does his homework while I hear Paula read. After that the children play or watch television until it's time for a bath and bed. But today with a baby now part of our family the old routine vanished and organized chaos reigned. It began on the driveway before we'd even entered the house.

I'd parked the car, got out and opened the rear doors of the car, which had child locks on so couldn't be opened from inside. Paula said she wanted to carry Harrison in his car seat into the house but I said it would be too heavy for her, so she sulked. Then Adrian opened the boot and began lifting out the chassis of the pram, which was helpful, except he accidentally caught Paula's shoulder with his elbow and she, not having recovered from her pique, hollered – out of all proportion to the small bump she'd received. Adrian apologized but added that Paula shouldn't have been standing in his way, so Paula retaliated by saying she hadn't been in his way and he should be more careful. Harrison, whom I was holding in the carry car seat and who until now had been asleep, clearly felt it was time he joined in the fray and, opening his mouth wide, began to cry.

The situation didn't improve indoors. I lay Harrison in the pram in the hall and began gently rocking him but without effect.

'Perhaps he's hungry,' Paula suggested, still rubbing her shoulder.

'I don't think so,' I said. 'I fed him just before I came to school.'

'Perhaps he's done a poo,' Adrian said. 'Josh says his brother poos all the time and it's runny and smells horrid.'

'It's possible,' I said. I undid a couple of buttons on Harrison's sleepsuit and checked his nappy but it was clean.

I continued rocking the pram but Harrison's cries grew and he became quite angry and red in the face. Adrian and Paula offered more suggestions, trying to outdo each other: Harrison was too hot, too cold, not tired or 'He wants his proper mummy,' which didn't help. Then they looked at me as though I should have known what was making Harrison cry and I started to feel inadequate that I didn't. Instinctively I picked him up and as I did he let out a large burp and his body relaxed.

'It's wind,' I said, as relieved as Harrison, and able to reclaim some of my parenting kudos. 'I should have thought of that sooner.'

'Yes,' Adrian and Paula agreed, as I massaged Harrison's back.

Once he was completely comfortable I returned him to the pram. 'We'll leave him to sleep,' I said.

Adrian and Paula went off to play – separately – while I began to make dinner, but fifteen minutes later the phone rang, which startled Harrison and he began to cry again. 'I'll answer it,' Adrian offered, seizing the opportunity. I didn't normally allow the children to answer the phone in case it was a nuisance call or a stranger but on this occasion I gratefully agreed.

'It's Nana,' Adrian called from the sitting room as I rocked the pram in the hall. 'She wants to know if you're coping all right.'

I thought she could probably hear the answer in Harrison's cries. 'Tell Nana I'll phone her back later,' I called, and Adrian relayed this to my mother.

A Baby's Cry

A few minutes later Harrison went back to sleep. I returned to the kitchen to make dinner, and Adrian and Paula followed me, complaining they were hungry. I gave them an apple each and told them to play in the garden, as it was a nice day. Then twenty minutes later Harrison woke again and screamed with a vengeance. This time I thought he was probably hungry, as it had been nearly three hours since he'd last been fed. Hearing his cries Adrian and Paula dashed in from the garden and I asked them to gently rock the pram while I made up a bottle, emphasizing the 'gently', which they did. Once I'd made up the bottle, remembering the bib, I carried Harrison into the sitting room, where I sat on the sofa, with Adrian and Paula either side of me, and gave him his bottle. I think the children were a little bit impressed that I knew how to make up a bottle and feed a baby, as they'd never seen me do it before: how to tilt the bottle at the right angle so that Harrison didn't take in air, and stopping every so often to sit him forward and wind him when he obligingly burped.

Then suddenly Adrian exclaimed: 'Mum, you are silly! It's not Monday!'

I looked at him. 'I know, love. It's Wednesday.'

'So why have you put Harrison in that bib with Monday on it?' Adrian said, laughing; Paula laughed too. The bibs I'd bought were embroidered with days of the week and I'd taken the wrong one from the packet.

'I've been busy,' I said. And I think they began to realize I wasn't as organized as I usually was and needed their help and cooperation.

'I'll get the right bib,' Adrian said, and went into the kitchen.

'Shall I get Harry's froggy rattle from upstairs?' Paula asked, also wanting to help.

'Yes please.'

Once Harrison had finished his bottle, Adrian and Paula came with me upstairs while I changed Harrison's nappy, and I remembered to use the disposable gloves this time. Then they followed me downstairs, where I lay Harrison in the pram to sleep while I finished making dinner. We ate eventually – over an hour later than usual – and I knew I needed to establish a new routine that incorporated Harrison's needs as well as Adrian's and Paula's. I also knew it was important that Adrian and Paula felt included by helping, which would reinforce that we were working together as a team.

That night I managed to get Paula into bed and off to sleep before Harrison woke for his eight o'clock feed. I'd noticed that he seemed to want feeding every three hours, as Adrian and Paula had done as babies, rather than four-hourly as suggested by some parenting guides. Fortunately his cries didn't wake Paula, and Adrian, who was still up, rocked the pram while I made up the bottle; then he sat beside me on the sofa, gently stroking Harrison's tiny hand while I fed him. Adrian, like many boys his age, put on a bit of male bravado in front of Paula (and other girls), but underneath he was a very kind and sensitive lad who tended to internalize his worries.

'Why isn't Harry with his mother?' Adrian asked quietly, as Harrison's little hand curled around Adrian's forefinger.

'She can't look after him?' I said. 'I don't know why.'

'That's very sad,' Adrian said. 'Can't someone help her to look after him?'

'I hope the social services will be able to suggest something, so she'll be able to,' I said.

Adrian went quiet and then suddenly kissed my cheek. 'I'm glad you can look after us,' he said. 'I love you so much. You're the best mother ever.'

My eyes immediately filled. 'Thank you, love,' I said, returning his kiss. 'You're the best son ever. You and Paula mean the world to me, which I hope you both know.'

Adrian nodded and, slipping his arm around my waist, rested his head on my shoulder, while Harrison took the rest of his bottle holding Adrian's finger.

Once Harrison had finished feeding I winded him and then I told Adrian he should get ready for bed while I settled Harrison in his cot for the night. I'd have to decide when would be the best time to incorporate a bath in Harrison's routine, but for tonight I wiped his face and hands with a flannel and cleaned his bottom thoroughly when I changed his nappy. The stump of the umbilical cord was still attached and, using a cotton bud, I also cleaned around Harrison's bellybutton. It was nearly nine o'clock by the time Harrison was in his cot and asleep, and Adrian was washed, changed into his pyjamas and in bed waiting for me to say goodnight.

As I entered Adrian's room he reminded me that I needed to phone Nana and Grandpa, to return their call.

'Thanks,' I said, giving him a hug. 'And thanks for all your help. I'll phone them now. You get off to sleep now, love. School tomorrow.'

'Only three weeks to the end of term!' Adrian said, snuggling down and grinning. He was looking forward to the end of the school year and the long summer holidays, and although we wouldn't be going away he knew I was planning days out, including some to the coast.

I kissed Adrian goodnight, went downstairs and then phoned my parents from the sitting room.

Mum answered. 'How's it going?' she asked a little anxiously as soon as she heard it was me.

'Good. Harrison's feeding well and is asleep now – in the cot in my room.' We chatted for a while and then we arranged for her and Dad to come to dinner on Sunday.

* * *

The Case

I knew Harrison would wake for feeding at least once in the night, if not more, and I wanted to be prepared. Going into the kitchen I checked I had enough sterilized bottles to see me through the night and then I took the tin of formula from the cupboard and placed it ready on the work surface. Wanting to make sure I also had everything ready for changing him at night, I went upstairs and into the spare bedroom. I would take Harrison in there to change him. The changing mat was on the bed and I put the baby wipes and nappy bags within reach. I also took a clean sleepsuit from the packet.

I went to the window to draw the curtains. The sun was just setting and the sky was clear. One lone star twinkled in the distance and I immediately thought of Michael, the little boy I'd fostered the year before (whose story I tell in *The Night the Angels Came*). He'd taken great comfort in looking at the night sky when his father had been very ill. Many nights we'd stood together at the window, gazing at the stars, which Michael had said made him think of heaven.

Slowly closing the curtains, I turned from the window. The trolley case, which I'd brought up earlier, stood in the corner of the room. Although I wouldn't need the clothes Harrison's mother had packed – I had plenty of first-size sleepsuits – I thought I should at least look in the case, if not unpack it tonight. I laid it flat on the floor. It was a good-quality case and appeared to be brand-new. Kneeling, I unzipped the top of the case and lifted the flap. I stared in amazement.

It was packed full of neatly arranged brand-new baby clothes, all taken from their packets and folded so that they wouldn't crease. As I moved some of those at the top I saw that in addition to the first-size clothes, 0–3 months, there were clothes to fit an older baby – in fact every size up to twelve months. Vests, socks, romper suits, little trousers with matching tops, sleepsuits, first-size shoes, slippers, boots, a coat and a woolly hat with matching mittens for winter. I noticed that all the clothes were for boys, so it appeared that Rihanna had known she was expecting a boy, presumably from the scan. There was also a small cuddly teddy bear and a panda.

I stayed where I was, kneeling on the floor, and stared at the open case, puzzled. A new case, possibly bought for the purpose of carrying Harrison's clothes, full of carefully selected and lovingly packed first-year clothes and two cuddly toys: it didn't make sense. Surely this wasn't the work of an abusive or negligent mother who was deemed to be unfit to parent her child? It couldn't be. Jill had said Harrison's mother wasn't drink or drug dependent, which really only left two alternatives for a newborn baby coming into foster care. Either Rihanna had mental health problems that stopped her from parenting, or she was a young teenage mother, pregnant by accident, who'd decided to give up her baby and continue her education (and life). Yet the expensive and stylish trolley case with its carefully and lovingly planned first-year clothes simply didn't fit either of these images. And why clothes for twelve months? Perhaps Harrison's mother had put her baby into foster care temporarily – for a year – and planned to return and parent him, although this was highly unlikely, as I knew the social services wouldn't tolerate a mother using the care service for extended babysitting. Usually I'm told why a child is brought into foster care, but all I had now was a healthy baby and a case of brand-new baby clothes.

Then I spotted a white envelope tucked into the pocket at the back of the case. I reached in and took it out. There was nothing written on the outside of the envelope but as I opened the handwritten letter I saw it began: *Dear Foster Carer.*

It was from Harrison's mother. I read on:

The Case

*This is a very sad time for me, as I'm sure you know. I have
cried every day since I first found out I was expecting and I am
crying now as I write this letter. I have prayed for a solution
that would allow me to keep my son, but there is none. In my
heart I always knew that would be true and I have had to be
very brave and plan for my son's future, as much as I'm allowed
to. Would you dress him in the clothes I have bought and put
the soft toys in his cot, please? I would be very grateful if you
would. Knowing Harrison is wearing the outfits I chose for him
and has the cuddly toys close by when he sleeps will be a
comfort to me. The social worker offered to send me some
photographs of my baby but I have refused. It would be too
painful for me to see them. I know I couldn't cope. I hope I've
bought enough clothes for Harrison's first year; after that his
adopted parents will decide what he is going to wear. You must
be a very good kind woman.*
    God bless you.
    Rihanna

I stopped reading and looked up, the letter in one hand and the
open case in front of me; tears stung the back of my eyes. I could
feel the love and concern that poor woman had for her child
reaching out to me from the words of her letter and the lovingly
packed clothes. I could also feel her sadness. But her letter raised
more questions than it answered. Although I now understood
why Rihanna had bought the clothes, and for the first year –
Harrison would be adopted by the end of the year – I still had
no understanding of why she couldn't keep her son. She obviously wanted to, and she sounded kind and loving. She appeared
articulate and educated, and something in the style of her words
suggested a mature woman, not a teenager. Yet for whatever
reason she had accepted that adoption was the only answer, and
her finality was chilling, for she would know that once Harri-

son was adopted there would be no going back and Harrison would become someone else's son for ever.

Slowly refolding the letter I returned it to the envelope and tucked it into my pocket. I then took the cuddly panda and teddy bear from the case and closed the lid. Standing, I carried the soft toys round the landing to my bedroom, where I placed them at the foot of Harrison's cot. Harrison was sleeping peacefully, lightly swaddled and on his side as I'd left him. Tomorrow I would follow his mother's wishes and dress him in the clothes she'd bought, and I would continue to do so every day until he left me to be adopted. When the social worker visited I would ask her to tell Harrison's mother I was carrying out her wishes. It was the least I could do, and I hoped it would give Rihanna some comfort.

Chapter Six

The Mystery Deepens

I fed and changed Harrison before I went to bed, and he woke at 2.00 a.m. for a feed. I heard his little whimper first, which allowed me enough time to go downstairs, make up his bottle and return before his cry really took hold. I sat on my bed, leaning against the pillows, as I fed him, as I used to when I'd fed Adrian and Paula. Once Harrison had finished his bottle I winded him and carried him round the landing to what would eventually be his bedroom, where I changed him before returning him to his cot in my room.

I lay in bed with the faint glow of the street lamp coming through the curtains and listened to Harrison's little snuffles of contentment as he slowly drifted back to sleep, just as I had lain there listening to Adrian and Paula when they'd been babies. I felt a warm glow from knowing Harrison was safe, fed and comfortable – the same nurturing instinct that bonds a mother with her baby. There's a lot of research that shows this bond (known as attachment) is not so much biological or genetic as a result of nurturing, after the baby is born. As I would be forming an attachment to Harrison so he would form an attachment to me, and he would transfer this attachment to his adopted parents when the time came. Babies who are not nurtured never form that first attachment and can develop emotional and physical difficulties in childhood and in adult life.

Harrison didn't wake again until six o'clock, which was considerate, as I was already surfacing from sleep by then. I heard his little cry and I was out of bed, downstairs and returning with his bottle before he was crying with hunger. As I had done during the night, I fed him in my bed and then carried him round to his bedroom, where I changed his nappy. I dressed him in one of the sleepsuits from the case Rihanna had sent. 'It's from your mum,' I said, picking him up and kissing his cheek. He wrinkled his little nose endearingly, so I kissed him again. He was a truly gorgeous baby, and also, so far, a very good baby. I returned him to his cot in my bedroom and he obligingly went straight back to sleep.

I showered and dressed so that when I woke Adrian and Paula at seven o'clock for school it was to a calm and well-ordered house. Paula wanted to see Harrison straightaway and tiptoed round to my bedroom in her nightdress. Adrian said he wanted his breakfast first but then couldn't resist a quick peep at Harrison en route to the bathroom.

I guessed that as Harrison had been fed at six o'clock he was likely to need feeding again at about nine o'clock, when I would be driving home from taking Adrian and Paula to school, so to be safe I took a carton of ready-made milk and a sterilized bottle with us in a bag. However, despite being moved in and out of the car, Harrison didn't wake until after I'd taken Adrian and Paula to school and had returned home. Once Harrison had finished his bottle and I'd changed his nappy he didn't want to go back to sleep immediately, so I sat him in the bouncing cradle in the sitting room and took the opportunity to take some photographs of him. While I knew from his mother's letter she didn't want photographs of Harrison, the pictures I took would be an important record of Harrison's first months both for him when he was older and for the adoptive parents, who obviously weren't here to see him as a baby. These photographs, together with his Life Story book, which I would put together – detailing his development and significant events – would go with him when he left and would be a record of his past. Children who are brought up by their own parents have a living record of shared memories in their family, but once a foster child leaves the foster home he or she leaves behind the family's collective history, which is why the photographs and Life Story book are so important.

As well as making a Life Story book all foster carers have to keep a daily record of the foster child's development and general well-being, which is filed at the social services when the child leaves the foster carer. Jill, as my support social worker, always checked this record when she visited; it was a fostering procedural requirement. I had already started a folder on Harrison the evening before and with him now sitting contentedly in his bouncing cradle I updated the record, making a note of his feeds during the night and that he had settled easily after feeding. I had put the letter from his mother in the folder and once I'd finished writing I placed the folder on the coffee table, ready for Jill's arrival at 10.30 – in half an hour. I was looking forward to Jill coming so that I could show her Harrison, of whom I was very proud, and also to hear what she had to tell me about Harrison's background and his mother. Never before had I fostered a child who had so much mystery surrounding him.

'Where is the little fellow?' Jill said, bustling past me as soon as I opened the front door, clearly more eager to see Harrison than me.

'In the sitting room,' I said, closing the door. 'Coffee?'

'Yes please.' She disappeared into the sitting room. There was a short pause before I heard her exclaim: 'Oh! What a lovely baby! What a darling! He's awake. Isn't he alert?'

'Yes,' I called back, going into the kitchen to make coffee.

'He looks older than a newborn, doesn't he?' Jill called.

'Yes. I think it's all that hair,' I returned. 'Are you having milk and sugar in your coffee today?' I was aware Jill's answer would depend on whether she was on a diet or not.

'Just milk, please.' So I thought she was.

'Biscuits?'

'Oh, go on then.'

I arranged the two mugs of coffee and a plate of biscuits on the tray and carried them through to the sitting room. Jill was kneeling in front of Harrison in his bouncing cradle, making all sorts of silly noises that adults manage to produce for babies. Harrison didn't seem to mind and was keeping Jill amused by appearing to smile at her and cutely wrinkling his little nose as he did for us.

'I'll put your coffee on the table,' I said to Jill.

'Who's a beautiful boy, then?' Jill replied, massaging Harrison's little foot through the sleepsuit. 'Are you being a good boy for Cathy? Are you eating and sleeping well?'

'Yes, he is,' I answered, taking my coffee to the armchair. 'He woke at two and six but went straight off to sleep again.'

'What a good boy! Coochicoo. Who's a sweetie-pie? Would you like a cuddle?'

'I'm sure he would,' I said.

Jill carefully lifted Harrison out of the bouncing cradle and then sat on the sofa with him cradled in her arms, grinning and talking to him. Clearly I was superfluous to needs and could have just easily got on with the housework. However, I appreciated the fascination a newborn baby held for Jill who, like most adults with the chance to see and hold one, found a tiny baby irresistible and was mesmerized by the incredible miracle of new life – so small but perfect in every way.

'I'll put your coffee within reach,' I said after a while, standing and moving the coffee table closer to the sofa.

'Thanks,' Jill said, and then she cooed and cuddled Harrison again, pausing briefly to sip her coffee.

'I didn't see Harrison's mother at the hospital yesterday,' I said after a moment. 'She'd left before I arrived.'

'Yes, Cheryl told me,' Jill said, glancing up. 'Pity you didn't get the chance to meet her. Apparently she's a lovely lady. Sad, isn't it?'

'Yes. She sent a case of new clothes for Harrison and there was a letter for me in the case.' I took the letter from the folder and passed it to Jill. With Harrison cradled in her left arm Jill held the letter out to the right and read it. Then she handed it back to me with a small sigh.

'I'm doing as she asked,' I said, returning the letter to the folder. 'It's the least I can do. The soft toys are in Harrison's cot and he's wearing one of the sleepsuits she bought.'

'Good,' Jill said, briefly glancing at me before returning her attention to Harrison.

'I'm guessing Harrison isn't in care because of concerns that Mum could abuse or neglect him?' I persisted.

'That's right,' Jill said, looking at Harrison.

'And I'm guessing Harrison's mother isn't a teenager either?'

'No.' Jill paused, and finally gave me her full attention. 'Cathy, Harrison is in care under a Section 20 – a Voluntary Care Order. It was his mother's decision to place him in care and she's been working with the social services. She has Harrison's best interests at heart and has requested that he be adopted. Cathy, what I'm going to tell you is highly confidential and I know you will respect that. Cheryl knows the full story and may share some more information with you tomorrow, but for now I need to tell you that Harrison's existence is a complete secret and has to remain so.'

I frowned, puzzled. 'What do you mean a complete secret? Surely that's impossible?'

'His birth will be registered by his mother in the normal way; it has to be by law. He will be known as Harrison Smith until he is adopted, when he will have the surname of his adoptive parents. Apart from his mother no one knows his true identity. His mother checked in and out of the hospital using the surname Smith. Rihanna agreed to cooperate with the social services only under the strictest confidentiality. If his birth were to be known it could have dire consequences.'

Jill stopped and I looked at her while I tried to make sense of what she was saying. I understood Section 20 of the Children's Act: it makes provision for parents voluntarily to place their child (or children) in foster care if there is a good reason. Harrison's mother wanting her son to be adopted would be a good enough reason. There are no court proceedings with a Section 20 and the parent(s) retains legal responsibility for the child, although the child lives with a foster carer. I understood this much; it was the rest I didn't understand.

'Why?' I asked at length. 'Why all the secrecy?'

'Harrison's parents are not married and cannot marry. Their relationship should never have happened.'

'But Jill!' I exclaimed. 'We live in the twenty-first century. I still don't understand. Lots of couples have babies without being married; some single women do too. And even if Harrison was a result of an affair I still don't see why all this secrecy and fuss.' I stopped and looked at Jill.

'Think about it. What reason can you think of for keeping it a secret?'

I continued to look at Jill, and the answer slowly dawned. 'One or both of the parents is a well-known public figure?'

Jill nodded. 'That was the conclusion my manager and I came to. And we guess it's Harrison's father who is famous – otherwise his mother would probably have booked into a private clinic to have her baby rather than an NHS hospital. If Cheryl does know the true identity of the father she won't be sharing it with us, and we don't need to know – it doesn't affect your care of Harrison. Both parents are healthy, as is Harrison: that's all we need to know.'

I nodded but my imagination was working overtime. A famous father – who could it be? A footballer? A film star or pop idol? A Member of Parliament? The Prime Minister? An archbishop? Royalty? There was no limit to my imagination and scenes from the historical novels I'd read flashed through my mind. I could be looking after a baby whose existence could alter the course of history!

'So I'm fostering a little superstar?' I said with a smile.

'Pretend you don't know that,' Jill said. 'If the press got wind of it they'd investigate until they found out.'

'I'll be careful,' I said. 'As far as everyone is concerned he's just Harrison Smith, the baby I'm fostering.' I paused thoughtfully, remembering Rihanna's letter. I looked at Jill. I was worried. 'I think Harrison's mother could have been put under pressure to give up her baby,' I said. 'She clearly wanted to keep him. She says in her letter she cried continuously and prayed for a solution that would allow her to keep him.'

'Yes,' Jill said. 'It sounds that way, but that's for Cheryl and the social services to look into. Show Cheryl that letter when she visits tomorrow, although I'm sure she's aware of how Mum feels.'

I nodded. 'I wonder if there is any way Rihanna could keep Harrison, with support?'

'No,' Jill said emphatically. 'Cheryl is very clear about that. It's out of the question. She's not allowed to.'

'Not allowed to?'

'They are Cheryl's words, not mine. You know as much as I do now. As I say, it's possible Cheryl may tell you more tomorrow, but I doubt it. If she does, tell me.'

I nodded. Harrison had fallen asleep in Jill's arms and she seemed content to leave him there while we talked. One of his little fists was resting on his chin as it did sometimes, giving him the appearance of being deep in thought, and I thought if he knew the mystery surrounding his birth he'd have a lot to think about.

We both finished our coffee and the biscuits and Jill asked to see my log notes. I lifted Harrison out of her arms and laid him, still asleep, in his pram in the hall. Returning to the sitting room, I gave Jill my folder and she read and signed the daily log. She asked if I had everything I needed to look after Harrison and I said I did; then, once we'd finished, she stood to leave. We went down the hall, past the pram where Harrison was still sleeping peacefully, and we both looked in.

'You know, Jill,' I said, 'despite all the precautions that are being taken to protect Harrison's true identity, it could still slip out. These things do have a habit of becoming known.'

Jill turned from the pram and looked at me, her expression deathly serious. 'It can't,' she said bluntly. 'Cheryl said that if it ever became known that Rihanna had had this baby and who the father was, she'd have to go into hiding. Her life would be in danger. I know it sounds incredible but we don't know all the details. Cheryl is adamant that Rihanna's worries are real and have to be acted on.'

Chapter Seven

Abandoned

After Jill's visit and her parting comments that Rihanna's life could be in danger if Harrison's existence became known, I had the unsettling feeling that I was becoming involved in something I would rather not have been. It seemed incredible to me that a mother could be in danger from simply having a baby. If it was all true, and Rihanna hadn't fabricated the story surrounding Harrison's paternity (for whatever reason), then I felt the sooner Harrison was adopted and settled into his new life the better for all concerned. I knew, however, that it was likely to take the best part of a year for the social services to find and vet a suitable adoptive family and for the legal process to be completed.

Fortunately I was busy for most of that day, so I didn't have too much time for speculation or worrying. Just after Jill left the health visitor telephoned and, introducing herself as Grace, asked if it would be possible for her to visit us that afternoon, so we arranged for her to come at 1.30. Harrison had a bottle at twelve noon and I had some lunch; then while he slept I went upstairs and unpacked the clothes his mother had sent. As I folded the items neatly into the wardrobe and drawers in his room my thoughts went again to Rihanna who, according to her letter, would find some comfort in knowing her baby was wearing these clothes. It touched me again, and I hoped Cheryl would make sure Rihanna knew I was carrying out her wishes when I told her the following day.

Once I'd finished unpacking the case I stowed it out of the way on top of the wardrobe and went downstairs, where Harrison was just waking.

'Hi, little man,' I said, gently lifting him out of the pram. 'Aren't you a good boy?' He wrinkled his nose and I kissed his cheek. 'What a little treasure you are!' I told him as I carried him into the sitting room. He didn't need feeding again, so I sat on the sofa and cuddled him.

When Grace, the health visitor, arrived at exactly 1.30 the house was tidy and Harrison was wide awake and sitting contently in the bouncing cradle in the sitting room. I hoped Grace was impressed.

'He's very alert for a newborn baby,' Grace said, going over and making a fuss of him. She then joined me on the sofa and asked me about Harrison's feeding and sleeping routine, before she took the red book from her bag and began talking me through it.

'I've filled in as much as I can,' she said, turning to the first page. 'But I've got quite a few blanks and some of it – about the mother – won't be relevant as he's in care.'

As I looked at the first page I saw that Harrison's name, date of birth, weight and length at birth had been filled in, together with the results of the standard tests that are performed on all newborn babies at the hospital just after they're born. But the next page – about the mother's contact details – was blank.

'I assume I put your contact details in here?' she asked me.

'I should think so,' I said. I gave Grace my full name, date of birth and GP's name and address. 'You'd better add "foster mother" at the top of the page,' I suggested, which she did.

The red book is quite an important document and includes health and development checks and immunizations. It is usually kept updated until the child is five years of age, sometimes for longer. Harrison's red book would go with him when he was adopted. There were now some questions about the mother's health during pregnancy, which I couldn't answer, and if the baby's birth was normal, which Cheryl had told Jill it was.

'As far as I know it was a normal birth,' I said, 'and I understand both parents were healthy and weren't addicts.' It was important that, as the health visitor, Grace knew this. 'But I'm afraid I don't know any more.'

'I'm concerned,' Grace said, suddenly frowning and looking from the red book to me. 'Health visitors are supposed to visit the mother when she is expecting to make sure she has the right health care, but I was never informed this mother was expecting. I'm going to look into it when I get back to the office. Clearly something has gone wrong here and I'm wondering how many other expectant mothers have been missed off the computer system. As soon as a mother goes to her GP or clinic,' Grace explained, 'and has a positive pregnancy test, her details are entered on the computer so that we can look after her and the baby. Also Harrison's mother will need a postpartum checkup – between four to six weeks after the birth – and very likely emotional support. It's not good enough. I'll ask my manager to look into it.'

I doubted it was a computer error that had led to Harrison's mother not appearing on the health-care system. But if I told Grace what I knew – that Smith probably wasn't Rihanna's real name, and her pregnancy and indeed Harrison's existence were a closely guarded secret and had to remain so – it would have sparked Grace's curiosity and led to more questions. I didn't want to be the one to send Grace on a hunt that might find Rihanna, even though she had the best of intentions.

'I suppose it's just one of those computer errors,' I said vaguely.

Grace shook her head, clearly worried. 'I'll look into it,' she said.

Setting the red book to one side, Grace took a set of portable scales from her large nurse's bag and assembled them. I remembered Adrian and Paula being weighed on similar scales and I gently lifted Harrison into the scales. Grace made a note of his weight on a form and also in the red book. 'He's the same as his birth weight,' Grace said. 'Which is good. That means he's already made up the weight he lost after the birth.' I also knew from having Adrian and Paula that babies often lose weight immediately after birth and can take a week or longer to regain it. Grace then measured Harrison from head to toe, and tested his reflexes and responses to light and sound. Reassuring me he was perfectly normal, she made a note of the results on her form and also in the red book.

'We carry out further developmental checks at eight weeks, six months, and then eighteen months,' Grace said. 'But obviously if you have any concerns about Harrison's development contact us or your GP straightaway.'

'I will,' I said.

'I'll send a copy of all my notes to the social services for their files,' Grace said. 'What's the care plan for Harrison? Rehab home?' Grace was referring to the care plan the social services would have drawn up for Harrison's long-term future; 'rehab home' was the term used for preparing a child to return home.

'I believe he's going to be adopted,' I said.

A look of pain and concern flickered across Grace's face. 'Oh dear. Is he really? And he's such a lovely baby. Oh well, I suppose it's for the best. At least he's young enough to have a fresh start.' I nodded. As a health visitor Grace would go into homes where babies and young children didn't have a very good start in life and one of her roles would be to monitor those children and alert the social services about her concerns. 'Why can't his mother look after him?' she asked after a moment.

'I don't know,' I said, which was the truth.

Grace then asked if I would like her to visit Harrison and me at home again or if I could take him to the clinic or GP to be weighed in future. I said I would go to the clinic and she made a note of this in her file. She then handed me the red book, which I knew I had to keep safe and take with me each time I went to the clinic, when the nurse would enter Harrison's weight, dates of vaccinations and also the results of the developmental checks.

'Well, if you haven't any questions I'll be off now,' Grace said, dismantling the scales and putting them in her nurse's bag together with her record sheets.

'I can't think of anything,' I said. 'I'll phone the clinic if I need advice.'

'You're doing a good job,' she said, smiling. 'I'll see you next week at the clinic, when you bring Harrison to be weighed.'

'Yes.' I thanked Grace and, leaving Harrison in his bouncing cradle for a minute, I saw her out.

Returning to the sitting room I lifted Harrison out of the bouncing cradle and carried him upstairs, where I changed his nappy. It was now 2.30 and time to be thinking about collecting Adrian and Paula from school.

Downstairs again I took a ready-made carton of milk and a sterilized bottle from the kitchen and at 2.45 began getting Harrison and the pram chassis into the car. I arrived in the playground with five minutes to spare and I joined a couple of friends. As we talked I gently rocked Harrison in the pram; I didn't feel quite so conspicuous now I was more confident in fostering a baby. Adrian and Paula came out of school with their news, including what each of them had liked and disliked of their school dinner, and I drove home.

A Baby's Cry

The evening ran more smoothly than the previous evening, as I began to establish a routine. Dinner was only a little late, and after dinner I gave Harrison his bath while Adrian and Paula played, so I had time to read Adrian and Paula a bedtime story once I'd settled Harrison in his cot. I gave Harrison a feed before I went to bed and he fell asleep immediately.

Later, as I lay in bed with Harrison asleep in his cot, I wondered again about Harrison's parents and if Grace would succeed in finding his mother. I doubted she would, without Rihanna's correct surname, date of birth or last known address. I'd no idea where Rihanna lived or what she looked like. The English in her letter was perfect and she'd made no cultural requests in respect of Harrison's care, so I assumed her family were very Westernized and that she'd probably been born in England. I'd already surmised she was well educated and mature, not a teenage mother. I knew nothing of Harrison's father other than that he was very likely a public figure, which didn't narrow it down much. I wondered if, in years to come, when Harrison was older, he would want to trace his natural parents, as some adopted children do, and what success he'd have. Would it be possible for him to find his parents when they'd gone to so much trouble to hide their identities? I didn't know.

I was used to children coming into foster care with information about their background arriving piecemeal, so their sad stories slowly came together like pieces in a jigsaw. But that wouldn't happen with Harrison. He was like a baby abandoned at a railway station with a note from his mother asking for him to be looked after, and I wondered what effect not knowing his origins would have on him as he grew older. Unless, of course, his adoptive parents didn't tell him he was adopted, in which case if he ever found out by accident he would be devastated.

Chapter Eight

Stranger at the Door

'Oh, isn't he gorgeous?' Cheryl, the social worker, enthused as I opened the front door with Harrison in my arms the following day. I'd just fed and changed him, so he was wide awake and contented. 'The nurses at the hospital said he was a lovely baby but this is my first chance to see him.'

Cheryl and I shook hands and I led the way down the hall and into the sitting room. I hadn't met Cheryl before; she was of medium height and build and I guessed in her mid-thirties. She was dressed smartly in black trousers and a white blouse. I'd no idea how long she'd been qualified as a social worker, nor how much experience she had, but she seemed very pleasant.

'Can I get you a tea or coffee?' I asked as we entered the sitting room. 'Or a cold drink?'

'A coffee would be lovely – thank you. I've come straight from a meeting and I'm gasping.'

'Would you like something to eat as well? I offered. 'I can soon make you a sandwich.' I'd had social workers arrive before having not had time to eat or even drink.

'That's kind of you, but a coffee will be lovely. I'll pick up something to eat on the way back to the office. I've another meeting at two o'clock. Can I hold him?' Cheryl asked, sitting on the sofa and looking longingly at Harrison in my arms.

'Of course.' I laid Harrison in her arms and went into the kitchen to make coffee. I could hear Cheryl talking to Harrison as Jill had done, only without all the funny noises: 'Aren't you a cute baby? Are you being a good boy? You certainly look very healthy' and so on.

'He's doing very well,' I said as I returned with Cheryl's coffee and a plate of biscuits, which I placed on the coffee table within her reach. 'The health visitor came yesterday,' I continued, updating her. 'She weighed and measured him and checked his hearing and sight; everything is fine. She's given me his red book and I'll be taking him to the clinic next week for weighing. She said she'd send you a copy of all her notes.'

'Thank you,' Cheryl said. 'Shall I put Harrison in his bouncing cradle while we talk and I have my coffee?'

'I usually put him in his pram for a sleep about now,' I said. 'Is that all right?'

'Yes, of course. Go ahead. Don't let me disrupt your routine.'

I carefully lifted Harrison from Cheryl's arms and carried him down the hall, where I settled him into his pram, before returning to the sitting room. Cheryl had taken a wad of forms – the paperwork I needed – from her briefcase and now handed them to me.

'I think everything is there,' she said. 'Although I'm afraid the information form doesn't tell you any more than you already know.'

I nodded and, sitting in the armchair, I looked through the paperwork as Cheryl sipped her coffee and ate a biscuit. The forms I needed were all here, although as Cheryl had already said there was nothing new to be learned from them. The essential information forms and placement forms, which usually contain background information and contact details of the child's natural family, were largely unfilled in. However, the last sheet – the medical consent form – contained a nearly illegible signature beginning with R, which I assumed to be Rihanna's signature. I needed this signed form in case I had to seek medical treatment for Harrison, including vaccinations. But it seemed strange to see Rihanna's signature on the form, given that she had severed all contact with Harrison.

'So you're still in contact with Harrison's mother?' I asked.

'Only through her solicitor now,' Cheryl clarified. 'She gives Rihanna any forms that need singing.'' I nodded. 'You understand why there is so little information in this case and why strict confidentiality has to be respected?' Cheryl now asked.

I hesitated. 'I only know what Jill has told me: that Harrison's birth has to be kept a secret. I don't know the reason. Were you aware that Rihanna sent a case of clothes for Harrison, together with a letter addressed to the foster carer?'

'No.'

Reaching over I took my fostering folder from the bookshelf and slid out Rihanna's letter, which I passed to Cheryl. While she read the letter I went down the hall and checked on Harrison in his pram; he was fast asleep. I returned to the sitting room and Cheryl handed me back the letter, with a small sigh.

'This is one of the saddest cases I've ever come across,' she said. 'As you realize from this letter, Rihanna wanted to keep her baby but couldn't – for reasons I am not allowed to go into.'

'Is she being forced into giving up her child?' I asked, worried. 'Her letter seems to suggest she could be. Jill thought so too.'

'Only by circumstances,' Cheryl said. She paused, as though collecting her thoughts, and I knew she was about to tell me what she could of Harrison's background. 'Rihanna first came to the attention of the social services four months ago,' Cheryl began. 'The duty social worker took a call from her on a private number late one evening. Rihanna was in a bad way, sobbing hysterically on the phone and saying she had done something terrible. She sounded desperate and the duty social was very concerned. He spent a long time talking to her and tried to persuade her to tell him where she was or come into the offices the following day, when she could be helped. But just as he thought he was getting through to her she severed the call. Then two days later Rihanna phoned the social services again during the day and I took the call. She was still very distressed but seemed to be more open to what I was saying – perhaps because I was a woman. After much persuading she finally agreed to meet me. She said she couldn't come to the offices in case she was seen but agreed to meet me in a coffee shop out of town.'

Cheryl paused to take a sip of her coffee and I sat, very quiet and still, waiting for her to continue.

'Rihanna was not what I expected,' Cheryl said. 'She is a mature woman with a successful career and a very responsible job. She is normally level-headed but because of the circumstances she found herself in she was very distressed and couldn't think straight. She was five months pregnant at the time, so it was too late for a termination and I doubt she could have gone through with that anyway. She said she wanted her baby adopted and agreed to cooperate with the social services as long as I was the only social worker she had to deal with. I had to explain there was certain information I would have to share with my manager – in the strictest confidence – and Rihanna accepted this. When she told me her situation I completely understood why she was so distressed and the strict rules she had put in place to protect her identity. Her fears for her safety are very real.'

'But are they really?' I asked, seizing the opportunity as Cheryl paused to finish her coffee. 'I appreciate you can't divulge the details but I find it incredible that a woman's life can be in danger because she has a baby, in this country in this day and age.'

Cheryl put down her coffee cup and met my gaze, her expression very serious. 'So did I to begin with, but once Rihanna had told me her full story I believed her. Her fears are real.' She paused, her gaze flickering around the room before returning to me. 'Cathy, I'm sure no one knows where Harrison is, and I've gone to great lengths to protect Rihanna's identity, but if you do see anyone acting suspiciously in the street outside your house you must call me immediately. And if anyone you don't know comes to the door and asks about Harrison or his mother, you need to phone the police.'

I looked at her, shocked. 'But you said no one knew he was here,' I said, a cold shiver running up my spine.

'That's right, and it should stay that way. I just want you to be aware.'

My unease grew. 'I have two young children,' I said. 'I'm not putting them in danger by looking after Harrison, am I?'

'No. If Harrison's whereabouts were to become known, which is highly unlikely, we'd move him straightaway. But I'm sure it won't come to that.'

I wasn't so sure. I knew of cases where the foster carer's address had been accidentally divulged to abusive and violent parents and the child had been moved immediately – to protect the child and also the foster family. Although in this case I didn't know where the threat would come from because Rihanna certainly wasn't an abusive parent; and Cheryl wasn't going to tell me, as she'd changed the subject.

'I met Rihanna a number of times during her pregnancy,' Cheryl said. 'I made sure she had her health-care check-ups and I'll make sure she has her postpartum check-up too.'

'Good,' I said, trying to get my thoughts back on track. 'The health visitor was worried about that. She was also concerned that Rihanna had been missed off the computer system and wasn't receiving the support she needs.'

'I'll phone the health visitor and tell her I'm taking care of it,' Cheryl said. I nodded. 'As you know, Harrison will be adopted,' Cheryl continued, 'and we're already pursuing that. We have plenty of approved prospective adoptive parents who have applied. He'll be an easy baby to place.'

'I see,' I said, surprised that the adoption process was moving so quickly. 'I'm taking plenty of photographs of Harrison, and I'm also beginning a Life Story book for the adoptive parents. Wouldn't Rihanna like a few photos too? She might feel differently now.'

Cheryl shook her head. 'I've spoken to her solicitor and she says Rihanna is still of the same mind and feels she couldn't cope with reminders.'

'Is she living alone?' I asked, worried for her.

'I believe so. As I said, Cathy, this is one of the saddest cases I've ever had to deal with. Rihanna is a lovely lady who would make a wonderful mother. It's such a pity she won't have that chance. I …' Her voice trailed off and she stared thoughtfully across the room as though she had been about to say more but had stopped herself. 'Anyway,' she said after a moment, checking her watch. 'If that's everything, I'd better be going. I've another meeting soon. Thanks for the coffee and biscuits, and thanks for looking after Harrison. I'll phone Rihanna's solicitor when I get back to the office and tell her that he is doing well.'

'Will you also tell her solicitor I am carrying out Rihanna's wishes and dressing Harrison in the clothes she bought for him?' I said. 'They fit perfectly and he looks very smart. The soft toys Rihanna bought are at the foot of his cot, and his cot is close to my bed so that I can hear him as soon as he wakes at night. Please ask the solicitor to tell Rihanna, Harrison is a very good baby and rarely cries. He's a delight to look after.' I stopped as a lump rose in my throat.

'I will, Cathy,' Cheryl said. 'I'll tell her solicitor and she'll pass it on to Rihanna. I know Rihanna would want me to thank you for looking after Harrison.'

'There's no need to thank me. I just wish things could be different for her.'

'So do I, Cathy; so do I.'

After I'd seen Cheryl out I pushed Harrison in the pram to the local shops for some groceries I needed. It was a beautiful summer's afternoon and a joy to walk in the warm air with the birds singing and gardens awash with colourful flowers. My thoughts went to Rihanna, as they often did when there was just Harrison and me, and I was sorry she would never be able to experience the simple pleasure of pushing her baby in his pram on a beautiful summer's day; or later, when he was a toddler, of taking him to the park, or seeing him open his presents on his birthday and at Christmas. All these occasions create the precious memories we, as parents, have of our children and carry in our hearts forever. Well, at least the adoptive parents, whoever they may be, will be able to enjoy Harrison, I told myself. But whether Rihanna would ever be able to truly forget her son as she'd told Cheryl she was trying to do I doubted. Learn to live without him as the bereaved have to do, maybe, but not forget him. I was sure that would be impossible, just as I never forgot any of the children I'd fostered, even those who'd only stayed for a few days.

When I returned home I put away the groceries and it was time to collect Adrian and Paula from school. I was pleased it was Friday, which meant a break from the school routine, and my parents were visiting on Sunday, when they would see Harrison for the first time. Although Harrison wasn't my baby my maternal instinct had resurfaced and I felt very proud and protective of him, which was just as well as he kept me up all

A Baby's Cry

Friday night for no obvious reason, so that by Saturday morning, far from feeling relaxed at the start of the weekend, I was exhausted from lack of sleep. Adrian and Paula had been woken by Harrison's cries in the night too, when I'd paced my bedroom with Harrison in my arms trying to settle him, so they were tired and irritable, and bickered at the breakfast table. Then to make matters worse I got the shock of my life when I answered the front door to find a man I didn't know asking me if I had a baby in the house!

Chapter Nine

Section 20

'A baby? Here?' I said. 'No, you've made a mistake.' Then Harrison let out a cry from his pram behind me in the hall. 'Well maybe – sort of. Why?' I asked, my heart starting to pound.

The man in his thirties looked at me oddly, which was hardly surprising considering I didn't appear to know if I owned a baby or not. 'It's just that I found this on the pavement outside your house,' he said. 'I thought it might be yours.' He held up a yellow toy duck, which I recognized as Paula's. She'd put it in Harrison's pram the day before and it must have fallen out.

'Oh yes, thank you,' I said, smiling. I felt utterly relieved and a complete idiot. 'That's kind of you. I'm looking after a baby temporarily,' I added, not sure if this made it look better or worse. 'Thank you so much,' I flustered.

'You're welcome,' he said. He handed me the soft toy, which was only a little dusty from a night on the pavement. 'I've got kids of my own, so I know how precious these toys can be.'

'Thanks again,' I said gratefully, closing the front door. But I knew that I needed to remember that, although I would be following Cheryl's advice to be vigilant, not every stranger who came to my house or I passed in the street posed a threat; otherwise I would soon become paranoid.

* * *

A Baby's Cry

Harrison was restless for the whole of Saturday morning for no obvious reason, as babies can be unsettled sometimes. I fed and changed him, winded him, and tried sitting him in the bouncing cradle, laying him in his pram and walking the house with him in my arms, but he refused to settle. Then I remembered that, following my mother's advice, when Adrian and Paula had been unsettled as babies I'd put their pram in the garden – not so that I couldn't hear them cry but because fresh air seemed to settle a fractious baby. I returned Harrison to his pram and then pushed it through the sitting room and out through the open French windows, and parked it on the patio. Almost immediately he stopped crying, placated by the new stimuli from being outside: the sights, sounds and smells of the garden and the feel of the fresh air on his face. I raised the pram hood so that the sun wasn't directly on him and, while Adrian and Paula played further down the garden, I went indoors and cleared away the breakfast things, which were still on the table at 11.00 a.m. With the windows and French doors open I could hear Harrison if he woke and cried, and Adrian and Paula would also tell me if he woke. But when Harrison did eventually wake he didn't cry but was content to lie in his pram and be entertained by all the different sensations from being outside. It was a good piece of advice from my mother and I know many mothers today do similar.

After lunch we went to our local park. It was a pleasant afternoon and I was looking forward to visiting the park more often when Adrian and Paula broke up from school for the summer holidays in two weeks' time.

That night Harrison woke at 2.00 a.m. and then again at 5.30. He settled straightaway after each feed so that I had two three-hour slots of sleep, which was fine for me. I went back to bed at 6.00 and dozed off. When I woke it was nearly nine o'clock and it was to the harmonious sounds of Harrison gurgling content-edly in his cot and Paula and Adrian playing in their bedrooms. All three children kept themselves amused while I showered and dressed. Sundays in our house, as in many households, are more leisurely than weekdays, so we didn't have breakfast until nearly ten o'clock, with Adrian and Paula still in their night-wear. After breakfast the children washed and dressed while I fed and changed Harrison, and by 12.30 p.m. we were all ready for my parents, who were coming for dinner.

Harrison was in the bouncing cradle at one end of the kitchen, watching me prepare the vegetables for later, while Adrian and Paula were in the front room, looking out of the window for their nana and grandpa, who were due any time. Whenever my parents visited Adrian and Paula would go into the front room and look out for them and then call me as soon as they saw their car pull up. They had been in the front room for about ten minutes when Adrian called, 'Mum!' But I instinc-tively knew his call wasn't because Nana and Grandpa had arrived: I heard excitement in his voice but also anxiety.

'Yes?' I called back from the kitchen, pausing from preparing the vegetables. 'What is it?'

'Someone's watching the house.'

I immediately put down what I was doing and went round to the front room. Although Adrian was a nine-year-old boy with a good imagination his worries needed to be taken seriously. I entered the front room and crossed to the bay window. 'Where?' I asked, joining him and Paula behind the net curtains.

'There!' Adrian pointed.

I looked across the road to the woman standing on the oppo-site side of the street a few houses up. She was of medium height and build and was dressed in beige summer trousers and a short-sleeved blouse. She wasn't looking at our house now, but up the street as if she might be waiting for someone. Her face was turned slightly away, so I could only see her profile, but it suggested someone in her late twenties or early thirties with chin-length dark hair.

'She's been standing there for ages,' Adrian said.

'She's probably waiting for someone,' I said. 'What makes you think she's watching our house?'

'She keeps staring over here,' Adrian said, with the same mixture of excitement and anxiety. 'She's stopped now. But she's been there all the time we've been watching for Nana and Grandpa.'

As I looked the woman did indeed look over and possibly at our house or the house next door, but it was no more than a cursory glance before she continued looking up and then down the street.

'There! Told you,' Adrian said.

'She just glanced over,' I said. 'I'm sure she's waiting for someone. There's nothing to worry about.'

'It's all those silly spy comics he reads,' Paula put in.

'No, it isn't,' Adrian returned.

At that moment my parents' car drew up and Adrian immediately forgot the woman as he and Paula rushed into the hall, where they waited for me to open the front door. Before my parents were out of the car we were on the pavement welcoming them, and the woman was walking up the street, presumably to meet the friend she'd been waiting for.

We had a lovely afternoon with my parents. Mum chatted to me in the kitchen as we put the finishing touches to dinner. Then after we'd eaten we all went in the garden, as the weather was warm and dry. Mum and Dad were soon as besotted with Harrison as we were, and Harrison spent most of the afternoon on one of their laps being cuddled and fussed over. Mum naturally asked me why Harrison's mother couldn't look after him and I replied honestly that I didn't know. Mum helped me bath

Harrison while Dad played badminton in the garden with Adrian and Paula. It was seven o'clock before my parents left, and once they'd gone the children began their bath and bedtime routine, ready for school the following day.

The following week was very busy and flew by. I drove Adrian and Paula to and from school each day. On Tuesday I took Harrison to the clinic to be weighed – he'd put on four ounces, which the health visitor entered in his red book. On Wednesday I had foster carer training run by Homefinders fostering agency, who also provided a crèche so that Harrison was looked after in the room next door while I attended the course. On Thursday I went to Adrian and Paula's school sports day with Harrison in his pram. He slept for a while and then when the cheering and applauding woke him I held him in my arms so that he could see what was going on. So many outdoor activities in the UK rely on the weather for their success and the weather stayed fine that afternoon, so the annual sports day was a great success.

By the end of the week I felt I had established a good working routine with Harrison and although I was tired – from having two three-hour sleeps instead of one of seven hours – I knew from the experience of having Adrian and Paula that in a few months Harrison should, I hoped, no longer need his 2.00 a.m. feed and sleep through. And to be honest I didn't mind the early-hours feed, as I hadn't minded it with Adrian and Paula. I found something quite serene and magical in sitting in bed by the light of the lamp with Harrison in my arms – the two of us quietly alone while the rest of the world slept. It was an oasis of calm and peace in an otherwise busy schedule and Harrison's little smile when he was full, and his gurgles of contentment as he lay in his cot before falling asleep, more than compensated for any tiredness I felt.

A Baby's Cry

I thought nothing more of the woman we'd seen in our street on Sunday and the week drew to a close with much excitement from Adrian and Paula, as there was only one week left until school ended for summer, or as Adrian put it: 'Freedom! For six whole weeks.' He was also in the end-of-year play, which the school staged in the final week. This year they were putting on *The Jungle Book* and Adrian was one of the vultures. He'd been practising his lines with a Liverpudlian accent at every opportunity: *What do you want to do? Don't know. What do you want to do? Don't know*, etc.

I was, therefore, starting to feel that life was running smoothly again and I needn't have worried so much about looking after a baby, as I'd successfully accommodated Harrison into our family with minimum disruption to Adrian and Paula. Indeed, they were enjoying helping me look after him and easily forgave him if he was fractious or woke them at night. However, on Saturday morning my complacency and feelings of well-being were shaken.

I opened the front door, ready to leave with the children to go shopping, and became vaguely aware that there was someone on the opposite side of the street. I didn't think anything of it to begin with, as I was concentrating on Harrison and checking I'd remembered to bring my shopping list, keys and purse, while Adrian and Paula stood behind me in the hall, ready to follow me out. Then I looked up and my heart missed a beat. Although she was dressed in different clothes, I was sure it was the same woman Adrian had spotted the previous Sunday. She was standing in the same place and seemed to be looking over at our house. As soon as she saw me she turned and headed up the street, walking quickly away just as she had done on Sunday.

Closing the front door and with my heart racing I put Harrison, who was in his car seat, on the floor. Could she be connected with Harrison? Had my contact details accidentally been released? It had happened before. Could she possibly be Harrison's mother? Then something else occurred to me that made my heart thump loudly and my mouth go dry. If a child is in care under an Emergency Protection Order or Full Care Order where there are concerns for the child's safety then the foster carer's contact details are not given to the parents. However, Harrison was in care under a Section 20 and I knew that usually with a Section 20 the parent(s) are given the foster carer's contact details. While Cheryl had stressed that no one knew where Harrison was, it now occurred to me that that might not have included Harrison's mother or father.

Adrian and Paula, who hadn't seen the woman this time but had seen me open and close the door, were now looking at me questioningly. 'Will you keep an eye on Harrison for a minute, please?' I said. 'I need to make a quick phone call.'

I left the children entertaining Harrison in his car seat, while I went down the hall to use the telephone in the sitting room. I closed the door to the sitting room so that the children couldn't hear, as I didn't want to worry them. Perching on the sofa and wondering if I was over-reacting I dialled Homefinders' office number. As it was Saturday I knew the call would be re-routed through to the agency's social worker who was on duty that weekend. A moment later a male voice answered and I recognized it as Michael's.

'Hello, Michael, it's Cathy Glass,' I said, trying to keep the anxiety from my voice.

'Hi, Cathy. What can I do for you?'

'Michael, am I right in thinking that with a Section 20 the parents are usually given the foster carer's address?'

'Yes. Usually. Why? Is there something wrong?'

'I'm not sure. How much do you know of Harrison's case?' I asked carefully.

'Not a lot, I'm afraid. If you explain the problem I can advise you, or I could phone Jill. She's not on duty this weekend but she won't mind if it's an emergency and I can't help.'

I hesitated. It wasn't exactly an emergency and while I didn't want to disturb Jill unnecessarily on her day off, I wasn't sure it was wise to explain Harrison's case to Michael. Given the level of confidentiality surrounding Harrison it was possible that only Jill and the manager at Homefinders were aware of his background.

'Michael, would you mind phoning Jill, please?' I said. 'It's not an emergency but I would appreciate her advice.'

'OK, if you're sure I can't help?'

'It's very complicated,' I said. 'It would be easier if I talked to Jill.'

'Of course. I'll phone her right away. Shall I tell her to phone your landline or mobile?'

I paused. 'Mobile, please. I'm just going out.'

'OK. Will do.'

I thanked him and, after replacing the handset, returned down the hall, where Adrian and Paula were still keeping Harrison amused. As I didn't know how long it would be before Jill returned my call I decided we'd continue with our shopping trip rather than wait in. I'd take Jill's call when it came through on my mobile.

I opened the front door and checked the street. The woman was nowhere to be seen. Adrian and Paula followed me out of the house and I closed and locked the front door. I checked the street again as the children got into the car and I strapped Harrison in his car seat under the seatbelt. With another glance around I climbed into the driver's seat and was about to start the engine when my mobile rang. I took the phone from my bag and saw it was Jill's number. I pressed to answer. At the same time I got out of the car and closed the driver's door so that Adrian and Paula couldn't hear what I was saying.

'What's the problem?' Jill asked straightaway.

'Jill, I'm sorry to disturb you at the weekend, and it may be nothing, but Cheryl said I should report any strangers hanging around in the street. Last Sunday and then again this morning I saw a woman standing across the road, just over from our house. The first time I thought she was waiting for someone but now I'm not so sure. Each time she walked off quickly when I came out of the house. Jill, Cheryl said no one knew where Harrison was but is it possible social services have given my details to Harrison's parents, as he's in care under a Section 20?'

'I shouldn't think so, given the level of confidentiality,' Jill said. 'What did the woman look like?'

'I didn't get a very good look at her because each time she rushed off. But I'd say late twenties or early thirties, smartly dressed, average height and build with dark hair and light brown skin.'

Jill went quiet for a moment as I looked in the car window to check on the children.

'I'll phone Cheryl first thing on Monday,' she said. 'It's no good me phoning now: their duty social worker won't know the case. Obviously if the woman or anyone else approaches you or comes to the house, don't take any chances: phone us or the police. We don't know who she is or why she's there.'

'All right, Jill.'

We said goodbye and I got into the car, slightly spooked by Jill's warning and her instruction to call the police if necessary.

We continued with our shopping trip but I was vigilant for the rest of the day and indeed that weekend. I checked the street every time we entered or left the house, but I saw no one acting suspiciously.

By Monday morning I was starting to think the woman's appearance was pure coincidence and was not connected with Harrison. That was until Jill phoned.

Chapter Ten
Shut in a Cupboard

It was just after midday on Monday and I was sitting on the sofa with Harrison in my arms, feeding him. It was raining outside and I was thinking I would need to take Adrian's and Paula's macs when I collected them from school if it hadn't stopped raining by home time. Harrison jumped when the phone rang and paused from sucking. I quickly reached over and picked up the handset.

'Hello,' I said, lodging the handset between my chin and shoulder so that I could continue holding Harrison's bottle.

'Cathy, it's Jill. Are you free to talk?'

I heard the seriousness in her voice. 'Yes, I'm feeding Harrison. What's the matter?'

'I hope you're sitting down,' Jill said. I felt my heart set up a strange little rhythm. 'I've just spoken to Cheryl on the phone and I'm afraid your address—'

'Has been released,' I interrupted, realizing the reason for her call and seriousness.

'Yes, you were right. Your address was included on the paperwork that was sent out. I've told Cheryl I'm very unhappy that we weren't informed and she sends her apologies. She said that as Harrison's mother was cooperating with the social services she saw no reason to withhold your address, and had assumed that as it is a Section 20 you and Homefinders would have

70

realized Rihanna would know where Harrison was, which clearly we didn't.'

'No. Cheryl went to such lengths to emphasize that no one must know where Harrison was, I assumed "no one" meant no one. It never crossed my mind anyone would have my contact details until Saturday, when I saw that woman in the street for the second time. Who else knows my address?'

'Only Rihanna's solicitor,' Jill said. 'There are no other parties involved in the case.'

'What about Harrison's father?'

'He's not involved.'

'You're sure?'

'That's what Cheryl said. She also assured me Harrison's mother won't cause you any problems. Rihanna's still cooperating fully with the social services and wishes only that Harrison can be found a good adoptive family. She doesn't want any contact with him.'

'So why was she outside my house?'

'Cheryl doesn't think it was her,' Jill said. 'Rihanna has told Cheryl she is trying to rebuild her life and has returned to work. But to put your mind at rest Cheryl said she'd write to Rihanna's solicitor and mention your concerns. Cathy, it could have been anyone in your road, although as Cheryl pointed out even if it was Harrison's mother she hasn't done anything wrong.'

'No,' I agreed thoughtfully. 'She hasn't.'

'Look, Cathy, if you are very worried I could try and find another carer to look after Harrison.'

'No,' I said quickly. 'There's no need for that.'

'Good. So let's assume for the time being that it wasn't Harrison's mother and see what her solicitor has to say – although it will probably be a few weeks before the social services receive a reply. In the meantime let me know if you have any more concerns, and please be assured that only his mother and solicitor have your contact details. All right?'

'All right.'

Jill apologized again for the oversight Cheryl had made in not telling me Harrison's mother would be aware of my address, and we wound up the conversation and said goodbye. I replaced the handset and remained where I was on the sofa, staring into space and deep in thought, as Harrison took the last of his bottle. Clearly Jill and Cheryl had decided that the woman outside my house wasn't Harrison's mother, but I wondered how they could be so sure. Cheryl had told Jill that Rihanna was trying to rebuild her life and had returned to work, but both sightings of the woman has been at the weekend when she wouldn't be at work. Or maybe, if it wasn't Harrison's mother, then it was someone his mother knew and had confided in: a sister or close friend. Clearly I didn't know, but I was annoyed that, not for the first time since I'd begun fostering, a social worker had forgotten to pass on a piece of vital information.

Harrison finished his bottle and I sat him upright on my lap and began massaging his back to release his wind, at the same time reassuring him (and myself) that he wouldn't be taken away: 'Naughty Jill,' I said, 'suggesting she could move you. Of course you're not leaving, not for a long, long time. You'll stay with us until the social services have found you a nice adoptive family, which will take most of the year.'

Harrison responded with a loud burp and I wiped the residue of milk from his lips with a bib. I then lifted him up and turned him round to face me so that I could kiss his nose, which he loved. He was such a cute little baby you couldn't help but pet and kiss him at every opportunity, and my thoughts went again to his mother and the fact that she would never know the joy of kissing her son or seeing him giggle.

Shut in a Cupboard

I sat Harrison in his bouncing cradle while I washed the bottle and put it in the sterilizer; then I wrote up my log notes, briefly including Jill's phone call and what Cheryl had said. Jill would have made more detailed notes in her records of the conversations she'd had with Cheryl and with me. When I'd finished updating my log notes I took some photographs of Harrison in his bouncing cradle, and was about to switch on the television for the one o'clock news when the phone rang again. Harrison frowned and looked in the direction of the ringing as I picked up the handset. I was surprised to hear Jill's voice again and immediately assumed it must be more bad news.

'What ever is it?' I said.

'Nothing to worry about. We were wondering if you could help us out with some respite care?'

I breathed a sigh of relief. Foster carers are often asked to help out other carers by offering respite. 'I should think so. Who and when?'

'It's little Ellie. She's six. Ava is her carer. I think you met them briefly on the agency's spring outing?'

'Yes, I remember. Ava and her husband are new carers.'

'That's right. Could you look after Ellie next week? I was thinking that as Harrison's cot is in your room Ellie could use the spare room? It's just for the week.'

'Yes, that should work out fine.'

'Thanks, Cathy. You're a gem. Ellie is a very quiet child, withdrawn, and just starting to talk about the abuse she suffered. Ava is doing a great job with her, but her brother is very ill and he lives in Scotland. Ava wants to go up to Scotland for a week to help. Her own two children are going to stay with her sister's family, who live close by. They offered to look after Ellie too but they're not police-checked, so I'm afraid they can't.' (Only families who are vetted by the social services and are police-checked can look after a foster child.)

'Ava would like to bring Ellie for a brief visit first,' Jill said, 'and then bring her to stay on Saturday morning, if that's all right with you. She'll collect her again the following Saturday.'

'Yes, that's fine.'

'I'll give Ava your telephone number, then, so she can phone you and arrange the visit. Thanks again.'

'You're welcome, Jill.'

I'd looked after children before on respite, so I didn't think there'd be a problem.

The rain had stopped and the sun had come out by the time I had to leave to collect Adrian and Paula from school. As I drove the strong summer sun, now shining from a clear blue sky, was causing the moisture from the garden fences and walls to evaporate and steam was spiralling into the air. I had the car window down a little and the air smelt fresh and vibrant. I parked in a side road and pushed Harrison in the pram into the playground.

Adrian and Paula were very excited when they came out of school. Adrian had spent the afternoon in a dress rehearsal for *The Jungle Book*, which they'd performed in front of an audience from the infant school, including Paula's class. Adrian was high on adrenalin and his performance continued in the playground with a rendition of 'The Vulture Song': *We're your friends, We're your friends, We're your friends to the bitter end* ...

'Are you singing that in the school play?' I asked, impressed, for I hadn't realized Adrian could sing.

'Maybe,' he replied shyly.

'He is,' Paula confirmed.

Then they both handed me a copy of the school newsletter and pointed to the line which stated: *School will finish early – at one o'clock – on Friday, the last day of term.*

'Noted,' I said.

Shut in a Cupboard

On the way home I mentioned to Adrian and Paula that I had agreed to look after little Ellie the following week for a week's respite and they just nodded. Having grown up with fostering they were used to children coming and going, staying sometimes only for a few days, although usually for a lot longer. Adrian's only comment was: 'It's a pity it's not a boy.' Which he said most times we fostered a girl.

'You had a boy last time,' Paula pointed out, making it sound as though I had a choice, which I didn't. Foster carers usually accept any child who needs a home within the age range for which they are approved; we were approved for the widest age range – birth to sixteen.

In the car I also reminded the children that they were going out with their father on Sunday, although they hadn't forgotten. Since John, my husband, had left he visited the children once a month, when he took them out for the day. He also telephoned a couple of times during the month. Adrian and Paula always had a nice time when they went out with their father, although Paula always asked, as she did now, 'Mum, can you come with us?'

As always her question tore at my heart and I had to put on a brave face when I replied: 'No, love, it's yours and Adrian's special time with your father. Don't worry about me: I'll have plenty to do and I've got Harrison for company.' For Paula had once told me that she worried I would be lonely while they were out.

The weather that evening was beautiful, as though making up for the heavy rain of the morning, and after dinner we all went in the garden. Adrian and Paula played on their bikes and then played bat and ball as Harrison sat contentedly in his bouncing cradle on the lawn watching them, and I did some gardening.

'It won't be long before you can join in,' I said to him,

smiling, for he looked as if he would have liked to join in the fun Adrian and Paula were having.

At 8.45 the children were in bed; Harrison had had his bath and bottle and was in his cot. I was downstairs, tidying up the sitting room, when the phone rang. It was Ava, Ellie's carer. She thanked me for agreeing to look after Ellie and then explained that her brother was receiving chemotherapy and his wife and young family were finding it very difficult to cope, so she was going to stay with them for a week to help out. Her husband couldn't take the time off work to look after the children, which was the reason her own two boys were going to stay with her sister and she'd asked for respite for Ellie. I said I was sorry to hear of her brother's illness and we arranged for her and Ellie to visit us on Friday. As Ellie's and her boys' schools also broke up early on Friday we made it three o'clock. Ava asked if she could bring her sons for the visit too and I said that was fine. Ava then told me a bit about Ellie so that I would be better able to cater for her needs when she stayed.

'Ellie's been with us for just over four months,' Ava said. 'She's a very sweet child but far too quiet. She came into care when her teacher saw what looked like burn marks on her back when she was changing for PE. She asked Ellie how she had got them and Ellie said her mother's boyfriend had made the marks with a cigarette. Then Ellie showed her some more burn marks on her bottom.'

'How awful!' I said, shocked.

'It was a real eye-opener for my husband and me,' Ava said. 'I mean you read about these things in the newspaper but it's not until you look after a child who's been badly abused that it really hits home. My sons are six and eight and I haven't told them the details. I've just said Ellie's family were not kind to her.'

'Yes, I protect Adrian and Paula as much as I can,' I said.

'When Ellie first arrived,' Ava continued, 'she hardly spoke at all, but now she's starting to trust me she's telling me some awful things. Last week she told me her mother's boyfriend used to hit her with a belt, and that her mother shut her in a cupboard. I told Jill and she told Ellie's social worker. They think there is probably more to come out. Unsurprisingly, Ellie is afraid of the dark and always sleeps with the light on.'

'I'll make sure that happens here too,' I said. 'And I always leave a night light on on the landing. Don't worry: I'll make sure Ellie's well looked after – day and night.'

'Thank you so much. I wish I didn't have to leave her but there's no choice.'

'Is there any contact while you're away?' I asked.

'Yes. Ellie sees her mother once a week. It's supervised at the family centre. I usually take and collect Ellie. Will you be doing that?'

'I expect so.'

Ava hesitated. 'You're a more experienced foster carer than I am, so perhaps you don't mind, but to be honest I find it really difficult meeting Ellie's mother and being polite to her when I know what she's done to her daughter.'

'It doesn't get any easier,' I said. 'I have to bite my tongue and put my own feelings to one side for the sake of the child when I meet parents who have abused their children. I take it Ellie still wants to see her mother?'

'Yes. That's the other thing I don't understand. Ellie still loves her mother and is so loyal to her despite all the abuse.'

'That's normal,' I said. 'It's very rare for a child, no matter how badly abused they've been, to reject their mother. There seems to be an underlying bond that continues, regardless. I suppose every child wants to believe that deep down their mother loves and cares for them.'

'I guess you're right,' Ava said thoughtfully.

I then reminded Ava to bring Ellie's favourite toys with her when she came to stay so that she would feel more settled and secure. We finished our conversation as we had begun with Ava thanking me for looking after Ellie. I put down the phone, but my thoughts stayed with little Ellie, whom I'd met briefly on the Homefinders spring outing. Another child abused by the very people who should have been loving and protecting her, I thought. It was sickening. Foster carers never get used to hearing about such atrocities, regardless of how long they have been fostering.

On Tuesday I took Harrison to the clinic for his weekly weigh-in and he'd put on another four ounces, which was good. The health visitor commented on how smartly dressed he always was and while I thanked her, I silently acknowledged that it wasn't to my credit but that of Harrison's mother, who'd so carefully chosen and packed all the clothes he needed for his first year. I received a small allowance from the social services towards the cost of Harrison's clothing and as I wasn't spending this money I was saving it so that he could take it with him when he was eventually adopted.

On Wednesday it was Adrian and Paula's school play and I sat in the audience, a very proud mother. Adrian didn't usually say much about his achievements and he wasn't an extrovert child, but he came into his own as the playful cheeky vulture in *The Jungle Book*. The vulture costumes the four boys had made in their art lessons at school were fantastic, with wings and feathers cut out of grey and black cardboard, and a cardboard vulture head with a large beak that protruded over their foreheads. The audience (of parents) laughed as the four vultures went through their spoken routine of: *What do you want to do? Don't know. What do you want to do?* etc.; but when they sang 'The Vulture Song', there was absolute silence. I hadn't really taken much notice of the words of the song before, but as the four boys sang *We're your friends ...* in harmony a lump rose in my throat. Adrian seemed to be looking straight at me as he sang: *When you're alone, Who comes around, To pluck you up, When you are down? And, when you're outside lookin' in, Who's there to open the door? That's what friends are for.*

I'd had doubts about taking Harrison with me to watch the show in case he became restless but, mindful that he might fret if I left him with another foster carer, I'd decided to take him with me and I'd chosen a chair at the end of a row so that I could slip out easily if he cried. However, he slept in my arms for most of the show despite the music, laughing and applause. When he did wake, fifteen minutes before the end of the show, I gave him some of his bottle and then he was content to lie in my arms, looking and listening at the new sights and sounds until the show finished.

When I met Paula and Adrian in the playground after the show I congratulated Adrian. 'You were fantastic!' I said. 'I didn't know you could sing and act. Have you thought about joining our local amateur dramatic society?'

'No.' Then looking at Paula he said with his dry humour: 'There's plenty of amateur dramatics at home.'

On Thursday both children took lemonade and snacks into school for their end-of-year class parties, and on Friday I was in the playground at one o'clock for the school's early finish. I was nearly as excited as the children by the arrival of the last day of term and the prospect of being out of the school routine for six whole weeks. I was planning activities and days out as well as simply allowing us time to relax at home and in the garden.

However, first we needed to welcome Ellie when she visited at three o'clock. I had already cleared the baby equipment from the spare room and I'd put a girly Minnie Mouse duvet cover on the bed and some cuddly toys on the chair. Aware that Ellie had suffered a lot in her six years and that she was probably going to miss Ava, I was expecting there might be occasions during the week when she would be upset, although I'd obviously try to make sure this didn't happen by keeping her occupied and keeping an eye on her. But nothing could have prepared me for the child who stood on my doorstep at three o'clock: with large brown eyes and tears streaming down her cheeks, she clung desperately to her carer's skirt and refused to come in.

Chapter Eleven

Ellie

'It's all right, Ellie,' I said gently. 'Take your time.' I smiled at Ava and then at Ellie, who took one look at me and buried her head in her carer's skirt.

'This is Cathy,' Ava reminded Ellie, lightly stroking her hair. 'You met her when we went on the coach to the zoo at Easter. She's a foster carer like me and has two children of her own.'

Adrian and Paula were standing behind me in the hall. 'Paula is five,' I said to Ellie. 'Nearly the same age as you.' I turned and looked at Paula, who nodded but didn't say anything, clearly worried by Ellie's crying. 'And Adrian is nine,' I added.

'Hi, Ellie,' Adrian said.

'Hello,' Ava replied. Ellie kept her head buried firmly in Ava's skirt and didn't say anything.

'And we're also looking after a little baby,' I said. 'He's called Harrison and is only a few weeks old. Would you like to see him, Ellie?' I tried.

Ellie shook her head.

'Don't forget our cat, Toscha,' Adrian added.

Ava smiled. 'We've got a cat as well, haven't we, Ellie?' she said encouragingly. Slipping one arm around Ellie's shoulder Ava tried to ease her forward over the doorstep, but Ellie stood firm. She kept her head buried in Ava's skirt and cried louder. I could see the whites of Ellie's knuckles as her little fists clung desperately to the material of Ava's skirt. 'Ellie, we've just come for a short visit,' Ava tried more firmly, but without effect. I knew that if we couldn't persuade Ellie to come in for a visit today it would be more difficult tomorrow when Ava had to leave her. Once before I'd had to take a sobbing child from her carer and it was heartbreaking, although she'd soon settled once the carer had left.

'We don't bite,' I said, trying a light-hearted approach, but only Ava smiled.

'I'm sorry, Cathy,' Ava said, now embarrassed and clearly made anxious by Ellie's behaviour. 'Come on, Ellie, we've got to go in.' But Ellie still didn't move. 'I don't know what to do,' Ava said desperately to me.

I thought this was the last thing Ava needed on top of all the worry of her brother's illness. I turned again to Paula and Adrian, who were still in the hall behind me, both of them looking at Ellie and Ava and also looking concerned. 'Paula,' I said. 'You're nearly the same age as Ellie. Do you think you could try? She might feel more comfortable with you.'

Although Paula was clearly unsettled by Ellie's crying, she slowly came forward and, stepping into the porch, put her hand on Ellie's arm. 'Hello,' she said bravely. 'I'm Paula, Cathy's daughter. I'd like you to come in. I have a doll's house but no one to play with. Will you come and play with me?'

Bless her, I thought. She'd said it so sweetly and sensitively, and used a touch of psychology too.

Ava smiled appreciatively at Paula. 'A doll's house!' she said. 'That's sounds fantastic. It's a pity Paula has no one to play with, isn't it, Ellie?'

It worked. Ellie slowly raised her head from Ava's skirt and, reaching out, took hold of Paula's hand. Then, concentrating on the ground, she allowed Paula to lead her over the doorstep and into the hall. Ava breathed a sigh of relief as I silently and quickly closed the front door.

'The doll's house is in my bedroom,' Paula said, holding Ellie's hand and leading her up the stairs.

'Why don't you go up too for a minute?' I said to Ava. 'Paula won't mind and it will help reassure Ellie.'

Ava followed Paula and Ellie up the stairs as Adrian said to me: 'Can I go and play in the garden?'

'Yes, of course.' He'd met Ava and Ellie and wouldn't want to play doll's houses with the two girls. Like many boys his age Adrian always found something to amuse himself within the garden even if he didn't have anyone to play with.

Adrian let himself out of the back door as I checked on Harrison, who was dozing in his bouncing cradle in the sitting room. Then I went into the kitchen, where I filled the kettle, guessing Ava would appreciate a drink. She appeared downstairs a few minutes later just as the kettle was boiling.

'Well timed,' I said. 'Would you like a tea or a coffee?'

'Tea would be lovely. Thanks.' Ava sighed gratefully. 'Paula's doing a good job. Ellie has stopped crying and is playing. Sorry about all that.'

'Don't worry. It's only natural that Ellie will have some worries about coming here and leaving you.' Then I suddenly realized that Ava didn't have her sons with her. 'You didn't bring your boys?'

'No, they had a last-minute invitation to play at a friend's house. I'll collect them later.'

I made the tea and carried it through to the sitting room, where Ava fussed over Harrison, who was now awake, before sitting down.

'What am I going to do tomorrow if Ellie is like she was earlier?' Ava asked, worried again. 'I can't take her with me and

I have to go to my brother's family. They desperately need some help.'

'I think Ellie will be far less worried tomorrow now she's seen our house and has met us. Before you go today we'll show her around so that she can see her bedroom and ask any questions she might have. And tomorrow when she stays she'll have her own things with her, which will help.'

'But supposing she's still very upset?' Ava persisted anxiously.

'Then I'll cuddle her until she recovers,' I said. 'Try not to worry. I've looked after lots of children, short and long term. She'll be fine. Has Jill suggested you phone mid-week to speak to her?'

'Yes, I'll do that.'

'Good. I'll keep Ellie busy and the week will fly by.'

'Thank you so much,' Ava said gratefully, and finally sipped her tea. 'We've had rather a rough time recently,' she confided. 'My brother was diagnosed with cancer in March and then Ellie arrived a week later, having been abused by her mother and her boyfriend. She didn't say much to begin with but now the floodgates have opened she keeps telling me new things. It's dreadful. Driving here she suddenly asked me if you had any kitchen knives. I said I thought you would have, but as at my house they would be kept safely.'

'That's right,' I said. 'The kitchen knives can't be reached by children. Why did Ellie ask you that?'

'That's what I asked her. She went quiet, as she does when she's about to tell me something bad. Then she said her mum had a big kitchen knife and Shane – that's the mother's boyfriend – used to hold it to her mother's throat and then cut her mother's arm with it. I mean, I ask you! What sort of people are they? I don't know why Ellie should suddenly think of that now.'

'It could have been triggered by feeling a bit insecure about coming here,' I said.

Ava nodded. 'I'll have to write what she said in my log notes when I get home and tell Jill.'

I nodded. 'And if Ellie makes any disclosures while she's staying with me I'll do the same and also update you.'

'Thanks, Cathy. There's more to this fostering than my husband and I ever thought.'

'I know,' I smiled. 'Looking after the child is only part of it. But you enjoy fostering?'

'Oh yes, and we love Ellie already. Goodness knows how we'll ever say goodbye.'

'That's one of the hardest parts of fostering,' I said. 'Having to say goodbye.'

Ava and I continued talking – mainly about fostering – while we finished our tea, and Adrian played in the garden and the girls played upstairs. Then after about half an hour Ava said, 'Well, I suppose we'd better be going now. Jill said to keep this visit short. Is it all right if I bring Ellie tomorrow at ten o'clock?'

'Yes, that's fine with me. Let's show Ellie around the house before you go.'

Not wishing to leave Harrison unattended in the bouncing cradle for any length of time, I scooped him up in my arms and then led the way out of the sitting room and down the hall, with Harrison gurgling at Ava over my shoulder and Ava making 'baby noises' to him as Jill had. Upstairs we went into Paula's room, where the girls had finished playing with the doll's house and were now looking at a book together.

'Time to go, love,' Ava said gently to Ellie. Ellie obediently stood and came to Ava's side. 'Thanks for looking after Ellie,' Ava said to Paula. Paula smiled.

'I'm going to show Ellie and Ava around the house,' I said to Paula. 'Are you coming too?'

Paula nodded; she was used to helping me show foster children around the house, whether they were staying for a few days or indefinitely, and it was important she felt included. Paula joined me at the bedroom door and the two of us led the way round the landing to what would be Ellie's bedroom for the week she stayed.

'This is where you will sleep,' Paula explained.

'This is nice, isn't it, Ellie?' Ava enthused.

Ellie gave a small nod and then took hold of a clump of Ava's skirt again as insecurity reasserted itself.

'I know you like to sleep with your bedroom light on,' I reassured Ellie. 'And you'll be bringing your favourite toys with you and your own clothes.' Which might not have been obvious to Ellie, as it was the first time she'd stayed away from Ava overnight.

Ellie didn't say anything. She held on to Ava's skirt as Paula and I led the way to Adrian's room, where I opened the door, and they both glanced in. Then we continued round to the bathroom and to my bedroom.

'This is where I sleep,' I said to Ellie. 'So if you wake in the night you know where to find me. I always leave a landing light on, so the house is never dark.'

'That's good, isn't it, Ellie?' Ava said encouragingly. 'Cathy's house is very similar upstairs to our house, isn't it?' But Ellie wasn't impressed.

We went downstairs and Paula and I showed Ellie and Ava the front room; then we went down the hall. I was going to turn right to show them the kitchen but Ellie stopped and pulled on Ava's skirt. Clearly Ellie didn't want to go into the kitchen and I wondered if it had anything to do with the kitchen knives that had been used to terrorize her mother. Who knew what pictures of abuse Ellie carried in her head?

There was no need for Ellie to see the kitchen, so we went straight into the sitting room instead. 'Look at this lovely garden,' Ava said to Ellie, encouraging her to go over to the

French windows. 'There's Adrian. You'll be able to play outside too on a fine day.'

Ellie, still holding Ava's skirt, gave a small nod but I saw her bottom lip tremble. Although Ellie was finding her visit difficult now she would have felt far more insecure and frightened had she just arrived the following morning without a preliminary visit and therefore completely unfamiliar with our house.

I opened the French windows and called to Adrian: 'Ellie and Ava are going now.'

He looked up from the sandpit, where he was filling a dumper truck with sand, and gave a little wave. 'Bye,' he called.

'Goodbye, Adrian,' Ava called brightly. 'See you tomorrow.'

Ellie didn't say anything but Harrison, still in my arms, gurgled happily. Paula and I then saw Ava and Ellie to the front door, where Ava thanked me again for agreeing to look after Ellie.

'You're welcome,' I said, and then to Ellie: 'We're all looking forward to you coming tomorrow.' But I could tell from Ellie's face she certainly wasn't.

I closed the front door and thanked Paula for her help, although I noticed she was now looking very serious too.

'Are you all right?' I asked.

'Mum,' she said frowning, 'Ellie said something really strange to me while we were playing. It was horrible.'

'What?' I asked, alarm bells ringing.

'She asked if we had a cupboard under the stairs,' Paula said. 'I said yes but it wasn't interesting. It just had junk in it. Then Ellie asked me if you ever shut me in there when I had been naughty. I said, "No, of course not." Then she said that's what happened at her mother's house.'

Paula (and Adrian) had heard other children we'd fostered disclose abuse and both children knew they had to tell me at the first opportunity.

'I'm pleased you told me,' I said. 'That was the right thing to do. Ellie was treated very badly at home. Ava told me Ellie's scared of the dark because she was shut in a dark cupboard. That could also explain why she didn't want to go into the kitchen,' I added, thinking aloud. 'You have to go past the cupboard under the stairs to go into the kitchen. I thought she was staring at that cupboard when she refused to see the kitchen.'

'It's horrible to shut someone in a dark cupboard,' Paula said, her brow creasing. 'Poor little Ellie.'

'Yes. And it's possible that when Ellie stays she may tell you other things that have happened to her. It's important you tell me so that Ellie can be helped to overcome what has happened to her,' I reminded her.

'I know,' Paula said, and then asked thoughtfully. 'Mum, why do some parents hurt their children when they are supposed to love them?'

'I wish I knew,' I sighed. I looked at Paula, so innocent, and like any child brought up in a normal loving family was unable to comprehend a parent hurting their child. Obviously I told off Paula (and Adrian) sometimes and occasionally got annoyed, just as most parents do, but that's a far cry from intentionally harming or scaring a child.

'Sometimes the parents were treated badly when they were children,' I offered, 'and they don't understand it's wrong.' But of course most adults who were abused as children do not go on to abuse their own children – just the opposite, in fact: aware that bad things can and do happen they go to great lengths to protect and cherish their children and keep them safe.

'I hope Ellie doesn't tell me any more bad things,' Paula said, as we went down the hall and to the garden. 'It makes me sad.'

'I know, love. I hope so too.'

Chapter Twelve
A Demon Exorcized

The following morning Adrian, Paula and I were up, showered and dressed in plenty of time for Ellie's arrival at ten o'clock. Harrison, or Harry as Paula always called him, had had his bottle and was awake in his bouncing cradle in the sitting room. I was finding that the periods during the day when he was awake were growing longer and that when he was awake he was alert and interested in everything around him. There'd been no further sighting of the woman in the street and, to be honest, my thoughts had been taken up with the busy end of term and now preparing for (and worrying about) Ellie's stay.

When the doorbell rang at 10.05 I asked Adrian, who was doing a puzzle in the sitting room, if he could watch Harrison while Paula came with me to answer the door, 'in case Ellie needs persuading to come in', I said.

But to my great relief when I opened the door Ellie wasn't crying; indeed she managed to look at me and even raised a tiny smile for Paula.

'Hi. Good to see you again,' I said, as Paula stepped forward and took Ellie's hand.

'And you,' Ava said. 'We've had a good morning so far.' So I guessed Ellie hadn't been too upset as they'd left home.

Ellie was holding a pretty glittering Cinderella bag while Ava was carrying a suitcase. 'That's a lovely bag,' I said to Ellie as they came into the hall. Ellie gave a small shy nod.

'There's a purse in her bag,' Ava said, putting down the suitcase. 'Ellie has some spending money and there are also some sweets in the bag. She just has a couple of sweets a day after her dinner. She's very good about rationing herself.'

'We'll do the same here,' I said, smiling at Ellie. I moved the suitcase to one side in the hall out of the walkway, to unpack later.

'I've written down Ellie's routine etc.,' Ava said, handing me a sheet of A4 paper. It's usual to give the respite carer a résumé of the child's routine; details of any medication the child might be taking; food preferences including special dietary requirements; allergies; doctor's and social worker's contact details; and anything else the carer might need to look after the child.

'Would you like a quick cup of coffee?' I offered.

'No, thank you,' Ava said. 'I'll say goodbye. I'm going straight to the station. Bob, my husband, is looking after the boys for the weekend and then taking them to my sister's tomorrow evening.'

'I hope your brother's a little better,' I said. 'And please don't worry about Ellie. She'll be fine with us.'

'Thank you, Cathy. I'll phone mid-week. Ellie's contact is on Wednesday,' Ava reminded me. 'I've put the time on the sheet.'

I nodded. As Ava now bent forward to hug and kiss Ellie goodbye, Ellie dropped Paula's hand and threw her arms around Ava's neck, hugging and kissing her for all she was worth. In the four months Ellie had lived with Ava she had clearly built up a strong bond with her and I could see there was a lot of affection from Ava for Ellie as well. After a few moments Ava slowly drew away and straightened, while not letting go of Ellie's hands. 'Now I want you to be a big brave girl when I go,' Ava said, standing in front of Ellie and looking her in the eyes. 'A week isn't a long time, so I would like a nice smile when you wave me off at the door. Do you think you can do that for me?'

Ellie nodded but I wasn't convinced she would. Ava gave Ellie a final hug and a kiss and then said 'Bye' to us all. She turned and went down the path while I put my hand lightly on Ellie's shoulder – partly to reassure her and also to stop her if she tried to run after Ava. But Ellie stood between Paula and me and smiled bravely and waved as Ava got in the car and then drove away.

It was only after I closed the door that Ellie burst into tears. 'I want Ava,' she sobbed. 'I want to go with her.'

I put my arms around her and, drawing her to me, sat with her on my lap on the bottom stair. 'You go into the sitting room with Adrian,' I said to Paula, for I knew Ellie's sobbing would soon upset Paula.

Paula did as I asked, while I cuddled and rocked Ellie. She was relaxed in my arms, rather like a large baby. 'Ava will be back in a week,' I soothed. 'And while she's away I'll look after you and keep you safe, just as she does.'

I stroked her hair, wiped the tears from her eyes and eventually Ellie's crying began to subside and then finally stopped. 'That's better,' I said. 'There's nothing to worry about. Let's find the box of tissues so you can blow your nose.'

I gave Ellie another hug and then eased her off my lap and on to her feet. She looked up at me, her eyes red from crying but also wide and watchful as though on the lookout for danger. I'd seen that look before in badly abused children. They never completely relax and are continually in a state of alert, as though expecting danger to strike at any moment. It's an inbuilt survival response and it can take years before the child feels safe enough to completely relax, especially in an unfamiliar setting.

I took Ellie's hand and gently led her down the hall, and was about to turn right to go into the kitchen, where I kept a box of tissues, when Ellie stopped dead. She stared at the cupboard under the stairs and refused to walk past, as she had done on her visit the day before, only now I was aware what the problem might be.

'You wait there, then,' I said to Ellie, 'while I fetch the tissues from the kitchen. Then we'll deal with that cupboard.'

I smiled at Ellie as she looked at me, wide-eyed and questioning, and I quickly went into the kitchen for the tissues. The understairs cupboard was similar to those in many other houses, although I guessed Ava's house didn't have one; otherwise I was certain Ava would have mentioned it to me and the reaction it would have caused in Ellie when she'd first arrived at Ava's house. Returning to the hall I found Ellie flattened back against the wall, staring at the cupboard door from a distance. I wiped her eyes and then gave her a tissue to blow her nose. She didn't say anything but all the time kept staring at the cupboard door and looking very fearful. Who knew what thoughts were going through Ellie's mind?

'Everything all right, Mum?' Adrian called from the sitting room.

'We'll be with you in a minute,' I returned.

I smiled again at Ellie and then knelt down so that I was at her eye level. 'I'm guessing there was a cupboard like this one where you lived with your mum and Shane?' I asked gently. 'Am I right?'

Ellie's eyes widened with a mixture of fear and surprise; then she gave a small nod.

'But I don't think Ava has a cupboard like this one, does she?' Ellie shook her head.

'Paula told me you asked her if I ever shut her in the cupboard and she told you no, never. I believe she also told you that I store things in the cupboard that we don't often use. So in a minute, when you are ready, I'm going to open the door and show you what's inside.'

Ellie's eyes widened even further as she looked from me to the cupboard and back again.

'Only when you are ready,' I said. 'First I need to tell you something very important.'

Ellie continued to stare at me, so small and vulnerable. A lump rose in my throat at the thought of what I was about to say, although I knew it needed to be said. 'Ellie, love,' I began, 'I would never shut you or any child in a cupboard. Not in this cupboard or any cupboard. It is a very bad thing to do, as I'm sure Ava has told you. Most adults would never do such a horrible thing. I want you to remember that.' This would have been obvious to most children but not to Ellie. She had lived in two houses (to my knowledge) – her mother's and Ava's. In one house she was shut in a dark cupboard and in the other she wasn't, so in Ellie's experience there was a 50 per cent chance it might happen again.

Ellie's gaze flickered to the cupboard and then returned to me as I continued: 'Adrian and Paula will tell you that if they are naughty, which isn't often, they lose some television time. That's all. They are never ever shut in anywhere, or hurt or frightened as a punishment. It is a bad thing to hurt or frighten a child. Most adults don't do it. Also, Ellie, it is impossible to get shut in this cupboard or any cupboard in this house by accident. All the doors can be opened from the inside.' (It was a fostering safety requirement.) 'Do you understand, love?'

She gave a small nod and I stood from kneeling. 'OK, I'm going to open the cupboard door now and show you what's inside.'

Ellie stared at me but didn't cry or say no. Then Paula, having heard us from the sitting room and realizing she could be of help, appeared in the hall and silently slid her hand into Ellie's. I smiled at her.

Turning, I took the couple of steps to the cupboard and opened the door, which had a magnetic surface catch. It opened with a small click as the two magnets separated and Ellie gasped. I looked at her and smiled reassuringly as Paula held her hand. I opened and closed the cupboard door a few times, showing her how easily it opened. Then I reached in and flicked on the switch for the light, which to my shame illuminated a real mess.

'It's got a light inside!' Ellie said quietly to Paula.

'Yes,' Paula said.

'Yes, it has,' I emphasized, as I gazed at the contents of the cupboard, which I kept meaning to clear out. 'The switch for the light is *in* the cupboard,' I pointed out. 'And the cupboard door can be opened from the inside simply by pushing the door. It's not a good idea to shut yourself in any cupboard,' I said, more to Paula than Ellie, who I was sure, after her experience, would never dream of playing hide and seek in a cupboard. 'But I am now going to shut myself in this cupboard to show you I can get out.' My amateur psychology said it would help exorcize Ellie's fear of not only this cupboard but, I hoped, cupboards in general.

Ellie watched dumbfounded as I stepped over a box of vinyl records and to the side of a pile of bathroom tiles and into the cupboard. Wedging myself between an upright hoover and an old standard lamp I pulled the door to. I didn't keep the door closed for long – only for a couple of seconds – and then I pushed it open. 'Hey presto!' I said, stepping out of the cupboard like a magician appearing from a magic box.

Ellie looked at me, still concerned (possibly for my sanity), while Paula laughed.

I repeated the performance. I stepped inside the cupboard, pulled the door to, and then pushed it open and leapt out, this time with a big 'Hello!' By the time I'd repeated the act a third and fourth time Ellie was actually laughing and Paula was saying, 'You are silly, Mum.'

'OK, show over,' I said.

I switched off the light in the cupboard and closed the door; then, leaving Paula and Ellie still holding hands in the hall, I went into the sitting room, where Harrison was now asleep. I lifted him from his bouncing cradle and took him down the hall, where I settled him in his pram. When I returned, Adrian, Paula and Ellie were in the kitchen and asking for a drink, with Ellie apparently having walked past the cupboard without a problem. One demon exorcized, I thought, but how many others lurked in that poor child's mind I could only guess.

I made the children a drink and a snack – they wanted a toasted cheese sandwich – which they ate at the table, while I looked at the notes Ava had given to me. Ellie's routine was similar to Adrian's and Paula's in the evening, with dinner, bath and bed. Ava said Ellie was usually in bed by 7.30 and reminded me she slept with the light on because she was afraid of the dark. Ava wrote that Ellie was a good eater and liked most food but not Marmite or anything very spicy, which I fully appreciated, as many young children don't like strong flavours. She said Ellie could take care of her own toileting, which was what I would have expected for a child of Ellie's age. Contact with Ellie's mother was at the family centre on Wednesday, from four o'clock to six o'clock. At the foot of the page Ava had written the contact details for Ellie's doctor and social worker in case I needed them in an emergency. Ava had signed off: *I hope you all have a good week. Thanks for everything. Ava.*

I folded the paper and put it safely in my 'fostering folder', where I also kept my log notes. Although Ellie was only staying for a week I would still keep log notes, which I would hand to

Jill when Ellie left. She would pass them to Ellie's social worker, who would put them on file at the social services. These records are kept and the child has a right to see them when they are adult.

Once the children had finished their snacks Ellie and Paula went up to Paula's room to play while Adrian went into the garden to ride his bike. Harrison was asleep in the pram, so I took the opportunity to go upstairs and unpack Ellie's suitcase, putting her clothes in the wardrobe and drawers in what would eventually be Harrison's bedroom. When I'd finished I came out and looked in Paula's bedroom before going downstairs. The girls were sitting on the floor in front of the doll's house, playing quietly. Paula was doing most of the talking but Ellie appeared to be involved and enjoying the game.

After lunch, as the weather was good, I suggested we walk to our local park and the children agreed. The park was busy, as it was a Saturday in mid-summer. I stood in the children's play area and rocked Harrison in his pram while Adrian, Paula and Ellie played on the apparatus. I noticed how timid and cautious Ellie was in her play. She went up to the swings or play equipment and spent some time watching other children playing before she was tempted to have a go herself. Even then she was very wary. Children who have been abused or neglected often have little self-confidence. Adrian and Paula, on the other hand, like most nurtured children, were confident in their playing, as they were in most things. Indeed Adrian had to be reminded sometimes to be careful, especially on the swings, which he worked far too high for my liking.

I was watching Paula as she ran back and forth across the rope bridge on the mini assault course, beckoning to Ellie to follow her. But Ellie had been standing at one end and watching for some minutes now, letting other children pass her and have a turn. I could see she wanted a go but daren't take that first step on to the rope bridge, which swayed but was only a foot or so above the ground.

I pushed the pram across to the assault course and parked it to one side; then I offered up my hand to Ellie and she took it. 'Come on. You can do it,' I said encouragingly.

Gripping my hand she hesitated and then tentatively stepped on to the bridge, and slowly walked across.

'Well done,' I said. 'Now you've done it once you'll be fine to do it again.'

And the smile on Ellie's face showed just how pleased she was with her achievement. Ellie, like most abused children, would gradually recover her confidence, although it would take years of love, support and possibly therapy. Emotional scars often run the deepest.

When we arrived home the children watched some television while I gave Harrison his bottle and then made dinner. Ellie was subdued, as she had been for most of the day, but had said she was all right each time I asked her. We ate around the table in the extension and then after dinner Ellie asked if she could have her sweets.

'Of course, love,' I said. 'Ava told me you had them after dinner.'

Ellie went into the sitting room (going past the cupboard under the stairs), where she'd left her Cinderella bag, and returning to the table took out a packet of Haribo mixed sweets. She carefully opened the packet and before she took a sweet herself she offered the packet to each of us, which was really touching.

'Good girl,' I said. 'It's nice of you to share.' Often when children have been badly neglected or abused they're over-protective of their possessions and have to be taught to share.

I continued to watch Ellie as she took out the two sweets she was allowed for herself, and then carefully refolded the top of the packet and tucked it into her Cinderella bag.

'Ava buys me a packet of sweets every week,' Ellie explained quietly. 'But I have to make them last, so I just have two a day.'

'That's very sensible,' I said. 'But as you have shared them with us they won't last as long, so I'll buy you another packet when that one runs out.'

Ellie looked appreciatively at me from across the table and then said in her quiet gentle voice: 'That's very kind of you, Cathy. Thank you. Everyone has been so nice to me since I came into foster care. I am lucky.'

I could have wept.

That evening, although I'd followed Ava's routine for Ellie, including a bedtime story, and leaving the light on in her room and her bedroom door open, Ellie was unsettled. When I'd said goodnight to her I'd told her to call me if she needed anything and she called me often, although when I went into her bedroom she didn't seem to need anything apart from another hug and goodnight kiss. Then she got out of bed a couple of times and came downstairs. The first time she asked for a drink of water but didn't appear very thirsty when I gave it to her; the second time she didn't really want anything and I took her back to bed and then sat with her until she fell asleep. It was nearly 10.30 by then and as I finally came out of Ellie's room, Harrison woke. I went into my bedroom and fed and changed him but he wouldn't settle. I guessed this was probably because he was aware there was someone new in the house and his routine was as a result a little different. Eventually he was asleep at 11.30 and then woke again at 2.30 for a feed. Then Ellie woke an hour later with a nightmare.

I heard her scream and was straight out of bed, rushing round the landing in my nightdress and into her room. Ellie was sitting upright in bed but not fully awake, so I eased her back down on to the pillow, tucked her in and then sat on the bed, stroking her forehead, until she fell asleep again. By the time I returned to my bed it was 4.30 and I was wide awake. I lay on my back, forcing my eyes to close and willing myself to go to sleep, aware that in just over an hour Harrison would be awake again for another feed.

It was probably because I was so tired that I didn't immediately understand what Ellie was trying to tell me the following day.

Chapter Thirteen

Pure Evil

It was Sunday afternoon and Adrian and Paula were out with their father. In the morning Ellie and I had walked to the corner shop for a newspaper and we were now having a relaxing day. Ellie seemed more at ease with me than she had done during her visit or when she'd arrived the day before, and was talking to me more. I'd opened the French windows and she was wandering in and out, familiarizing herself with the house and garden. After lunch I spread a blanket on the ground under the shade of the tree. Harrison was in his bouncing cradle, watching the leaves stir gently overhead; I was flicking through the newspaper, and Ellie was stroking Toscha, who was stretched leisurely beside her, enjoying the attention and showing her appreciation by purring loudly.

'Cats can make a lot of noise,' Ellie announced after a while.

'Yes,' I said absently, while still reading. 'She's purring because she's happy you're stroking her.'

A few moments passed as Ellie continued stroking and petting Toscha, and I read; then Ellie said: 'Cats make a horrible noise if they're hurt.'

'They do,' I agreed, glancing up. I remembered an incident when, not realizing Toscha was behind me, I'd accidentally stepped back and trodden on her paw. 'I think it's called a yowl.'

'They have claws,' Ellie said. 'Not like us.'

'No, we have nails.'

A minute or so passed, during which I closed the paper and opened the colour supplement, before Ellie said: 'Cats can scratch you if they are angry.'

'Yes,' I agreed. 'But Toscha won't scratch you. She's only ever scratched once and that was when Adrian was younger and pulled her tail.' I turned the page of the colour supplement.

'Did you take away Toscha's claws when she scratched Adrian?' Ellie then asked.

I looked up and smiled. 'No, you can't take away a cat's claws. They're joined on and are part of the cat, like your nails are part of you.'

Ellie met my gaze. 'Shane did,' she said, referring to her mother's boyfriend. 'He took our cat's claws away when she scratched him.'

I looked at her, puzzled. 'You mean he cut her claws?' I asked.

Ellie shook her head. 'No. Mum and me had a cat called Mog. It was our cat, not Shane's. He didn't like Mog and he was horrid to her. When Mog scratched him, he took her nails away.'

'I'm sorry, love,' I said. 'I don't understand.' I was still looking at Ellie, who was concentrating on Toscha as she rubbed behind the cat's ears, which Toscha loved. Ellie didn't look at me as she spoke but concentrated on lovingly petting Toscha; and her gentle kindness seemed to highlight the shocking horror of what she now described.

'Mog scratched Shane with her claws,' Ellie began, 'because he pulled her whiskers. He grabbed Mog by the neck and told Mum to get the pliers. Mum was crying and said she didn't know where they were. I was crying because he'd just hit me. Shane shouted to Mum that the pliers were in his toolbox. I didn't know what pliers were. He said if Mum didn't get the pliers he'd do the same to her when he'd finished with the bloody cat. Mum went into the kitchen and came back with some metal things, which she gave to Shane.'

Ellie paused, as though summoning the strength to continue, while her hand moved slowly over Toscha's fur and down her back.

'Shane put Mog on the floor and turned her over so she was on her back,' Ellie continued quietly. 'But she kept struggling to get the right way up. He knelt on her with his knee so she couldn't move. Mog was struggling and making a lot of noise. Then he held her front paw and pulled out her claw with the pliers. Mog screamed and then he did it again and she was screaming all the time. There was blood all over Mog's fur and on Shane and on the floor. Mum was screaming and begging him to stop, but he didn't. When he'd pulled all the claws out of one paw he started to do it to her other paw. I felt sick and angry. I was crying and shouting at him to stop. I couldn't do anything to help Mog, so I ran into the toilet and shut the door. But I could still hear Mog screaming and Mum crying. Even when I put my hands over my ears I could still hear them. I can hear them now sometimes.'

Ellie stopped and her hand grew still and lightly rested on Toscha's head. It was as though a shard of pure evil had pierced the beauty of the garden that afternoon; the air chilled, the birds stopped singing and nothing seemed to move. I stared at Ellie, my heart racing and nausea rising in my throat. I didn't want to believe what I'd heard but I knew immediately from the simple child-like language she'd used and the look on her face that it was true.

'I can still hear them screaming sometimes,' Ellie said again. 'I could hear them last night and they're coming again now.' Taking her hand from Toscha's head she pressed both hands to her ears, as if trying to block out the sound of her mum and the cat screaming.

I quickly moved across the blanket and took Ellie in my arms. She didn't say anything, but with her hands covering her ears she rested her head against my chest. I held her tightly. If a child fell over and hurt themselves I instinctively found the words to comfort and reassure them, but presented with such barbaric cruelty I couldn't think of anything that would come close to reassuring Ellie. What she had told me was so shocking that I was out of my depth. All I could do was hold her. The two of us sat in silence under the shade of the tree on that glorious summer's afternoon with Ellie trying to block out the sound of her mother screaming and her cat being tortured.

After a while Ellie slowly took her hands from her ears and put them around my waist. 'It's gone,' she said quietly. 'I can't hear them now, but it will come back again. It always does. Only before I didn't know why I heard the screaming, and now I do.'

I held Ellie close to me. 'Have you told Ava what Shane did?' I asked gently after a moment.

'No. I didn't know. I've only just remembered why she was screaming. Ava's cat is different to Mog. Toscha looks the same as Mog.' Being with Toscha had therefore triggered the memory of Shane's cruelty; previously Ellie had only heard screaming without knowing its source. This can happen with post-traumatic stress: a buried memory is released by something similar, which results in a flashback.

'We didn't see Mog again,' Ellie said sadly, her head still resting on my chest and her arms around my waist. 'Mum said she'd gone to heaven, but I think Shane took her away.' I guessed the poor cat had died, for I doubted she could have survived the trauma of having her nails pulled out, and that Shane had probably disposed of the body.

'Mog will be at peace now. She won't suffer any more,' I said, as much for my benefit as Ellie's. Ellie was sad but seemed to be coping with the recollection calmly – better than I was. She was relatively composed, while I was still reeling from the shock of what she'd told me. Perhaps Ellie had found some release in identifying the cause of the screaming that had plagued her; or possibly she'd become slightly desensitized from seeing this and other abuse, which can happen. I tried to imagine how Adrian and Paula would have reacted to witnessing such cruelty but I couldn't – my mind recoiled.

'Shane is a very cruel and wicked person, Ellie,' I said at last.

'Mum says he's evil.'

'Yes,' I agreed, wondering why on earth her mother stayed with him.

'He did other bad things,' Ellie said. 'He cut Mum with a big knife and he burnt me with his cigarette. When I was naughty he locked me in a cupboard in the dark.' I already knew this, although Ava had said it had been Ellie's mother who'd locked her in the cupboard. Given Ellie's loyalty to her mother it was possible she was transferring the blame to Shane, but I didn't know. 'It's because of him I'm in foster care,' Ellie added.

'Yes, you're safe in foster care,' I said.

I was still holding Ellie, and she now raised her head and moved slightly away so that she could stroke Toscha again. I felt I hadn't really been much help but at least Ellie had been able to tell me. 'Has Shane always lived with you and your mum?' I asked presently, as Ellie stroked Toscha and normality began to return. Had I been Ellie's permanent foster carer I would have known more about Ellie's background but as a respite carer – just looking after Ellie for a week – and in line with guidelines on sharing confidential information I had been told only what I needed to know.

Ellie shook her head. 'No, it was just me and Mum, and we were happy. Then when I was four Shane came to live with us and it was horrible. He was horrible and he made Mum horrible too.'

From what Ellie said, therefore, it appeared that Ellie's mother had successfully looked after Ellie for four years until Shane had moved in, so it seemed that in some ways Ellie's mother was a victim too – terrorized by an abusive partner and possibly behaving in a way she wouldn't otherwise have done. But allowing a child to be caught up in domestic violence is considered an abuse in itself. The courts take a firm line with mothers who fail to protect their children, often not returning the child to the mother even when the abuser has left the home.

'I love my mum, but I hate Shane,' Ellie added.

I nodded. 'Ellie, I'm going to tell Ava and your social worker what Shane did so that they can help you, all right?'

'Will they be able to stop the screaming in my head?' she asked, glancing up from Toscha. 'It makes me cry when I hear Mog and Mum scream. I want them to stop.'

'Yes. There is a person called a psychologist at the hospital who can help you. Some of the children I've looked after have been to her. She's a very nice lady and you see her once a week and do lots of nice things, like painting and making models, but at the same time she helps you to get rid of the bad memories and the screaming.' The referral would need to be made by Ellie's social worker and I knew there was a waiting list, so it would be some weeks before Ellie could begin therapy. Also therapy is sometimes purposely delayed if there is a court case pending and the child's evidence could be diluted by issues explored in therapy.

Harrison was now restless in his bouncing cradle, so I lifted him out and laid him on the blanket next to me, where he grinned and kicked his feet happily. Presently Toscha finally had enough of being petted and, stretching and yawning, slowly stood and sauntered off down the garden. Ellie also stood and went to play in the sandpit. I hoped she didn't tell Adrian and Paula what she'd told me about Shane torturing her cat. I knew how upset they'd be and I wanted to protect them. They'd been told horrible things before by children we'd fostered and had been upset for a long while afterwards, as I had. Although I recognized that Adrian's and Paula's upset from hearing cruelty described was little compared to that of the abused child who'd been there or had it done to them.

I knew I should write up my log notes covering what Ellie had told me while it was still fresh in my mind, so a little while later when Ellie was still playing in the sandpit, I carried Harrison indoors for his afternoon nap and at the same time took my fostering folder and a pen from the front room. Returning to the garden I sat on the blanket beneath the tree and wrote in detail what Ellie had told me, using her words as much as possible. This verbatim report was important so that I could accurately tell Jill what Ellie had told me, when I phoned her on Monday, and also for the social services, who would put a copy of my record on their file and use it accordingly – possibly in court. I would also update Ava when she returned.

I finished writing and returned the folder to the front room. As Harrison was still asleep I took the opportunity to play with Ellie in the garden: first we played bat and ball, and then we took turns on the mini trampoline, Ellie finding my efforts on it quite amusing.

Adrian and Paula returned from seeing their father at five o'clock and both gave me a big hug. They waved goodbye to their father at the door and then Paula gave me another hug and said: 'I've missed you. What did you do today?'

I told her Ellie and I had pushed Harrison in his pram to the corner shop for a newspaper and then we'd spent the rest of the day relaxing and playing in the garden. Satisfied, Paula ran off with Adrian to join Ellie in the garden, while I gave Harrison a bottle and then began preparing dinner. Our kitchen was at the rear of the house and I had a clear view of the garden from the kitchen window. As I worked I kept glancing out to make sure the children were all right. Adrian was practising his goal-keeping skills and had positioned himself in front of the mini goal posts at the bottom of the garden, and the girls were taking it in turns to kick the ball and try to score a goal. So far they hadn't succeeded.

As I watched my thoughts went again to the atrocity Ellie had witnessed. The image of that poor cat being tortured and Ellie having to watch was fresh in my mind. Not only was the act depraved and carried out by someone with a depraved and warped mind, but I knew from my training that research had shown that adults who are cruel to animals are often cruel to children too. Ellie had already admitted that Shane had burnt her with a cigarette, hit her with a belt, locked her in a cupboard and tortured her cat. What else had that evil man done to that poor child? I was soon to find out.

That night when Ellie said she didn't want a bath I wasn't concerned. She hadn't had a bath the night before either, but as that had been her first night with us I hadn't thought much of it. She would have had a bath or shower before she left Ava's so it wouldn't matter for another night. She'd already mentioned our bathroom was very different to Ava's, so I thought she might have been feeling a bit insecure, or possibly uncomfortable about taking off her clothes, although I'd said I'd run the bath and then leave her to undress and wash. It was only when Ellie was in bed and I'd read her a story and was about to say goodnight that she said something that made me think there could be more to it.

'You won't *make* me have a bath, will you, Cathy?' Ellie asked.

'No, not if you really don't want one,' I said, perching on her bed. 'But I think you should. A week is a long time to go without a bath. Don't you like having a bath?'

There was a small silence, which Ava had said usually preceded a disclosure and I'd seen that afternoon before she'd told me about Mog. Then Ellie said: 'Shane made me have baths but the water was cold, so I don't like baths.' She said it so matter-of-factly that I could have missed the point had I not now been alert.

'Do you mean the water was warm and then went cold while you were sitting in the bath?' I asked.

'No,' Ellie said. 'It came from the cold tap and was freezing. I had to sit in it for a long time. I shivered and my skin went blue and wrinkly, then Mummy got me out. Every Friday I had to have a cold bath. Ava knows I don't like baths so I have a shower there.'

'You can have a shower here too,' I quickly reassured her, as I again struggled with the cruelty of this man. 'Adrian has a shower but Paula prefers a bath so she can play in the water. That's why I thought you would want a bath. Does Ava know why you don't like baths?'

Ellie shrugged. 'I don't know.'

'Have you told her the reason?'

'I don't know.'

'All right, don't worry.' I guessed Ellie hadn't told Ava; otherwise Ava would have made a point of telling me. There seemed to be much undisclosed abuse in this poor child's life but now she'd started remembering and telling (a process begun at Ava's) it was as though a damn had burst and all the horrors she'd witnessed and had been subjected to were pouring out.

'You won't have a bath here unless you want one,' I said. 'You can have a shower tomorrow. But in our house and in Ava's house and most other houses, we put nice warm water in the bath, not cold. It was very wrong of Shane to make you sit in a cold bath. I'll tell Ava and your social worker this as well.'

Ellie threw me a little smile from beneath the duvet. She was such a sweet and gentle-natured child it seemed to make the cruelty inflicted on her all the worse. 'You're going to be telling Ava and my social worker lots of things,' she said.

'Yes,' I said sadly. 'It's good that you are able to tell me, like you told Ava, but I'm so sorry you have suffered.'

'I'm safe now,' she said, repeating what I (and Ava) had told her.

'Yes, love, thankfully you are.'

I kissed her cheek, said goodnight and came out, my heart aching for all little Ellie had suffered.

Chapter Fourteen
Shane

Monday was the first day of the school holidays and I settled Adrian, Paula and Ellie with paints and paper at the table in the kitchen before I collected my log notes from the front room and phoned Jill. I used the phone in the hall – on the hall table – where the children couldn't hear me but I could keep an eye on Harrison, who was asleep in his pram. It was nearly 10.30 and Jill was in the Homefinders' office. She answered with a bright 'Good morning.'

'Hello, Jill,' I said. 'I hate to start your week badly but Ellie told us some awful things over the weekend. Some of the disclosures were new.' Jill then listened carefully as I began with Ellie's visit on Friday, when she'd asked Paula if I ever shut her in a cupboard for being naughty, and then continued with Ellie's fear of cupboards, Shane's shocking cruelty to their cat and, finally, his forcing her to have a cold bath every Friday. I read from my log notes the words Ellie had used, my questions and replies, and included where and when Ellie had made the disclosures.

'Monster,' Jill said as I finished. 'Evil bastard.' Which, while lacking professional detachment, summed up exactly what she and I felt. 'I'll pass all this on to Ellie's social worker,' Jill said, 'together with a copy of your notes, please. How is Ellie now?'

'Not too bad, considering,' I said. 'She's painting pictures with Adrian and Paula. We're going out for the day tomorrow and then she has contact on Wednesday.'

'Are you able to take and collect Ellie from contact?'

'Yes. Do you know Ellie's mother?' I asked with some trepidation. I thought that she might, as Jill was Ava's support social worker too.

'I've met her once,' Jill said. 'She's young – twenty-two, I think. She was very angry when Ellie was first taken into care and used to shout at Ava. She's calmed down a bit now, but the staff at the family centre will be watchful. She wants Ellie back but I can't see that happening.'

'Does she still see Shane?' I asked.

'The last I heard they were still living together.'

'No!' I gasped, horrified.

'So I believe. Anyway, how's Harrison?' Jill asked, changing the subject.

'A real treasure,' I said, glancing in the pram. 'He's fitted into our family so well it's like he's always been here. Can I keep him?' It was said as a joke, sort of.

'In your dreams,' Jill said. 'He's very popular. They' – she meant the social services – 'already have a shortlist of ten possible adopters for him. Speaking of which, Cheryl has asked if you can attend a planning meeting a week on Tuesday to discuss Harrison's adoption. There's a letter in the post to you with the details. I know it's the summer holidays, so can you find someone to look after Adrian and Paula?'

'Yes, I should think so. I might have to bring Harrison with me.'

'Not a problem. We can all have a cuddle, then.'

Jill finished the conversation as she usually did by thanking me for all I was doing and telling me to phone her if I needed any help or advice. We said goodbye and I went through to the kitchen, where the children were still happily painting. It may seem strange that Ellie was able to enjoy herself, given what she had suffered, but children who have been abused often compartmentalize their experiences, hiving off the abuse, which allows them to function in everyday life. Therapy encourages the young person to bring out and deal with their memories of abuse, so that they can move on with life. If the abuse isn't dealt with it can resurface in adulthood, triggering all sorts of problems, including eating disorders, self-harming, depression and mental health problems. Fortunately most children brought into care in the UK now receive some therapeutic help.

After lunch on Monday we went to a local park, where we stayed for the afternoon, and that evening on returning Ellie happily had a shower. On Tuesday I put together a picnic and, packing Harrison's bottles and nappies in a bag, we went out for the day. I'd asked Ellie which local attractions Ava had taken her to so that I could take her to something different. Ava and her family had taken Ellie to quite a few local places of interest but eventually I discovered she hadn't been to the castle ruins that were about a forty-five-minute drive away. When we arrived I bought a guidebook and, leaving Harrison's pram in the car, I strapped him to me in a baby sling, and we had a lovely time exploring the ruins and imagining life in medieval times. We ate our picnic at a picnic table where the moat used to be, and the ham sandwiches, salad, crisps, biscuits and fruit were so much tastier in the country than they would have been at home. It was a nice day, enjoyed by us all. The only downside was that later, when we were home, Ellie decided to share some more bad memories from her past with Paula, which upset her dreadfully.

The two of them were in the sitting room, stroking Toscha, while I was in the kitchen, making a late supper. The first I knew there was anything wrong was when Paula came into the kitchen, close to tears, and said, 'Ellie's saying horrid things again. She said Shane pulled her cat's claws out with pliers.'

My heart sank and I stopped what I was doing. Paula stared at me, horrified, wanting me to tell her it wasn't true, which I couldn't. I tried to lessen the impact by avoiding the details and telling Paula that Shane did some very wicked things that had hurt Ellie, her mum and their cat, but that Ellie was safe now and would be kept safe in the future which helped a little.

Then later, as I was bathing Harrison, Paula came to me again and said Ellie had told her that Shane had pulled out a clump of her hair and her mum had seen him do it but couldn't stop him. This was a new disclosure as far as I knew, so I quickly finished bathing Harrison and, settling him in his cot, I went downstairs to the dining-room table, where the girls were doing a large puzzle. It was bedtime, so I asked Paula to go to the bathroom and start her wash while I spoke to Ellie.

I sat in the chair Paula had vacated, next to Ellie, as she put another piece of the puzzle into place. She continued doing the puzzle as I spoke to her. I said calmly and gently that I was worried because of what she'd just told Paula about Shane pulling out her hair. Ellie nodded without looking up and, still doing the puzzle, repeated what she'd told Paula, adding some more details. It seemed that Shane had drunk a lot of beer and had then got angry – she didn't know why – and had shouted at her to get out of the room. But before she'd had a chance to get out he'd grabbed her by the hair and pulled her towards the door, when a clump of her hair had come away in his hand. Ellie said her mother was in the room, but she couldn't help her because Shane had hit her and she was bleeding.

It was sickening but, as with Ellie's previous disclosures, all I could do was reassure her that she was safe now, tell her it was a very bad thing for Shane to do and cuddle her; then later when she was in bed I wrote up my log notes, detailing what she had told me. I obviously couldn't tell Ellie not to talk to Paula (or Adrian) about the abuse she'd suffered, and I didn't blame Ellie for telling Paula, but I tried to protect them as much as possible and I wished she'd just tell me.

That night, despite Ellie's disclosures, and tired from our day out exploring the castle ruins, we all slept well, including Harrison, who had a bottle at eleven o'clock and then didn't wake again for a feed until four o'clock. Once Ellie was awake she immediately remembered it was Wednesday and she would be seeing her mother at the family centre that afternoon. She told me as soon as I opened her bedroom curtains and then she told Adrian and Paula at breakfast.

Paula, acutely aware that Ellie's mother hadn't protected her from Shane's cruelty, found Ellie's excitement at seeing her mother confusing, which was understandable.

'Why does Ellie want to see her mum?' she asked me quietly, later, when Ellie couldn't hear.

'Because she still loves her,' I said. 'I know it's difficult to understand with everything that's happened to her. But Ellie has some happy memories of the time when there was just her and her mother.'

'I see,' Paula said, and went off to play, although I doubted she did 'see'. I, as an adult, found it confusing and had mixed feelings towards Ellie's mother, even though I'd never met her. While, on the one hand, I appreciated she was a victim too – young and terrorized by Shane – I also thought that as a mother she should have protected Ellie, and the fact that she was still living with Shane compounded my mixed feelings. But I also realized that my life experience was so different from Ellie's mother's that it was wrong of me to judge her, and there was no way of knowing how I would have reacted in her situation.

Shane

Ava telephoned from Scotland just after lunch, and the first thing she asked was how was Ellie. I said she was playing really nicely with Adrian and Paula and we'd kept her busy, so she was fine. I thought Ava had enough to worry about with her brother's illness, so I would leave updating her until she returned. I asked her how her brother was and she said he was staying positive and hadn't been so sick with the second lot of chemotherapy, which was good. When I passed the phone to Ellie I was pleased she told Ava about all the nice things she'd been doing with us – especially our trip to the castle – and didn't mention Shane, dark cupboards or any of the other horrors she had remembered. When Ellie had finished she handed the phone to me and Ava sounded relieved that Ellie was all right and enjoying herself. Ava reminded me that contact was four o'clock to six o'clock, that afternoon, and then said she would be home late on Friday, so she would collect Ellie on Saturday morning at ten o'clock if that was all right. She finished by thanking me again for looking after Ellie and we said goodbye.

At 3.15 p.m. I began getting us all in the car, ready to make the trip to the family centre for Ellie's contact. From previous visits I knew there was a small car park at the very front of the centre where I could leave Adrian, Paula and Harrison in the car for a minute while I took Ellie in. I wouldn't be inside long and it was easier to take Adrian, Paula and Harrison with me to the centre rather than finding a sitter. The children sat in the rear of the car and Harrison was in his reverse-facing car seat on the passenger seat. During the journey the children chatted, and Adrian asked Ellie if she ever saw her real father. (Shane was her mother's partner.) I was slightly surprised when Ellie replied, 'Yes, sometimes. When he's on leave.' For I hadn't heard Ellie's father mentioned before.

'What's "on leave"?' Paula asked.

'I'm not sure,' Ellie said. 'That's what Mum used to say to me. She said my dad goes away on a big ship and then he comes home to this country. It's called on leave and that's when I see him.'

'I think he could work on a cruise liner or be in the navy,' I suggested, but Ellie didn't know.

'Did your dad live with you?' Adrian asked. I glanced at Ellie in the rear-view mirror to make sure she wasn't uncomfortable with the questioning, but she seemed happy to answer. Adrian and Paula were only being curious.

'Mummy told me Daddy lived with us when I was little,' Ellie said, 'but I don't remember. When I see my daddy it's at Nana's house. That's my daddy's mummy,' Ellie explained quaintly. 'I like my daddy and my nana. I hope I see them again soon.'

'When did you last see them?' Paula asked.

I glanced in the rear-view mirror again and saw Ellie shake her head. 'A long time ago,' she said. 'Shane wouldn't let me go.'

I didn't know what arrangements, if any, were being made for Ellie to see her father and paternal grandmother. As Ellie was only with me for a week and there was no contact scheduled for her to see her father during that week there was no reason why I would be told. Ellie's social worker should be aware of Ellie's father and if it was felt appropriate for Ellie to keep in touch with him and her paternal grandmother, then the social services would make the necessary contact arrangements, whether Shane liked it or not.

'Has your social worker talked to you about seeing your dad?' I asked, aware that sometimes these things were overlooked.

'Yes,' Ellie said. 'My dad is away, so I can't see him now. But when he comes home on leave I will.'

'Good,' I said, for I had formed the impression from what Ellie said that her father and grandmother were a positive factor in Ellie's life.

When we arrived at the family centre I found that the small car park at the front of the building was full, so I had to park in the road. I wasn't going to leave Adrian, Paula and Harrison in the car and out of sight, even for a couple of minutes, so I told Adrian and Paula they would come in with me, which they had done before and didn't mind. It was 3.55 and I hoped Ellie's mother would be inside the family centre by now, or arrive after we'd entered. I'd been in situations before when the child's parent(s) had arrived at the same time as us and it was always difficult. The child, pleased to see the parent, rushes over, oblivious to the traffic or the fact that the contact that follows is unsupervised until they are all safely in the centre. I was even more concerned now that I had Adrian and Paula with me, for while I knew Shane couldn't go into the family centre – the contact was for Ellie and her mother only – there was nothing to stop him waiting outside, and I really didn't want to meet him. However, we entered the building without incident and as I said hello to the receptionist, who knew me from previous visits, the security door closed protectively behind us. The receptionist said 'Hi' to the children, and then to Ellie: 'Your mum's in the waiting room.'

As Ellie turned to look in the direction of the waiting room a young woman, fashionably dressed in jeans and a T-shirt, and with long fair hair, appeared, together with the contact supervisor, who would stay with Ellie and her mother throughout the two hours' contact. Ellie rushed over to her mother and they hugged.

'See you later,' I called, ready to leave. 'Have a nice time.'

'Thank you, we will,' Ellie's mother said. 'And thanks for looking after Ellie while Ava's away.'

I looked over to Ellie's mother and smiled at her. 'You're very welcome,' I said. 'Ellie's been fine.'

Once outside Paula summed up exactly what I (and probably Adrian) had been thinking: 'Ellie's mum doesn't look horrid,' Paula said. 'She looks normal, like a mummy.'

'Yes,' I agreed sadly. 'She does.' And I wondered whatever had gone wrong in that poor woman's life to keep her in an abusive relationship that had ultimately led to her having her child taken away.

We went home for an hour and then it was time to return and collect Ellie from contact. When we arrived at the family centre I was able to park in the car park at the front of the building but I decided not to leave the children in the car. I don't know why: it wasn't dark, I'd only be in the centre for a minute and I could see the car from reception, but something told me it was better not to leave them unattended.

With Harrison in my arms and Adrian and Paula either side of me we went up the path and the security door clicked open. Ellie was waiting in reception, having said goodbye to her mother in the contact room, as was normal practice. We said goodbye to the staff and left. In the car park it took me a few minutes to strap Harrison into his seat and for the children to climb into the rear seat and fasten their belts. I then checked that everyone had their belts on, closed the rear door and went round the back of the car to get into the driver's seat. As I did Ellie's mother came out of the family centre and walked down the path to where a man was now waiting on the pavement. As she approached him I heard her say, 'That's the one that's looking after Ellie this week.'

I glanced over and met the gaze not of Ellie's mother but of the man. He was short, thickly set, with a shaven head and tattoos on his neck and both arms, and his stance emanated pure aggression. I instinctively knew it was Shane. I quickly got into the car, closed the door and clicked the internal locking system. Ellie's mother and Shane were now walking along the pavement, side by side and talking. Ellie hadn't seen them and I wondered how she would react when I drove past them. I reversed out of the parking bay and began down the road.

'There's your mummy,' Paula said innocently.

I glanced in the rear-view mirror and saw Ellie sink low in her seat so that she couldn't be seen from outside, and then bury her head in Adrian's shoulder. Such was her fear of Shane.

Chapter Fifteen

No Wiser

On Thursday I planned another day out and, armed with bottles and nappies, I took the children to an animal sanctuary, which was about half an hour's drive away. Adrian and Paula had been to the sanctuary before on a school outing but were happy to go again. The sanctuary was home to all types of animals that had been abandoned or maltreated. A rather eccentric elderly lady owned and ran the sanctuary and could be seen wandering around the paddocks in wellington boots and an old waxed jacket, talking to the animals. She used all her own money and then relied on public donations to fund the sanctuary, whose residents included turtles that had outgrown their tanks, birds that couldn't fly, a sheep with three legs and an albino pig that couldn't go out in the sun without sunscreen.

Beside each enclosure was a plaque that gave the name of the animal; information about the breed of animal; the date the animal had arrived; and the reason the animal was in the sanctuary. Adrian, aged nine and able to read well, appointed himself our tour leader and read aloud from each plaque as we grouped around him; Ellie, at six, could read some sentences, and Paula, five, could read some of the words. There were other families in the sanctuary who were doing something similar; it was an educational and fun day out, and the children (and I) learnt a lot about animals without actually realizing it. There was a small café, where we had a sandwich lunch and I gave Harrison his bottle. Then when the children had had enough of looking at the animals they played in the activity corner with rope ladders and swings, while Harrison slept in the sling. The sky was overcast but it didn't rain, so we had an enjoyable day, and unlike our previous day out – to the castle – when we returned home Ellie didn't disclose any further abuse.

Friday was Ellie's last full day with us and Ava was due to collect her the following morning. Having had the outing to the sanctuary the day before, I planned for the children to play at home today, but first I needed to go to the local shops for some groceries. The weather was fine, so rather than use the car we walked to the local supermarket, with Paula and Ellie taking turns to push Harrison in his pram (I was right beside them), and Adrian on his scooter. In the supermarket I told the children they could choose something for dinner and they were soon peering through the door of the chiller cabinet containing chips, pizzas, burgers, pies and other processed food, which I only allowed occasionally.

'Cathy, you eat lots of food, don't you?' Ellie said, standing between Adrian and Paula and peering in the chiller.

'We do,' I said, guessing Ellie meant our family rather than me personally.

'Ava has lots of food in her house too,' Ellie said. 'I like Ava's food and I like yours.'

'Good,' I said.

Adrian and Paula had now opened the chiller door and were trying to decide between potato waffles, chips or alphabet potato shapes to go with the pizza they'd chosen.

'What do you want, Ellie?' I asked. 'You help choose.'

'I don't mind,' Ellie said with a small smile. 'I like any food. We didn't have much at my house.'

'The house where you lived with your mother?' I clarified.

121

Ellie nodded. 'Mum never had any money to buy food,' she said. 'We had one cupboard in the kitchen but it only had cans of beer in it.'

'Didn't you have a fridge?' Paula asked, unable to comprehend a house without limitless food and therefore assuming the food must have been kept in the fridge.

'There was beer in the fridge too,' Ellie said. 'Then the fridge broke and Shane got angry because his beer wasn't cold.'

'So what did you eat?' Adrian asked, his attention now diverted from the chiller cabinet to Ellie.

'Sometimes bread and sometimes cat food, but I had a school dinner as well.'

'Cat food!' Adrian said, turning his back on the chiller to give Ellie his full attention. 'You can't eat cat food!'

Ellie nodded. 'At the weekend when I didn't go to school and have a school dinner I did. You can't go to sleep if you're very hungry. It hurts your tummy. So I waited until Shane was asleep and went into the kitchen and ate the cat's food.'

'What! From the bowl?' Adrian asked, unable to believe his ears. Paula stared at Ellie in disbelief.

'No, I used a spoon, silly!' Ellie said. 'I'm not a cat – I don't eat from a cat bowl!' And she laughed. Despite all she'd been through she was still able to laugh at Adrian's suggestion that she ate from the cat bowl.

Adrian and Paula didn't laugh or smile, though; neither did I.

'That's horrid,' Paula said, pulling a face.

'Didn't it make you sick?' Adrian asked.

'Yes, and then I didn't eat it any more. Shane was angry about the smell I made.'

Adrian and Paula both had their backs to the chiller, all interest in what they were going to eat gone. My appetite had disappeared too.

'That's dreadful,' I said. 'Absolutely dreadful.' I pulled a bag of chips from the chiller and dumped it in the basket.

That evening Ellie told Paula that she'd also eaten the remains of Shane's takeaways, which she'd pulled out of the dustbin, and sometimes her mother sent her next door to ask the neighbour for food. Jill had been right when she'd told Ava that now Ellie was starting to talk about her life at home there'd be more to come out, and what that poor child had been through sickened me to the core.

Once the children were in bed that night I typed up my log notes and printed out copies for Ava and Jill. If I had to add anything before Ava collected Ellie the following morning I'd do so in at the foot of the paper. When I'd finished I shut down the computer and put Toscha out for her run; then I went upstairs and gave Harrison his late-night feed. As I sat on my bed by the light of the lamp, with Harrison in my arms sucking contentedly, I breathed a small sigh of relief: very soon normality would return and I'd just have Adrian, Paula and Harrison again. For while Ellie was a darling child and I felt dreadfully sorry for her, I also felt weighed down by her suffering and all the abuse she'd told us about. I was very grateful that Harrison didn't know what it was to suffer and would eventually leave us for a loving adoptive family. How different his life would be to Ellie's!

The following morning when we opened the door to Ava I could see how pleased Ellie was to see her and to be returning home, which was how it should be. Ava stepped into the hall for a few minutes but said she wouldn't stay for a coffee, as her boys were waiting at home, having also missed her. I'd already packed Ellie's case and had brought it down to the hall, and I now handed Ava a copy of the notes I'd printed out the night before and had put in an envelope. She thanked me and, not wishing to discuss what I'd written in front of Ellie, Adrian and

Paula, I said I'd phone her later in the evening. The children and I said goodbye to Ava and Ellie and we waved them off at the door.

'I'll miss Ellie,' Paula said wistfully, as I closed the door.

'Yes, you two played very nicely together,' I said. 'But Ellie is very happy with Ava,' which Paula appreciated.

However, although Ellie had returned to live with Ava the legacy of Ellie's suffering would stay with us for some time to come. Every so often for the rest of that day and in the following weeks, Adrian or Paula would suddenly break from what they were doing and ask me: 'Do you really think Ellie was ...' and then repeat something she had told us – shut in a dark cupboard, ate cat food, etc. – finding the abuse too awful to believe; and I would answer: 'Sadly, yes, I do.'

That Saturday evening when Adrian, Paula and Harrison were in bed I telephoned Ava, as I'd said I would. She'd had time to read my notes and was horrified by the disclosures Ellie had made, but not wholly surprised. She believed, as did Jill, that Ellie had suffered a lot more than the social services had realized. I then asked Ava if she'd ever seen Shane waiting outside the family centre after contact as I had and which I'd mentioned in my notes.

'Yes,' Ava said. 'Sorry, I should have warned you. He's not there often but when he is, it scares Ellie. I told the social services he waits outside the family centre sometimes but there's nothing they can do. If he tries to go into the centre or approaches or threatens Ellie, then they can call the police or take out an injunction, but they can't stop him standing in the street.'

'No,' I agreed. 'They can't. But Ellie clearly feels threatened just seeing him.'

'I know,' Ava said. 'That man gives me the creeps. I dread to think of the effect he has on Ellie.'

I then confirmed with Ava that I would give a copy of my notes to Jill, who'd pass them to Ellie's social worker. She thanked me and we said goodbye, adding that we'd probably see each other at one of the fostering training course or social events Homefinders organized.

The children and I went to my parents for the day on Sunday. On Monday, Adrian and Paula had friends in to play and on Tuesday they were invited to friends' houses, which worked out very well, as it meant I didn't have to find a sitter for them while I attended the planning meeting for Harrison which Jill had previously informed me of. It was the first week in August and Harrison had been with us for just over a month, although it seemed much longer, so easily had he fitted into our family and we'd all bonded.

The meeting was scheduled to begin at 11.30 a.m. and was at the council offices. So at eleven o'clock, armed with the 'baby bag', as it had become known, which contained all I might need for Harrison, including sterilized bottles, a carton of milk, nappies, baby wipes and nappy bags, I dropped off Adrian and Paula at their respective friends' houses and continued to the council offices.

I hadn't been to an adoption planning meeting before, as none of the children I'd previously fostered had left me to go to adoptive parents, although some had subsequently been adopted after they'd left me. Others had returned home or gone to live with a relative in their extended family. I therefore wasn't sure exactly what to expect at the meeting, although I'd attended other planning meetings before and I guessed they all followed a similar format. But any format or formality disappeared as soon as I walked into the room with Harrison in my arms.

'Oh! You've brought him with you! Fantastic!' Cheryl, Harrison's social worker, exclaimed.

'Let's have a look,' one of the two women there I didn't know cried in delight.

The four of them – Jill, Cheryl and the two women I didn't know – immediately rose and, coming over, began making a big fuss of Harrison, baby-talking and touching his little hands and feet. Harrison didn't mind – far from it. He grinned, gurgled, wrinkled his nose and then reached out one little hand as if trying to hold their hands. I felt sure he was playing to the audience.

'He's the cutest baby I've ever seen,' the first woman exclaimed.

'He's simply gorgeous,' the other woman said.

'He's grown,' Jill said, and Cheryl agreed.

'Can I hold him?' the first woman asked, holding out her arms to receive him. 'We haven't met before. I'm Viera from the adoption team.'

'Hello,' I said as I placed Harrison in Viera's outstretched arms.

'And I'm Jessica, acting team manager,' the other woman said, offering her hand for shaking.

'I'm Cathy. Pleased to meet you.'

Jessica, Jill and Cheryl now regrouped around Harrison in Viera's arms and continued admiring and baby-talking to Harrison as he grinned and wrinkled his nose endearingly. I was clearly superfluous to needs but I didn't mind; I felt very proud, as any mother does when her baby is admired.

Eventually, Jessica, as acting team manager, glanced at the wall clock, which was now showing 11.45. 'Ladies,' she said, 'I think we need to start this meeting. I have another meeting straight afterwards.'

'Oh, must we?' Viera joked, giving Harrison one last hug before returning him to me.

We eventually settled around the table and I tucked the baby bag on the floor beside my feet so that I could easily reach in for a bottle if Harrison became restless during the meeting.

'Welcome, everyone,' Jessica began, picking up a pen and opening a large notepad. Jill also opened a notepad, while Viera and Cheryl had folders on the table in front of them. 'This meeting is to plan for Harrison's future, and review our progress in finding suitable adopters for him,' Jessica said. 'I shall be chairing and minuting the meeting. Although we have already introduced ourselves, could we do so again, please, for the sake of the minutes? I'll begin: I'm Jessica Laming, acting team manager.'

Introductions, a chairperson and minuting are usual practice at any social services meeting, and we now went round the table stating our name and role: Viera, social worker from the adoption team; Cheryl, Harrison's and Rihanna's social worker; Jill, support social worker from Homefinders fostering agency; Cathy Glass, Harrison's foster carer. Then after a short pause I added: 'And this is Harrison, my foster child.'

'Yes, we mustn't forget to minute that he's present,' Jessica said with a smile. 'Although I guess you'll be speaking for him on this occasion?' I laughed and nodded.

Following the format of previous planning meetings I'd attended I would now have expected Jessica, as acting team manager, to give a brief résumé of Harrison's case: a little bit about his family history, the circumstances that had brought him into care, as well as the care plan for his future, which I knew to be adoption. Given the secrecy surrounding Harrison's case I was intrigued to hear what Jessica would have to say about Harrison's background and family history, and I thought I might learn something – possibly why his mother had had to give him up. I guessed Jill felt the same, for as Jessica began to speak Jill glanced at me and then sat forward in anticipation, pen poised over her pad. However, we were both quickly disappointed.

'Harrison's case is very straightforward,' Jessica began. 'Rihanna, Harrison's mother, made the decision while she was expecting that she couldn't keep her baby and that he should be adopted as soon as possible. Sad though this is, it has meant that the department has been able to start forward planning so that Harrison needn't be kept in foster care any longer than is necessary.' This wasn't a slight on me but an acknowledgement that the sooner Harrison was bonding with his adoptive family the better it would be for him.

'Harrison is in care under a Section 20,' Jessica continued. 'We have his mother's full cooperation, and I would hope to have him settled with his adoptive parents within the year. Before we hear from Viera, who will give us an update on how our plans are progressing, Cathy, perhaps you would like to say a few words about Harrison – his routine and how he's settled in with you. He's obviously doing very well.'

'Yes, he is,' I said, while thinking, So you're not saying anything about Harrison's family or the secrecy surrounding his case? But it wasn't for me to pry, so I began the update on Harrison. 'Harrison has settled very well,' I said. 'I feed him on demand – every three to four hours during the day, and he wakes once at night: between two and three o'clock. He then sleeps until nearly six o'clock, which is good.'

All three women nodded and Jessica wrote on her notepad.

'I take Harrison to the clinic every week to be weighed and measured,' I continued. 'The results are entered in the red book, which I've brought with me.' Dipping my hand into the baby bag I took out the red book and handed it to Jessica. She opened it, made a note of Harrison's most recent weight and then sent the book round the table for the others to look at as I continued. 'Harrison will start the baby immunization programme when he is two months old,' I said. 'The booster injections follow at three and four months of age. I see the health visitor at the clinic and she is happy with Harrison's progress, as I am.' I stopped, unable to think what else to say. When I foster older children, who often have special needs and behavioural problems, there is always plenty to say, but now it seemed I'd covered everything.

'Thank you, Cathy,' Jessica said, glancing up from writing. 'Harrison's certainly looking very healthy.'

'And smart,' Viera added. 'I love his little romper suit.'

'Thank you,' I said. 'I always dress him in the outfits his mother sent.'

Viera looked puzzled.

'Rihanna sent a suitcase full of clothes for his first year,' Cheryl clarified, so I guessed Viera didn't know.

Jessica had finished writing and now looked at me. 'And there's been no more sightings of Mum in the street where you live?'

'No,' I said. 'Not as far as I'm aware.'

'We are not even sure it was Rihanna,' Cheryl said. 'I'm still waiting to hear back from her solicitor.'

Jessica made a note and then said to me, 'Of course you appreciate that under a Section 20, until Harrison is adopted Rihanna has a right to see her son, but we would obviously arrange contact rather than have her just arrive on your doorstep.'

'Yes, I understand,' I said.

'Well, thank you, Cathy,' Jessica said again. 'Is there anything you wish to add?'

'I don't think so. Harrison is alert and doing everything a baby of his age should be doing. My family and I are enjoying looking after him.'

Harrison gurgled his approval and everyone smiled.

'Viera,' Jessica said, turning to her, 'could you give us your update please, on how your search for an adoptive family for Harrison is progressing?'

Viera nodded and glanced at the top sheet of the file open on the table in front of her. 'We've been very busy,' she began. 'We've had a lot of interest in Harrison, and we received over seventy applications to adopt him.'

I let out a small gasp and Jill and Jessica raised their eyes in astonishment.

'He's a very popular young man,' Viera continued. 'We examined each application carefully and have now shortlisted five couples who seem to be the most suitable. Four of the couples are childless and the other couple has one adopted child who is six: they would like to adopt again so that their daughter has a sibling. All five couples are vetted and approved adopters, so we won't be waiting for approval – you know how long the adoption process can take. These five are also partial matches for Harrison's cultural identity. We knew we wouldn't find an exact match because Harrison's father is—' Viera stopped and I knew she had been about to give away a detail that could have identified Harrison's father. I assumed this detail was already known to Cheryl (as Harrison's social worker) and Jessica (as acting team manager), but it clearly wasn't to be disclosed to Jill or me.

Viera quickly rephrased: 'I am sure the adoption panel will consider any one of these couples a good match for Harrison. When I return from leave I shall meet all the couples in their homes and then write my recommendation.'

'When will that be?' Jessica asked, glancing up from note taking.

'I'm on leave for the next two weeks,' Viera said. 'I shall begin visiting the couples on my return. I hope to have seen them all by the end of September, and my report should be ready by the end of October.'

'So you'll be able to go to the matching panel in November?' Jessica asked. 'Then the adoption panel in January? I don't think they sit in December.'

'That's right,' Viera confirmed. 'Assuming the panel approves the adoption we can start the introduction of the lucky couple to Harrison straight after the panel meets, with a move in February.'

'Excellent,' Jessica said.

'Cathy,' Viera now said to me, 'could you let me have some photographs of Harrison so that I can show the prospective adoptive couples when I visit them?'

'Yes, I've taken plenty.'

'Good. Also, could you complete these forms so that I can write up Harrison's profile? The forms are used for children of all ages, so some of the questions won't be entirely relevant, but if you could put something in each box, that would be good.'

I took the forms Viera now passed across the table and slid them into the baby bag to look at later.

'Is that everything?' Jessica asked Viera.

'Yes, I think so.'

'Cheryl,' Jessica now said, looking at Harrison's social worker, 'would you like to give us your update, please?'

Cheryl moved slightly closer to the table, and Jill and I exchanged a glance, wondering if Cheryl would give any more details that might explain the mystery surrounding Harrison, but we didn't wonder for long.

'There isn't much to say, really,' Cheryl began. 'As you know, all correspondence goes through Rihanna's solicitor and we haven't heard from her since Harrison came into care. Our legal department has sent the paperwork for the Section 20 to the solicitor; they'll also send a copy of the minutes of this meeting when it becomes available. The search for an adoptive family for

Harrison is going well, as we've just heard. I'm not expecting any problems, as we have Mum's full cooperation and consent.'

'And the LAC review?' Jessica asked.

'It's due,' Cheryl said. 'Shall we arrange a date now?'

'Yes, I think we should,' Jessica said a little firmly.

The LAC (Looked After Children) review is a legal require-ment to make sure the care plan is appropriate and the child's needs are being met. The first review has to be held four weeks after the child comes into care.

'Can we make it next Wednesday?' Cheryl asked, taking her diary from her bag and opening it.

'I'm on leave,' Viera said.

'I can give your report,' Cheryl said.

'I can make next Wednesday,' Jill said, and I agreed I could too.

'We're obliged to send an invitation to the review to Rihanna,' Cheryl said to us all. 'But she won't attend.' Then, looking at me: 'Cathy, on a Section 20, it is usual to have the review in the child's home. Is that all right with you?'

'Yes,' I said. I'd had review meetings in my house before, so I knew what to expect, and it would also save me having to find a sitter for Adrian and Paula as they would simply play in another room.

'Shall we set the time for eleven o'clock?' Jessica said, glanc-ing up from minuting.

'Fine with me,' Cheryl and Jill agreed, and made a note in their diaries; while I said yes, and made a note in my head.

'I won't attend, but an independent chairperson will,' Jessica added, which was normal procedure.

There being no further business Jessica thanked us all for coming and the meeting ended as it had begun: with the four women fussing over Harrison, and Jill and me none the wiser as to why Harrison's mother couldn't keep him and why all the secrecy was necessary.

Chapter Sixteen

The Woman in the Street

CHILD'S PROFILE
To be completed by the child's main carer in black ink.

Name of Child   Date of Birth   Age   M/F

_____   _____   _____   ____

Once the children were in bed I decided to tackle the forms Viera had given to me so that they wouldn't get forgotten and I would have them ready to hand to Cheryl at the LAC review the following Wednesday. Using a black biro I filled in the first row of boxes, although I stumbled over 'age', uncertain if it meant Harrison's age now or at the time of the adoption; I opted for now. The next questions were relatively straightforward too: *How long have you known the child? Are there any other siblings in the family? Is the child normally healthy? Does the child have a registered disability? If so, for what? Is the child registered blind? Is the child registered as deaf or hearing impaired?* These questions were largely single word *Yes/No* answers, and having completed them I turned to the next page. The first box was headed: *Describe the child's daily routine*, which I did; it took me about fifteen minutes to choose the best words, for I knew the contents of this form would be sent to all the professionals connected with Harrison's case and the prospective adoptive parents, so I wanted my description to be clear and well written.

The question in the next box asked: *Does the child have any special needs? If so, please describe what these are.* I wrote *None*. The box below asked: *Does the child have any behavioural difficulties? If so, describe what these are and the strategies you are using for dealing with them.* I smiled at the thought of little Harrison with behavioural difficulties and again wrote: *None*. Turning the page, the first question was: *Does the child have age-appropriate self-care skills – for example, can he wash and dress himself?* Viera had said the form was for children of all ages and she had asked that I put something in each box, but many of the questions weren't relevant at all. I thought it would have made more sense to have had two forms – one for infants and one for school-aged children. I decided to write *N/A* in the box – short for Not Applicable.

The next box related to the one above and asked: *If the child does not have age-appropriate self-care skills, what are you doing to teach them?* The answer could have been *Nothing*, for even though Harrison was alert and intelligent I wouldn't be teaching a baby how to wash and dress himself, so I wrote *N/A* again and then added: *The child is a baby*, to clarify. The questions continued with: *Are the child's language skills appropriate for the child's age?* I was tempted to write: *Yes*, because Harrison's gurgles were age-appropriate, but I opted again for *N/A – The child is a baby*. The next question was: *What does the child like to eat and drink?* I wrote *Formula milk*. Then I laughed at the next two questions: *What does the child like to do in his or her leisure time?* And *Does the child belong to any after school activities?* I again entered *N/A – The child is a baby* in both the boxes and continued down the page.

It wasn't until I reached the final box on the last page that I had the opportunity to give a realistic appraisal of Harrison:

Describe in your own words the child you are looking after. This was a large box, nearly half the page, and I carefully filled it in. I said that I'd collected Harrison from hospital when he was one day old and he had quickly settled into a routine (which I'd described in a previous question). I said he was a contented baby, alert, responsive and interested in all that was going on around him. I gave his current weight, and I described his physical appearance and also his little mannerisms which were so endearing – like the way he wrinkled his nose. As I finished filling in the last box I realized I knew Harrison as well as I knew my own children. I felt a stab of sadness as I acknowledged that at some point, in the not-too-distant future, Harrison would be leaving us for his adoptive family and would no longer be one of my family.

I signed and dated the last page and then tucked the set of forms into my fostering folder, where I'd already put the photographs Viera had asked for. Viera would use the information I'd given on the forms together with the photographs when she compiled Harrison's profile, which would be shown to the prospective adopters and members of the matching and adoption panels. I wondered what the prospective adoptive parents were like. The adoption team had certainly had a huge response and I knew it was because Harrison was a healthy baby. Had he been an older child or a child with special needs the response would have been very different; often such children are never adopted and stay in foster care until they are eighteen, when they come out of care and are essentially on their own, which is very sad.

The following day, armed with the baby bag, buckets and spades, swimming costumes and towels, we went to the seaside for the day. The nearest coast was about seventy miles from my house, and in high summer it was a popular destination. The road to the coast was very busy and when we arrived it took me twenty minutes to find somewhere to park, by which time Harrison was protesting that he needed his bottle and Adrian and Paula were protesting about how long it was taking. But as soon as I'd parked and we were out of the car and on the beach, Harrison had his bottle, Adrian and Paula changed into their swimming costumes and everyone was happy. The sun shone in a clear blue sky and there was a gentle sea breeze causing little waves to ripple on to the shore. The air was alive with happy children playing and shouting and I was pleased I'd made the effort to come. Adrian and Paula paddled in the sea and jumped the waves and then made sandcastles on the beach. Harrison, bemused by all the new sights and sounds, lay either in my arms or on the blanket, gurgling and waving his hands in excitement. He seemed to be taking it all in and his face was a picture when Adrian filled up a bucket of wet sand and dipped his hand in.

At one o'clock everyone was hungry, so I bought fish and chips from the beach café, and we ate them straight from the paper on the beach; then later in the afternoon we had ice-cream, and later still Adrian and Paula had a burger each and then candy floss. It was after six o'clock – when other families were also leaving the beach – when I said we really needed to be going. I gave Harrison a bottle before we left; then, having gathered together our belongings and shaken the sand off the blanket, we returned to the car, pleasantly exhausted from a great day.

The following day we awoke to wind and rain, which continued for the next two days and largely confined us to the house, so I was pleased we'd gone to the seaside when we had.

The weekend arrived and the rain finally stopped, but on Saturday morning I told Adrian and Paula that before we did anything else we needed to do a big supermarket shop. The children had good appetites and it seemed I was continuously low on food and having to restock. Adrian and Paula weren't over-enthusiastic supermarket shoppers and it took a lot of coercing from me and moaning from them before they finally stopped playing and came into the hall to put on their sandals as I'd asked them to do. Adrian was still wearing a rather sulky expression, so that when he opened the front door and then slammed it shut I thought he was messing around and making a statement about not wanting to go shopping.

'Adrian,' I said, not best pleased, 'the sooner we go to the supermarket, the sooner you can come home and play.'

'It's not that,' he said. 'There's someone watching our house.'

'What? A spy?' Paula teased.

'No,' Adrian said. 'It's that woman. The one who was there before.'

It took me a moment to realize that Adrian wasn't fooling around and was probably referring to the woman we'd seen before, waiting across the street. The door was closed and Adrian still had his hand on the doorknob.

'Let me see,' I said, setting down Harrison's car seat in the hall.

'I bet she's gone now,' Adrian said, pulling a face at Paula for doubting him.

I turned the doorknob and slowly opened the front door, expecting to see an empty street, because on the two previous occasions the woman had fled as soon as she'd seen us. Perhaps she hadn't seen Adrian – he'd opened and closed the door very quickly – so perhaps that was the reason she hadn't run away. For as I opened the door and looked across the road I saw the woman on the pavement opposite before she saw me; then she turned and fled. And whereas on the other occasions I'd had doubts as to whether she'd been looking at our house or the house next door, or was just waiting for a friend, now I had no doubts at all. She had definitely been watching our house and I had a feeling she'd been there for some time.

I went down the front garden path to the gate and watched the woman running up the road, quickly disappearing out of sight. I returned inside, where Adrian and Paula were looking at me anxiously.

'It's nothing to worry about,' I reassured them. 'Honestly. I'll mention it to Jill, but she'll say the same, and the woman's gone now.'

'Is it Harrison's mother?' Adrian suddenly asked.

'What makes you say that?' I asked surprised.

'She looks like Harrison,' Adrian said. 'I saw her face when I first opened the door, when she didn't know I was watching, and their faces are similar.'

'I'm not sure,' I said, which was true. For while Adrian might have had a good look at her face to see a likeness, I hadn't, and I wasn't going to fuel Adrian's imagination by making links where there might be none. Also, I wasn't concerned for our safety at that time; the woman hadn't shown us any aggression – indeed she'd always fled when she saw us. So I reassured the children that there was nothing to worry about and we continued into the car and to the supermarket.

I didn't consider this third sighting of the woman in our street to be an emergency or even urgent, so I didn't phone the out-of-hours cover at the fostering agency over the weekend. I waited until Monday to phone the office and then I was surprised by Jill's reaction.

'Not again!' she said. 'I'll phone Cheryl straightaway and find out what's going on. We'll also raise the matter at the LAC review. This is not acceptable.'

'There wasn't a problem,' I said, a little bemused. 'The woman ran off as soon as she saw me. I just thought you should know.'

'You did right. It's not fair on you or the kids. Who knows what frame of mind Rihanna is in? If Cheryl hasn't had a reply from Rihanna's solicitor about this then she needs to be chasing it up. I'll phone Cheryl now and get back to you.'

'All right. Thank you, Jill,' I said, but I was now worried by the seriousness with which she was taking this sighting.

Jill phoned back later on Monday afternoon, having spoken twice to Cheryl. In between Cheryl had phoned Rihanna's solicitor, who'd said Rihanna hadn't been in touch with her for nearly three weeks. The solicitor said she had left two messages on Rihanna's voicemail but as Rihanna hadn't returned the calls she had assumed she must be away. The solicitor said she'd phone Cheryl as soon as she'd spoken to Rihanna and had ascertained if it was her client we had seen in the vicinity of my house.

'Sorry,' Jill said as she finished. 'I've done what I can but it's not satisfactory. Cheryl said she'd phone me as soon as she heard from the solicitor, and I said we'll also raise it at the LAC review on Wednesday.'

'Thanks, Jill,' I said again. 'See you Wednesday.'

We said goodbye and hung up, and I continued with Monday, still feeling that Jill might have over-reacted, but aware that as my support social worker she had my family and my best interests at heart. However, the following morning – Tuesday – something happened which forced me to acknowledge that Jill had been right to be concerned. At 7.45 a.m., before the children were up, I opened the front door to bring in the milk and had the shock of my life. As I glanced up I saw the woman on the pavement right outside my front gate. I started and she did, presumably not expecting the door to open so early; then she turned and fled up the road.

I ran the few steps up the garden path and on to the pavement, but the woman was already halfway up the street and disappearing fast. It crossed my mind to run after her, but I couldn't leave the children alone in the house, and was it really the wise thing to do? Although I'd previously felt she meant me no harm, now I couldn't be certain. She'd been close enough for me to see the likeness Adrian had seen, and I now knew for certain it was Harrison's mother. And if she wasn't away, as her solicitor had said, why wasn't she returning her solicitor's phone calls?

With my heart racing I returned inside the house and shut the front door. Adrian and Paula were still asleep, fortunately, and I wouldn't be telling them I'd seen her. It would unnerve them, as it had me. I went through to the kitchen and continued as best I could with my normal early morning routine: I fed Toscha; I filled the kettle for coffee; I loaded the washing machine; and then when the children came downstairs I made them breakfast as usual.

As soon as Homefinders' office opened, at nine o'clock, I left the children finishing their breakfasts and went into the sitting room and phoned. A colleague of Jill's answered.

'Could I speak to Jill, please?' I said, keeping my voice even.

'I'll put you straight through.'

'Is everything all right?' Jill asked, as soon as she answered.

'No. Not really.' I paused and lowered my voice so that the children couldn't hear me. 'The woman was outside my house again – right outside, by the gate, at seven forty-five this morning. I'm sure it was Harrison's mother.'

'How can you be certain? I thought she was away.'

'Harrison is the image of his mother. He has the same nose and eyes. I'm positive it was her.'

'Did she approach you? Or say anything?' Jill asked, concerned.

'No. As soon as she saw me she ran off. She looked scared but not half as scared as I was. It gave me a dreadful shock.'

Jill paused in thought and then said, 'Cathy, let me speak to Cheryl and then I'll get back to you. Are you in today or shall I phone your mobile?'

'I'll be in this morning. Then I thought we'd go out this afternoon.'

'OK, I'll try to get back to you this morning; otherwise I'll phone your mobile later. And Cathy, if she appears again today call the police. Explain you're a foster carer and there's a woman loitering in the street outside your house, and let them deal with it.'

'All right, but hopefully it won't come to that.'

'Hopefully, but don't take any chances. We don't know what's going on here.'

I was on edge all morning. I kept going into the front room and peering out from behind the net curtains to check the street, but there was no sign of her. I was pleased; I didn't want Adrian and Paula upset, or to involve the police unless it was absolutely necessary. In the afternoon when we left the house to walk to the park I was vigilant; likewise when we returned to the house later in the afternoon I kept a lookout, but the street was clear. Jill hadn't phoned back, although I'd repeatedly checked my mobile while we'd been in the park. It wasn't until the children and I were having dinner at six o'clock that the phone rang.

'You two stay at the table and finish your meal,' I said to Adrian and Paula as I stood. 'And keep an eye on Harrison for me, please.'

I went into the sitting room and picked up the handset.

'Sorry I didn't phone sooner,' Jill said. 'I've been waiting for Cheryl to get back to me.' Jill paused and took a deep breath, as though she had a lot to tell me and was slightly stressed. 'Rihanna's solicitor has finally managed to speak to Rihanna,' Jill began. 'It *was* Rihanna who was outside your house. And not just the few times you've seen her; she's been there at other times as well – over a number of weeks. I don't know how many exactly, but it was certainly her.'

'She admitted it?' I asked, immediately concerned.

'Yes. However, Rihanna has told her solicitor that she promises she won't do it again. She just wanted a glimpse of Harrison to make sure he was being well looked after. She asked her solicitor to tell you that she was sorry she scared you this morning. She hopes you understand she didn't mean any harm but it's been difficult for her. She thought that seeing Harrison and the people who were looking after him might help her. Cheryl did remind her solicitor that Rihanna could have contact with Harrison until he's adopted but Rihanna is still saying she couldn't cope. She also asked her solicitor to thank you for looking after Harrison, and for dressing him in the clothes she bought. She said it means a lot to her.'

'Oh, Jill!' I exclaimed, a lump rising in my throat. 'This is so upsetting. Why ever is Rihanna having to give up her son? She seems a lovely person and obviously cares a lot for Harrison. I just don't understand it.'

'Neither do I,' Jill said. 'You have all the information I have. I'm not holding anything back.'

'I know you're not,' I said with a sigh.

'I'm afraid we just have to accept what we're told, and I hope that once the adoption is finalized Rihanna will be able to move on with her life. Cheryl suggested again to Rihanna's solicitor that it might help Rihanna if she had some photographs of Harrison and Rihanna has now agreed to this.'

'Good,' I said.

'Cathy, I know you've got to give Viera some photos for the adoption profile, but have you a few more you could give to Cheryl at the review tomorrow so she can pass them on?'

'Yes, I've got plenty. I'll sort out some ready.'

'Thanks. Well, at least we have an explanation for the woman in the street, and hopefully that will be the end of it.'

'Yes,' I said, subdued.

That evening while the house was quiet and the children slept I sat on the sofa, surrounded by all the photographs I'd taken of Harrison, and tried to decide which ones to give to Cheryl to pass to his mother. It was proving very difficult, as Harrison looked lovely in all of them and there were over thirty photographs. The pictures showed Harrison in his pram, bouncing cradle and cot (the cuddly toys Rihanna had packed for him visible at the foot of the cot), at home, in the garden, in the park, on the beach, on my lap, on the sofa – in fact I'd captured Harrison on camera everywhere he'd been. The photos also showed him awake, asleep, laughing, waving his arms, wrinkling his nose, having his bottle; and always dressed smartly in the clothes his mother had sent. As well as being for myself to keep and for Harrison's Life Story book, so that he and his adoptive family would be able to share the first year of his life when they hadn't been together, the pictures would now also give Harrison's mother a window into Harrison's first year. And they would probably be the only photographs she would have of him for very rarely do adoptive parents send photographs of the child to the natural mother.

I continued to look through the photographs and, still unable to decide which ones to select for Rihanna, I decided to send the whole set. I'd already taken out some for Viera for the adoption profile and I could have another set printed for me and to go in his Life Story book. Yet as I tucked the photographs into the envelope ready to give to Cheryl at the review meeting I wondered how Rihanna would feel when she saw the pictures of Harrison. Would it really help her to come to terms with losing her baby, as Cheryl had said? Or would looking at pictures of her darling little boy keep the wound open for longer? I tried to imagine how I would feel in her position but the thought of having to give up Adrian or Paula and rely on photographs was beyond my comprehension.

Chapter Seventeen

Information Sharing

The following morning I prepared for the LAC review, which was to be held in my house. After I'd cleared away the breakfast dishes and cleaned and tidied the kitchen, I vacuumed and tidied the rest of the downstairs of the house; gave the toilet an extra clean; took my fostering folder and pen from the front room into the sitting room; laid out activities for Adrian and Paula to do at the kitchen table; filled the kettle; arranged biscuits on a plate; gave Harrison his bottle; and then settled him in his bouncing cradle in the sitting room. I was now ready.

Jill arrived first at 10.50 and was in very good spirits. 'Hi! How's my favourite foster carer?' she said, greeting me with a big smile at the door.

'Very good,' I said, aware that Jill called all her foster carers 'my favourite'. 'Come in. You look happy.'

'I am. I've just been promoted. I'm a senior practitioner now.'

'Well done,' I said. 'Congratulations. You deserve it.' Jill was an excellent support social worker who did far more than her contract required.

'Thanks, Cathy. I'm pleased.'

Jill knew the layout of my house (from all her previous visits) and she also knew that if there was a meeting scheduled and the children were not at school then they would be settled at the kitchen table with plenty of activities. She went down the hall and into the kitchen. 'Hi, kids!' she said, entering. 'How are you? Enjoying the school holidays?'

'Yep!' Adrian said.

'I like school,' Paula said, 'but I like being home better.'

'That's how it should be,' Jill said, and I agreed.

'Coffee?' I asked Jill.

'Please. Where's the little fellow?'

'Waiting for you in the sitting room,' I said.

Jill immediately disappeared and a moment later we heard weird and wonderful baby-talk noises coming from the sitting room: 'Coochicoo. Who's Jill's cutikams? Who's a clever little smookams? Harry's not ready for sleepbize yet, are you?' The last of which we understood. Adrian sniggered and Paula laughed out loud.

I took Jill's coffee and a plate of biscuits into the sitting room, where Jill was kneeling in front of Harrison in his bouncing cradle, ticking his little feet through his socks, while baby-talking to him. Harrison was enjoying the attention and when Jill stopped to take a sip of her coffee he looked as though he was going to cry.

The doorbell rang, so leaving Jill entertaining Harrison I went to answer it. Cheryl was with a man I hadn't met before. 'I'm Tom Gray, the reviewing officer,' he said, offering his hand for shaking. The independent chairperson is also known as the reviewing officer at a LAC review.

I showed Cheryl and Tom through to the sitting room and offered them coffee, which they both accepted. Leaving Tom Gray introducing himself to Jill, I went into the kitchen and made coffee for them and for me. I also poured a glass of juice each for Adrian and Paula, which I placed on the table at which they were working, together with the biscuit tin. 'No more than two biscuits each,' I reminded them. Then added: 'I'm going to close the sitting-room door but if you need me call or knock on the door.' Adrian and Paula knew the importance of the meetings we had at home and they knew they weren't to interrupt unless it was urgent.

In the sitting room Tom and Cheryl were seated on the sofa. I passed them their coffees and then offered the sugar, which they both refused.

'Are we expecting anyone else?' Tom asked, taking a sip of his coffee and then opening a large black notebook on his lap.

'No,' Cheryl said. 'Viera from the adoption team sends her apologies. She's on annual leave so I will give her report. The health visitor was invited but she's on holiday too. Cathy will be able to update us on Harrison's health and development.'

Tom made a note of the apologies for absence, and Jill finally rose from the floor and sat on the chair nearest to Harrison's bouncing cradle where she tucked her foot under the rim so that she could still rock him. I sat in the remaining chair.

'And Mother?' Tom asked, glancing sideways at Cheryl. 'Is Harrison's mother coming?'

'No,' Cheryl said. 'An invitation was sent to her through her solicitor but Rihanna won't be coming.'

The reviewing officer made a note of this and then opened the meeting with introductions, and said this was the first review for Harrison Smith. I was wondering what Cheryl would say about Harrison's background when she was asked to give her report, for the first LAC review would normally cover the reasons the child had been brought into care. Following the format of the previous reviews I'd attended, I, as the child's foster carer, was asked to speak first, and I gave an update on Harrison, very similar to the one I'd given at the planning meeting the week before, covering his arrival from hospital, routine, health and development. This took about ten minutes and I then handed the red book to Tom so that he could verify what

I'd said and make a note of Harrison's weight. Tom then asked Jill to give her report and she stated her title and role – support social worker to me – and then confirmed what I'd said about Harrison's health and development, and that he was doing well. Tom thanked her and then looked at Cheryl.

'Would you like to give your report and then the report from the adoption team?' he said.

'Yes,' Cheryl began, and I listened hard. She also had Jill's complete attention too. 'Harrison is in care under a Section 20. His mother, Rihanna, is single and cannot look after him. She made the decision to place her baby for adoption early on in her pregnancy, and she has been working with the department to allow us to facilitate this. We have her complete cooperation, although since the birth of Harrison all communication has been through her solicitor.'

'Why is all communication through her solicitor?' Tom asked, glancing up from writing. The reviewing officer is independent of the social services and relies on the social services for his information.

'It's at the mother's request,' Cheryl said.

Tom nodded and wrote as Cheryl continued: 'Although I haven't seen Rihanna since just before the birth, our legal department is in contact with her solicitor. I spoke to the solicitor personally yesterday – on another matter – and Rihanna is happy with the way the department is handling her case, and the progress we are making in finding a suitable adoptive family for Harrison.'

'I can't imagine the mother is "happy" at giving up her child,' Tom said dryly without looking up from writing. 'Perhaps "satisfied" with the department's progress would be a better word.'

'Yes,' Cheryl agreed quickly, slightly embarrassed by the reviewing officer's criticism.

'We'll hear about the progress of the adoption in a minute,' Tom said. 'I need to know more about the mother first. How old is she?'

I saw Cheryl hesitate before answering. 'Thirty-five,' Cheryl said. Which was new information for Jill and me and I caught Jill's gaze.

'So she's not a teenage mother, then?' Tom said to Cheryl, having assumed as I had initially that this was the most likely reason.

'No,' Cheryl replied.

'And is Rihanna having contact with the child?' Tom now asked.

'No,' Cheryl said again.

'Has she had any contact at all?'

'No,' Cheryl said. 'At her request. The department offered contact but Rihanna has refused. She feels it would be too upsetting to see her son knowing he is to be adopted.'

'But she has seen him from this street,' Jill put in.

The reviewing officer looked at Cheryl for explanation. Cheryl briefly explained that I had seen Rihanna in the road outside my house, when she'd been hoping to catch a glimpse of Harrison, and that she had now promised – through her solicitor – she wouldn't do it again.

'And Rihanna is still definite she doesn't want contact with her child?' Tom asked Cheryl.

'Yes,' Cheryl said. 'But I've persuaded her to accept some photographs of Harrison, which I think may help.'

'I have them ready,' I said, and I handed Cheryl the two envelopes, which I'd marked: *Adoption profile photos* and *Photos for Mum*.

'Thank you, Cathy,' Cheryl said, and tucked them into her briefcase.

Tom finished the sentence he was writing and glanced sideways again at Cheryl, who was sitting on the sofa beside him.

'And Harrison's father? Grandparents? Other family members? Do they have contact?' Jill and I exchanged a pointed glance.

'No,' Cheryl said. 'There is no contact at all.'

'Has contact been offered to the father?' Tom asked.

'No.'

'Why not?'

Although I was very intrigued by Tom's questions and the answers they were producing I was starting to feel sorry for Cheryl. She was looking increasingly uncomfortable, but part of the reviewing officer's role is to have a clear understanding of the case and be satisfied that everything that can be done is being done for the child, and in the case of a young baby, the mother too.

'It wasn't felt appropriate to offer contact to the father,' Cheryl said a little guardedly.

'Why not?' Tom asked.

'He will never play a part in the child's life.'

'So where is the father?' Tom persisted.

'We don't know exactly,' Cheryl said.

'Does he know he is the father of the child?' Tom now asked, writing as he spoke.

Cheryl hesitated as Jill and I exchanged another glance; then Cheryl replied carefully: 'There has been no indication from the mother to make us think the father knows he has a child, although Harrison has his father's surname.'

'So does a large proportion of the population,' Tom remarked dryly. 'Smith is a very common name.' Cheryl nodded but didn't say anything. 'Is the father's name on the child's birth certificate?' Tom now asked. 'If so he will need to give his permission to free the child for adoption.'

'The department is aware of that,' Cheryl said. 'And we are in the process of obtaining a copy of Harrison's birth certificate.'

Information Sharing

Tom wrote while Jill gave Harrison a little rock in his bouncing cradle and Cheryl shifted uncomfortably on the sofa.

'So why is the mother giving her child up for adoption?' Tom now asked, pausing from writing to look at Cheryl. 'Most single mothers can keep their children in this country. We have a benefit system.' It was a direct question and Tom was clearly looking for an equally direct answer.

Jill and I looked at each other as Cheryl concentrated on the notepad on her lap as she spoke. 'Rihanna approached the social services when she was five months pregnant, and asked us to find an adoptive home for her child when it was born. Since then she has been working with the department to—'

'Yes, I understand that,' Tom cut in. 'But my question is, why? Why is the mother giving up her child? What is the reason?' I was holding my breath now, waiting for the reply, and I think Jill was too, for this was the question I'd asked myself time and time again: why was Rihanna having to give up her child when she clearly cared so much about him? Even little Harrison was quiet, seeming to sense the enormity of the moment.

Cheryl turned slightly on the sofa to meet Tom's gaze, and when she spoke her voice was even and controlled. 'There are highly sensitive and confidential issues surrounding this case,' she said. 'They cannot form part of this review. I think you will need to meet my manager to discuss the background details further.'

'And that meeting can take place straight after this meeting?' Tom said, clearly irritated by the lack of information.

'I will need to phone my manager to find out if she is free,' Cheryl said, reaching into her briefcase for her phone.

'Not now,' Tom said sharply. 'We'll finish this meeting first and then you can phone your manager. I'm sure Jill and Cathy have other things to do. And in future if there are confidentiality issues surrounding a case that stop information that should have been included in the review from being included, then I need to be told beforehand. Is that clear?' Cheryl nodded. 'I can't come to a review not properly prepared and then be expected to write my report.'

'I'm sorry,' Cheryl said, flustered. 'I didn't realize. I don't think my manager thought of this either – otherwise she would have raised it with me.'

'No, well,' Tom said, more conciliatorily. 'This degree of confidentiality is unusual but not unheard of.'

There was silence as Tom wrote.

Then Cheryl asked quietly, 'Shall I give Viera's report now on the progress of the adoption?'

'Yes please,' Tom said.

Slightly relieved that she was no longer under scrutiny Cheryl took a typed sheet of paper from her briefcase and began to read Viera's report, which essentially covered all the information Viera had given at the adoption meeting the week before. Tom made notes as Cheryl spoke and because Viera's report was straightforward – there were no ambiguities – Tom didn't need to interrupt to clarify any points, so Cheryl continued uninterrupted to the end, when Tom thanked her and finished writing.

'There is good progress in finding a suitable adoptive family, then,' Tom confirmed, and Cheryl nodded. 'Does anyone want to add anything to Harrison's review?' Tom now asked, glancing at Jill, Cheryl and me.

Jill and Cheryl shook their heads. 'Only that Harrison is a lovely child and doing very well,' I said.

'Thank you,' Tom said. He then closed the meeting by thanking us all for attending. 'And thank you for the coffee,' he said to me. 'It was most welcome.'

He and Cheryl stood and made their way down the hall and towards the door, calling goodbye to Jill as they left. I went with them to see them out. They went down the front path, talking quietly, with Cheryl taking her phone from her bag, presumably to speak to her manager and arrange the meeting with Tom. I closed the front door and returned to the sitting room, where Jill was trying to pacify Harrison, who'd finally had enough of sitting in the bouncing cradle. I lifted him out and kissed his nose. 'You were such a good boy this morning,' I said, and Jill agreed.

'Wouldn't we like to be flies on the wall at their meeting?' Jill said to me, meaning wouldn't we like to know what Cheryl's manager would be telling Tom.

'I'm not so sure,' I said. 'It's all a bit scary, and sad, for whatever the background information is has resulted in Rihanna loosing her child. I'd probably rather not know.'

'You may be right,' Jill said, standing ready to leave. 'And very likely we'll never know. Anyway, I need to be going. I've got another meeting this afternoon.'

Having tickled Harrison under his chin Jill went into the kitchen and said goodbye to Adrian and Paula; then with Harrison in my arms I went with her to the front door, where I saw her out. I returned to Adrian and Paula, who were still at the kitchen table.

'Can we stop painting now?' Paula asked, making it sound like a penance.

'Yes, of course,' I smiled. 'Thanks for keeping yourselves amused. You were both very good.'

'What's for lunch?' Adrian asked.

I didn't know; my thoughts had been preoccupied with the meeting. 'Shall we take a picnic to the park?' I suggested. The children immediately began packing away the paints. 'I'll change and feed Harrison while you clear up the table,' I said. 'Then we'll make some sandwiches for our picnic.'

I went upstairs, changed Harrison's nappy and then came down and gave him his bottle. By the time he'd finished it he was asleep – exhausted, I suspected, from being subjected to all the adult chatter at the meeting. I knew how he felt! I settled him in his pram and then went through to the kitchen, where Adrian and Paula had finished clearing up. Taking the picnic hamper from the cupboard under the stairs, Adrian and Paula then helped me to make sandwiches and put together a picnic from whatever was in the cupboard.

Half an hour later we were in our local park, sitting on a blanket under the shade of the tree and enjoying our picnic. I wondered what Cheryl's manager was now telling Tom, which thankfully wasn't my concern and need never be. As a foster carer my role was to care and nurture Harrison until a suitable adoptive family was found, when my involvement would come to an end. Later I realized just how naïve these thoughts had been.

Chapter Eighteen
Staying Safe

August and the long vacation from school flew by, with days out, time at home and in the garden, a weekly visit to the clinic to have Harrison weighed; and then suddenly we were buying Adrian's and Paula's new school uniforms, ready for the start of the autumn term. Rihanna kept her promise and we didn't see her in the street again. I heard nothing further from Cheryl or Jill, who were both away on holiday until the beginning of September, although I knew I could phone Homefinders or the social services and speak to one of their colleagues if I needed help or advice while they were away.

Harrison continued to grow and flourish and was much loved, not only by Adrian, Paula and me but also by my parents, and my brother and his wife, who were trying to start a family. All too soon it was 4 September and the first day of the new school term. That day stands out in my memory for three reasons: it was the first day of the new term and we were struggling to get back into the school routine; Harrison was due to have his first vaccination that afternoon; and when I returned home from taking the children to school Cheryl phoned and asked me if I would meet Harrison's mother.

It was mid-morning and I was already feeling apprehensive, because I had to take Harrison to be vaccinated. Jill was still on holiday and wasn't due to return to the office until the following day, so Cheryl phoned me directly instead of discussing the matter with Jill first. Cheryl began by asking how we all were and then said: 'I've just had a request from Rihanna's solicitor, asking if you would be willing to meet Rihanna before the adoption is finalized. Rihanna feels meeting you in person would help her.'

'What, just her and me?' I asked, very surprised.

'No. Jill and I would be present. It would be here at the council offices.'

'I see,' I said slowly, not fully understanding what was being asked of me. 'She wants to see Harrison?'

'Oh no,' Cheryl said, as though I should have realized. 'Rihanna would find that far too upsetting. She just wants to meet you and hear first hand how Harrison is doing and maybe ask you some questions. She knows that once the adoption goes through there won't be this opportunity.'

'I see,' I said.

'The meeting would reassure Rihanna,' Cheryl said. 'It would be no longer than an hour, and I'm sure Jill will be able to arrange for someone to babysit Harrison.'

'Yes, I am sure she will,' I said apprehensively. But that wasn't the reason I was reluctant. I could already picture how upsetting it would be to sit in a room with Rihanna and tell her about Harrison, both of us aware that very soon he would be with his adoptive parents and someone else's son forever. But I also knew I couldn't refuse Rihanna's request – not professionally or personally. I couldn't deny her this opportunity to hear about Harrison first hand if it would help her adjust to losing him and allow her to move on with her life.

'All right,' I said.

'Thank you, Cathy. I'll speak to Jill as soon as she returns to the office and arrange the meeting.' Cheryl thanked me again; we said goodbye and she hung up.

Staying Safe

I stood for moment, deep in thought, with the phone still in my hand, as the line went dead and then buzzed with the disconnected tone. I hoped Rihanna was being honest when she'd told her solicitor she wanted to meet me simply to hear how Harrison was doing; I hoped there wasn't an ulterior motive – possibly to criticize me, threaten me or even (if she was unstable through grief) attack me. With so little background information all this seemed possible, apart from the upset from such an emotionally charged meeting.

I slowly replaced the handset and then went to tend to Harrison, my worries about meeting his mother temporarily overtaken by my worries about the injection he would shortly be receiving. Having a needle stuck in your arm as an adult is uncomfortable (if not painful), but an adult is able to appreciate the benefits gained from a vaccination and a baby can't. As far as Harrison was concerned he would be hurt and I was responsible for allowing it to happen. I could still remember the look of accusation on the faces of Adrian and Paula as they'd sat on my lap and I'd held their arms for the injection, and their smiles had crumpled into pain. Now I was about to do the same to Harrison.

'Sorry, Harry,' I said as I gave him his bottle before we left. 'The vaccination is for your own good.' But he didn't look convinced.

I dressed him in the zip-up suit his mother had sent to go to the doctor. Now he was bigger I was using the stroller rather than the pram, so he didn't have the all-round protection from the wind the pram offered, and although it was a clear day the air was starting to freshen, suggesting autumn wasn't far away. Harrison preferred the stroller to the pram, as he was able to see where he was going, and be seen. Alert and engaging, he attracted the attention of those we passed in the street and I lost count of the number of passers-by who paused to make a fuss of him whenever we were out. But while Harrison was busy watching everything and everyone around him as I pushed him up the road and towards the doctor's surgery, my thoughts returned to his mother. While part of me said Rihanna's request to meet me was simply as it appeared – to reassure her and help her come to terms with losing Harrison – another part of me said that given the secrecy surrounding this case, I had every right to be concerned. I was pleased Jill was returning to the office the following day, for when it came to fostering matters Jill was always the voice of reason and good sense. I knew she wouldn't allow me to go into a situation she thought might be dangerous.

As predicted Harrison cried when the nurse gave him the injection and glared at me accusingly. I felt awful for allowing him to be hurt, but as with Adrian and Paula, his upset was short-lived and a hug and kiss soon put him right. Later, when I collected Adrian and Paula from school and told them Harrison had had his first injection, they sympathized and made a fuss of him, for they'd both recently had booster injections and could empathize with him.

Harrison was restless that night, possibly as a result of the injection, and I didn't sleep well either. In between settling him, making him a bottle and myself a cup of tea, then trying to go back to sleep, my thoughts kept returning to Rihanna and the meeting Cheryl was going to arrange. With little sleep I didn't hear the alarm go off the following morning and I then had to rush to get the children to school on time. Having begun the day disorganized the rest of the day seemed to follow suit and nothing went as it should. However, it seemed I wasn't the only one who wasn't having the best of days, for when Jill phoned it was after 5.50 p.m. and she didn't sound at all relaxed after her holiday.

'Cathy, it's Jill,' she said, as soon as she heard my voice, and then continued before I had a chance to ask her if she'd had a nice time. 'I've just been on the phone to Cheryl. I've told her we will attend the meeting with Rihanna but it is to be kept to one hour, the content regulated and minuted by Cheryl and me, and that Cheryl must arrange for a security guard to be posted outside the meeting room. If the social services are not prepared to share information with us, I am not prepared to allow one of my foster carers to go into a situation that could put her at risk. I am not being unreasonable – I discussed it with my manager first – and Cheryl has agreed to my requests.'

Dear Jill, I knew she would know what to do. 'Thank you so much,' I said. 'I have been worried.'

'You had every right to be. There are too many unknowns here. And goodness knows why Cheryl phoned you yesterday instead of waiting until I returned and discussing it with me first. Are you all right about attending the meeting with these safeguards in place?'

'Yes, I feel much better about it now.' I was very grateful that Jill wasn't afraid to challenge the social services and make stipulations where necessary.

'OK,' she said with a small sigh. 'I'll get back to Cheryl tomorrow and confirm; it's too late now – she'll have gone home. Rihanna doesn't want Harrison at the meeting, which I suppose is understandable, so I'll find a carer to look after him for the time you are there.'

'Thank you,' I said again, and I finally got the chance to ask her if she'd had a nice holiday.

'I think so,' she said. 'It seems a long time ago now. I'll need another one to get over the day I've had!'

* * *

Now we were back in the school routine the week disappeared. On Wednesday I took Harrison to the clinic to be weighed; on Thursday I attended a foster carer support group where, over a cup of coffee, I met other carers, which gave us a chance to socialize as well as discuss any fostering difficulties we might be experiencing. Ava, Ellie's carer, was there and she said Ellie was well, although still disclosing more abuse. I was relieved Ava didn't tell me exactly what Ellie had disclosed and I asked Ava to give Ellie my love. Then it was Friday and the end of the week. Jill phoned on Friday afternoon and said she was still waiting to hear from Cheryl about a date for the meeting with Rihanna, but in the meantime she (Jill) needed to arrange to visit me. This was one of the routine four-weekly supervisory meetings that all foster carers have with their support social worker (who can also be known as a supervising social worker or link worker).

Supervisory meetings are semi-formal and take place at the foster carer's home, and are in addition to any other meetings or telephone conversations the carer might have with her support social worker (Jill in my case). During the meeting the support social worker checks the carer's records, discusses any difficulties he or she may be experiencing and generally monitors the foster carer to ensure he or she is doing everything as it should be done for the good of the child.

Jill and I set the date for her visit for the following Thursday, by which time Jill said she hoped to have the date for the meeting with Rihanna. It seemed to me that the urgency of the meeting with Rihanna had diminished somewhat and I wondered if Rihanna had had second thoughts, perhaps deciding it wouldn't help her to meet me, which I could understand, for I did wonder what she would really gain from it.

However, when Jill arrived the following Thursday she was holding a piece of paper on which were scribbled two dates.

'Cheryl's just left a message on my mobile,' Jill said, coming in. 'Rihanna has suggested the second or fourth of October to meet. Cheryl can do either of these dates, and so can I.'

As Jill went into the sitting room, where Harrison was in the bouncing cradle, I fetched my diary and, opening it, found I too had both these dates free.

'Let's make it the second of October, then,' Jill said, grinning and making faces at Harrison. 'Cheryl suggested eleven o'clock. Is that all right with you?'

'Yes, fine.' I noted the meeting in my diary.

'I'll arrange for your sitter to arrive just after ten o'clock so that you have plenty of time to show her where everything is and then drive to the council offices.'

'Thank you, Jill,' I said, adding a note in my diary of the time the sitter would arrive. 'Coffee?'

'Yes please.'

While Jill baby-talked and fussed over Harrison I went into the kitchen and made coffee for us both. Returning to the sitting room I placed the coffee on the table within our reach and we sat on the sofa. Jill took the supervisory forms from her bag and began filling in the top sheet with my name, the date of the meeting, and the name and age of the child I was fostering. Then, as we drank our coffee Jill made notes from the update I gave her on Harrison's progress and development since her last supervisory visit, including his weight gain and his first vaccination, both of which I showed her recorded in the red book. Jill then checked and signed my log notes; she also asked me if there were any changes to my household, which she knew there weren't but was still obliged to ask. As there was nothing else to discuss Jill thanked me and tucked the supervisory forms in her bag. When she returned to the office she would type up her notes and print two copies, which we would both sign; one copy would go on the agency's files and the other was

A Baby's Cry

for me to keep. Jill finished by saying she would phone with the details of the carer who would babysit Harrison when it was confirmed; then, coochicooing a goodbye to Harrison, she told me not to worry about meeting Rihanna, and left to go to another carer.

Although I was reassured by the safeguards Jill had put in place for my meeting with Rihanna, which was now less than two weeks away, I was still concerned. As a foster carer I'd had a lot of experience meeting parents of the child or children I was fostering and it was never easy. Sometimes the parents were very angry that their child or children had been taken into care; sometimes they were upset and cried, and in the case of Michael's father who had been terminally ill when I'd met him, it had been me who'd cried. But until now I'd never met a mother who had been separated from her child at birth and had no hope of being reunited with him or ever seeing him again. I tried not to think about the meeting but it kept creeping into my thoughts, and I'd suddenly catch myself trying to imagine what Rihanna would be like in person: her tone of voice, her mannerisms, what she would say, the questions she would ask and of course how she would react to me. I was still taking lots of photographs of Harrison and I wondered if I should take some of the recent photographs with me to give to Rihanna at the meeting. Babies grow so quickly and the ones I'd previously sent to her via Cheryl were already old. Would Rihanna appreciate up-to-date photographs of her son or would they be too upsetting for her? I didn't know. I couldn't decide what to do for the best, so when Jill next phoned – with details of the carer, Chris, who would be babysitting Harrison – I asked her for advice.

'Take some of the photographs with you,' she said. 'Keep them in your bag, and then we can decide at the meeting if it's appropriate to give them to Rihanna.'

Simple really, but so often when we are in the middle of a situation and emotionally involved in it, logic and common sense disappear.

That evening I telephoned Chris to thank her for agreeing to babysit Harrison and also to check she knew where I lived, which she did. On Sunday Adrian and Paula spent the day out with their father and all too soon it was the evening of 1 October, and the eve of my meeting with Rihanna. Before I went to bed that night I placed the photographs I was taking with me in an envelope and put it in my handbag; then upstairs in my bedroom I laid out the clothes I had chosen to wear – a smart skirt and blouse. In the morning when I returned from taking Adrian and Paula to school I wouldn't have much time and I needed to be ready for when Chris arrived to babysit Harrison at ten o'clock.

I gave Harrison his late-night feed and he was soon sleeping peacefully in his cot. He was three months old and had just started sleeping through the night, not waking for another feed until five o'clock. Soon I would move him into his own room, as I had done with Adrian and Paula when they'd started sleeping through the night. Before I got into bed I stood by his cot and gazed down at him. The faint glow from the street lamp meant that my room was never completely dark. I could see Harrison's little face completely relaxed in sleep and his mouth slightly open. I could hear the faintest whisper of his light breathing, and one of his little hands lay characteristically against his chin as though he was deep in thought. I wondered what Rihanna was thinking and doing now – on the eve of meeting me. Was she nervous, upset, trying to imagine what I would say or do? Or had she resigned herself to letting go of Harrison and moving on with her life? I'd no idea.

Chapter Nineteen
A Right to Cry

'Have I explained everything?' I asked Chris, the babysitter, the following morning as we stood in the kitchen and I looked anxiously around.

'Yes, I'm sure you have,' Chris reassured me. 'Harrison's feeds are made up and are in the fridge. All I need for changing him is upstairs in the spare bedroom. He is likely to wake at eleven o'clock for a feed and then he's quite often up for the rest of the morning, so we'll play.'

I smiled. 'Thanks. I'll leave my mobile on silent, so if you need me, call.'

'All right, but I'm sure we will be fine. I've had lots of experience looking after babies and young children.'

'I know you have,' I said. 'I'm sorry. It's just that this is the first time I've left Harrison with anyone.'

Chris smiled kindly. 'I'm exactly the same with my babies, but please don't worry. Now off you go – you don't want to be late.'

It was now 10.25 and it was just as well Jill had arranged for Chris to arrive early, as it had taken me over twenty minutes to show her where everything she might need was kept and talk her through Harrison's routine, although that was probably due to my fussing. Chris came with me down the hall to see me out and as we passed the pram I checked on Harrison one last time.

He'd been awake when Chris had first arrived and now he was having his morning nap.

'Bye, little fellow,' I said quietly. 'Be good.' Then to Chris: 'I should be back by twelve-thirty.'

'OK, but don't worry it your meeting overruns. I've nothing planned for this afternoon.'

Thanking Chris again, I came out and she closed the door quietly behind me so as not to disturb Harrison. I unlocked my car, climbed in and reversed off the driveway; then I headed for the council offices. I now realized I should have had something to eat before I left. I'd had very little breakfast and my stomach was churning – partly from hunger but also, I suspected, from nerves. My thoughts went again to Rihanna and I wondered how she was feeling as she too approached our meeting.

I arrived at the council offices at 10.50, parked the car and entered reception, where I'd arranged to meet Jill. She was already there and looking out for me. Seeing me she immediately came over.

'All right?' she asked, touching my arm reassuringly.

'Yes, I think so.'

'Good. I've just seen Cheryl and Rihanna go up. We're in Room 3 on the first floor.'

I felt my stomach churn again as we crossed reception and made our way up the stone steps. As we went up Jill tried to make light conversation, asking me how Adrian, Paula and Harrison were, did we have a nice weekend, wasn't the weather good; and had I remembered to bring the photographs? But my thoughts were elsewhere and I answered all her well-meaning questions with 'Yes, fine, thank you.' Or just 'Yes.'

We arrived on the landing and turned left into the corridor where the meeting rooms were and my anxiety soared; my mouth went dry and my heart began thumping loudly in my chest. The door to Room 3 was closed and Jill gave a brief knock, threw me a reassuring smile and, turning the door handle, pushed the door open. I took a deep breath and followed her in. My gaze went immediately to the right of the room where, away from the main conference table, there was an informal circle of four chairs. Cheryl and Rihanna were sitting in two of the chairs, next to each other, and looked up as we entered. I closed the door and followed Jill across the room. Rihanna stood to shake our hands.

'Hello, Rihanna. Pleased to meet you,' Jill said, shaking her hand first. 'I'm Jill, Cathy's support social worker.'

'Hello, Jill,' Rihanna said softly, with a small fragile smile.

Lowering Jill's hand Rihanna turned to me and as our eyes met I saw Harrison – so strong was the likeness.

'I'm very pleased to meet you,' I said, taking Rihanna's hand.

'And you, Cathy,' she said quietly. 'Thank you so much for coming. It was very kind of you.'

I felt her hand warm in mine. A little taller than me, she was dressed in a pale blue summer suit, and was slim despite her recent pregnancy. My immediate impression was how elegant and gentle she appeared and also how very sad. Her black hair was cut neatly to chin length, as it had been when I'd seen her outside my house; she wore no make-up but her light brown skin and large eyes had a beauty of their own. Outwardly composed, she thanked me again for coming before she finally dropped my hand.

The four of us sat in the small circle of chairs; I was opposite Rihanna and Jill and Cheryl were either side of us. Now I was in the room and had met Rihanna I was starting to feel less anxious. Jill and Cheryl were taking notepads from their bags and opening them on their laps. Rihanna stole a glance at me and I smiled reassuringly; she returned a small sad smile before looking away.

'OK,' Cheryl said, straightening in her chair. 'I'll open this meeting by thanking everyone for coming. I am sure we will find it very helpful. Although this meeting is informal, Jill and I will be taking a few notes. I wasn't going to produce minutes unless anyone present requests them.' She looked up and then around at each of us.

Rihanna shook her head and I did likewise. 'My agency will be satisfied with my notes,' Jill confirmed.

'Good. That's one less piece of paperwork,' Cheryl said, trying to lighten the mood. Rihanna briefly smiled again but it was a smile of politeness and I could see the tension beneath.

I'd no idea what to expect now in respect of the format the meeting would take, as I'd never attended a meeting like this before, but I guessed that as Rihanna had come here to learn about Harrison, I'd be asked to speak first and tell her about him. I was nearly right.

'As you asked for this meeting,' Cheryl said, looking at Rihanna, 'perhaps you would like to tell us what would be most beneficial for you? I would suggest we hear from Cathy first and then you ask her any questions you have.'

Rihanna met my gaze and said quietly, almost timidly: 'I just want you to tell me about Harrison, please.'

'Yes, of course,' I said.

'Jill and I will be writing,' Cheryl said to me, 'but don't let that put you off.'

I nodded, and then looked at Rihanna. 'Shall I start with Harrison's routine?' I asked. 'From when he wakes in the morning?'

I saw Rihanna hesitate and then she said quietly. 'Could you go back and tell me about when you collected him from the hospital, please? I'd like to hear that. I should have stayed to meet you. I was sorry I didn't, but at the time I couldn't face it. I was so upset.'

'Yes,' I said, touched she wanted this detail. 'I'll have to think back and remember. Stop me if you have any questions.' And I wondered what I could possibly have been afraid of in meeting this gentle, quietly spoken woman who wanted nothing more than to hear about her son.

'I was told I should collect Harrison at one o'clock,' I began, looking at Rihanna as I spoke. 'I made sure I was prepared. I had the carry car seat to take Harrison home in ready and also a bag with a bottle of milk in case he needed feeding. If I'm honest I was quite nervous driving to the hospital because I thought you and Harrison's father might be there. I wasn't sure how you would react to me or what I could say to you. When I arrived on the ward and found you weren't there I was relieved but also a little disappointed; I would have liked to have met you too.' A small flash of gratitude crossed Rihanna's face in acknowledgement that we'd both had similar feelings about meeting.

'I went to the end of the ward,' I continued, 'where Harrison's crib was, and when I saw him my heart melted. He was such a cute baby – he still is. The nurses were making a fuss of him. He looked gorgeous in the little white hat and shawl you wrapped him in. He was asleep but he had one little hand pressed to his chin. He still does that when he's in a deep sleep as though he's thinking hard.'

'Yes,' Rihanna said softly. 'One of the photographs you sent me shows him doing that. I have that photo and some others propped up by my bed.' I saw her eyes mist, and my heart went out to her.

'The nurse told me you'd fed and changed Harrison before you left,' I said, continuing. 'So I knew he wouldn't need feeding again until we were home. I remember I was reluctant to pick him up to begin with, as he seemed so small and fragile. But I carefully lifted him into the baby seat and he didn't wake.

I noticed he was wearing a blue sleepsuit very similar to the one I'd bought. I haven't used any of those I bought as I always make sure he's dressed in the clothes you sent.'

'Thank you, Cathy,' Rihanna said quietly. 'That means a lot to me.' Jill and Cheryl nodded as they wrote.

I hoped I wasn't giving Rihanna too much detail but I was trying to give her a clear picture of her son, which is what I thought she wanted, so I continued with my recollections of that day. 'I left the hospital and then spent a long time in the car park making sure the car straps were fastened and Harrison's car seat was secure. I still do that now – double check his harness and seatbelt very carefully. Harrison slept all the way home and then once we arrived he woke and I gave him a bottle and changed him. We very quickly fell into a routine which has largely continued today,' I said. Then I talked about Harrison's average day – beginning with his five o'clock bottle and finishing with his late-night feed. 'Harrison sleeps well,' I said. 'But when he's awake he is very alert, and interested in all that is going on around him. He is a bright baby and I know he is going to be very intelligent when he grows up. He gurgles a lot as though he's trying to talk, and also has a funny little habit of wrinkling up his nose, which is so cute.'

'Does he?' Rihanna asked suddenly, interrupting me. 'My father does that – wrinkles his nose. It's a family trait. I've been told my grandfather did it too.'

I paused, wondering if Rihanna was going to say any more about this inherited characteristic, which had obviously taken her by surprise and touched her, but she didn't, so after a moment I continued.

'I have Harrison weighed and checked every week at the clinic and I update Jill and Cheryl on his progress. I understand Cheryl passes that information on to your solicitor, who tells you.'

Rihanna nodded.

'I've given Rihanna an update today,' Cheryl added.

I now wanted to reassure Rihanna that as well as looking after Harrison's physical needs – feeding, changing and bathing him, etc. – we were also looking after his emotional needs, and indeed we were very attached to him. I thought Rihanna would find it reassuring to know Harrison was loved and cherished. 'Harrison fitted very easily into my family,' I said. 'He soon became one of our family and we all adore him. My children treat him as their little brother, and my parents, and my brother and his wife, think the world of him. Harrison's adorable and we love him, although we appreciate that at some point he will leave us to go to his forever family.' I saw Rihanna's eyes mist and I realized I'd said too much or the wrong thing.

'I wish you could keep him,' she blurted, her face creasing. 'You would take such good care of him. You would love him as I would have done, I know you would.'

A lump rose in my throat and I didn't know what to say. Jill came to my rescue. 'Sadly, that won't be possible,' she said kindly. 'Cathy is a foster carer and has two children of her own. Her job is to give Harrison the best possible care until he is adopted, and she does that very well.'

'But it's more than a job to Cathy,' Rihanna said. 'I can tell she loves him. I know if you asked her to keep Harrison and adopt him she would.'

I didn't say anything. I looked at Rihanna as her tears fell and I felt my own eyes mist.

'Plans for Harrison's adoption are progressing well,' Cheryl said evenly to Rihanna. 'The adoption team will be finalizing their choice of a family for Harrison shortly and then he will be settled.'

'But I don't know the family,' Rihanna said, desperation in her voice and wiping her hand over her eyes. 'And from what you've told me I am unlikely to know them, or even meet them. I feel I know Cathy and her family, and I know they will love and care for Harrison just as I would have done. I can tell: I can see it in her face, hear it in her voice. She loves Harrison as she loves her own children. Why don't you ask her to adopt him?'

There was silence as Rihanna's words hung in the air; then Cheryl said: 'It is not possible.'

Rihanna delved into her handbag and, taking out a tissue, wiped her eyes and blew her nose. I sniffed and just about managed to stem my own tears. I couldn't look at Rihanna; I couldn't bear to see her pain. Rihanna was right: of course I would have kept Harrison had the social services asked me to. But Harrison was being found a two-parent family to match his cultural identity and I knew I would never be asked to adopt him. There was a list of prospective adopters who were far better-suited than me.

Rihanna was still crying openly while dabbing her eyes and I wondered why no one was comforting her. Reaching across the circle I took her hand. 'Don't cry,' I said. 'Please don't cry. Harrison is doing very well. I know you love him. I love him too, but so will his permanent family. I know he will be well looked after and happy wherever he is. Please try not to upset yourself …' My voice trailed off and I swallowed hard.

Rihanna had one hand in mine and was holding a tissue to her face with the other. I couldn't just sit there and watch her cry; it was not in my nature. Rising from my chair I stood beside her and put my arm around her shoulders. She rested her head against me like a child and continued to cry openly. All that could be heard for some moments was the sound of Rihanna's sobs. Jill looked close to tears herself while Cheryl, not knowing what to say or do, looked embarrassed. I held Rihanna, feeling her pain and sorrow personally, and with no idea why this woman with so much love to give her child could not keep him.

After a few minutes Rihanna's tears began to subside and she slowly lifted her head. 'I'm sorry,' she said, wiping her eyes on the tissue. 'I told myself I wouldn't cry. I am so sorry.'

'There's no need to be sorry,' Jill said kindly. 'You have a right to cry.'

I returned to my chair and sat down, very close to tears myself.

'We can speak further after this meeting,' Cheryl said to Rihanna, finally patting her arm.

'There's no point,' Rihanna said bluntly, without looking at Cheryl. 'You and I both know that.'

There was an awkward silence and I wondered if Rihanna would elaborate and give a clue as to why there was no other path open to her apart from having Harrison adopted, but she didn't.

Presently Cheryl said to Rihanna: 'Is there anything else you'd like to ask Cathy about Harrison while she's here?'

Rihanna looked at me, her eyes now dry but still very, very sad. 'Could you send me a few more photographs, please, before he leaves you? I won't be allowed any once he is adopted.'

'Yes, of course,' I said, and drawing my bag on to my lap, I took out the envelope containing the recent photographs.

'No sooner said than done,' Jill quipped, but no one smiled.

I handed the envelope to Rihanna and watched as she lifted the flap and, taking out the photos, flicked through. 'Thank you so much,' she said gratefully, brightening a little. 'They're lovely. Hasn't he grown! I thought he had when I saw him with you in the street. Oh, and doesn't he look smart in that navy romper suit?'

'Yes,' I said. 'You chose his clothes well. Everyone we meet remarks on how smart he looks. And the cuddly panda and teddy you sent are at the foot of his cot,' I added.

'Thank you,' Rihanna said quietly, and her face clouded again.

'I'll send more photos – for as long as Harrison is with me,' I said.

'And, Rihanna, you'll have the one of you and Harrison together at the goodbye contact,' Cheryl added.

Immediately I knew that was the wrong thing to say; so too did Cheryl and Jill. Rihanna stuffed the photographs back into the envelope and, jumping up, fled from the room in tears.

'That was tactless of me,' Cheryl said. 'But I thought it might help.'

Cheryl had been referring to the photograph that would be taken at what is known as the 'goodbye contact'. This is the last time the parent (or parents) of a child who is being adopted is allowed to see their child.

Jill shook her head sadly. 'I don't think Rihanna will be up to attending a goodbye contact,' she said. Cheryl agreed.

'I know I couldn't,' I said. 'It's the stuff of nightmares: to have to smile for a photograph knowing you are saying goodbye to your child forever.'

Chapter Twenty
An Ideal World

The three of us, Jill, Cheryl and me, stayed where we were – in the meeting room – for a few minutes, to see if Rihanna would return, but she didn't. Jill and Cheryl then put away their notepads and pens and I checked my mobile; there were no missed calls but one reassuring text message from Chris: *Harrison is fine.* I thought it was sweet of her to text. Cheryl then thanked Jill and me for coming and left the room to go to her office, which was in another part of the building. Jill and I also left the room and slowly made our way down the stairs, across reception and into the car park, both of us sombre and subdued.

'At least I was able to give Rihanna the photographs,' I said in the car park, wishing I'd been able to do more.

'Yes,' Jill agreed. 'And you were able to reassure her that Harrison is doing well and is contented, which should ease her worries.'

I shrugged despondently. I could tell that Jill thought as I did – that my meagre reassurance was small recompense for the huge loss and grief Rihanna was feeling.

'Anyway, thanks for arranging Chris to babysit,' I said as we prepared to part.

'You're welcome,' Jill said. 'Take care, and phone me if you need me.'

An Ideal World

'I will.' We went our separate ways, downcast and deep in thought.

The picture of Rihanna – so dignified yet so very upset – stayed with me for the rest of the day, and indeed for most of that week. Sometimes an image is so poignant that it can seal itself into your mind and it is very difficult to shake it off, and so it was with Rihanna: polite, gentle, quietly spoken, grateful, but so desperately unhappy. I was sure I would have liked Rihanna anyway, but as she was the mother of the child I was looking after my affinity and empathy towards her were even stronger. I felt she would have made a wonderful mother – kind, caring and loving – and not knowing why she couldn't keep Harrison made her grief almost impossible for me to come to terms with.

By the end of the week I'd worried myself so much that I telephoned Jill and said: 'Rihanna wouldn't do anything silly and harm herself, would she? I think she's desperate.'

Jill took a more professional and objective approach. 'I'm sure Cheryl is aware of Rihanna's emotional state,' she said. 'And she'll offer appropriate help if and when she feels it is necessary.'

I knew I had to try to let go of my worries for Rihanna and concentrate on Harrison, but it wasn't easy.

By this time Harrison was regularly sleeping through the night, so at the end of the week I moved his cot into his own bedroom as I'd planned. The first two nights he took a while to settle, clearly realizing there'd been a big change in his surroundings, but on the third night he settled more easily and after that he was fine. It was strange for me too, not having Harrison in my bedroom and hearing his little sighs and movements during the night. But like Harrison I adjusted, although I often checked on him during the night, just to make sure he was covered and comfortable.

A Baby's Cry

The same week Harrison had his second vaccination and as before he cried when the needle went in but soon recovered after a cuddle. I continued to have him weighed every week at the clinic and he continued to grow and flourish. I took plenty of photographs – for Harrison's Life Story book, for his adoptive family, for Rihanna and for me to keep. During October the sun lost its warmth and the air began to chill as autumn set in. I put away the light jacket Harrison had been wearing and began using the thicker padded suit Rihanna has sent in the case.

I was stacking the clothes Harrison had outgrown in the bottom of the wardrobe in his bedroom. Usually when a child is in care any clothes the child outgrows that have been bought by their natural family are offered back to the family, as legally the clothes belong to them. However, while I appreciated why this was done it had always seemed cruel to me: to return the child's clothes to the parents but not the child – what an upsetting reminder of the child they had lost! And to return Harrison's first-year clothes to Rihanna, which she'd so lovingly chosen but had never seen him wear, when he would shortly be adopted, was a cruelty I couldn't contemplate. So I continued to stack his outgrown clothes at the bottom of his wardrobe in the hope that they might simply disappear.

In November Harrison had his third vaccination, which completed the first course. The next vaccination wasn't due for another eight months, when he would be one year old and very likely settled with his adoptive family. Harrison's second LAC review was also scheduled for November and, as before, it was held at my house.

It began at eleven o'clock, when Harrison had just woken from his mid-morning nap, and he was very pleased to see everyone. Jill arrived first, then five minutes later Cheryl and Viera (from the adoption team) arrived together, followed by Tom Gray, who was chairing the meeting as he had before.

An Ideal World

I made us all coffee and took it through to the sitting room, where once everyone had finished making a fuss of Harrison, Tom opened the meeting with introductions. He asked me to speak first and I gave an update on Harrison – his progress, development and any significant events since his last review. Tom made notes as I spoke, and I said Harrison was alert, reaching the developmental milestones as he should; was eating and sleeping well; and was now in a room of his own and sleeping through the night. I said that following the health visitor's advice I would be introducing solid food into Harrison's diet soon, and that he had completed the first series of vaccinations in the childhood immunization programme. I then passed Tom the red book and he noted the dates Harrison had had his vaccinations and also his current weight.

Thanking me, Tom then asked Jill if she had anything to add, and she said that as my support social worker she visited regularly and that Harrison was being well looked after.

'Yes, I can see he is,' Tom said, unable to resist a smile at Harrison, who was waving his arms as though trying to attract Tom's attention.

Tom then asked Cheryl for her report and also asked if there had been any contact between Harrison and his mother since the last review. Cheryl said there hadn't, but that Rihanna had received photographs of Harrison and had also – at her request – met me at the beginning of October.

'So you have met Harrison's mother?' Tom said to me. 'How did that meeting go?'

'All right,' I said. 'Although Rihanna was very upset.'

'And she hasn't been in your street again?' he asked me.

'Not as far as I'm aware.'

Tom nodded and made a note, and then Cheryl gave the rest of her report, which was short. As at the previous review her report contained many omissions (due to the high level of confidentiality), but this time Tom didn't question Cheryl or press her for the missing information, so I guessed he'd met Cheryl and her team manager prior to the review and had been updated on any confidential information. I also knew that this information, as before, would not be appearing in the minutes of the LAC review, which were circulated to all those involved in Harrison's case.

Tom thanked Cheryl and then asked Viera to give her report, which was on the progress of the adoption. Viera said she had seen all the couples who had been shortlisted – as being suitable to adopt Harrison – and she had now narrowed the list down to two. She said both couples were excellent matches for Harrison and she hoped to finalize her decision and have her report ready by the end of November.

'So you won't be taking it to the matching panel this month?' Tom queried, aware that that had been Viera's original plan.

'No,' she said. 'We're slightly behind. The panel doesn't meet in December, so I anticipate going to the matching panel in January, and the adoption panel in February. We can then start introducing Harrison to his adoptive family straight after the adoption panel meets. So he should be living with his family by the end of February or beginning of March at the latest.'

Tom made a note and then, glancing from Viera to Cheryl, asked: 'Will you be offering Rihanna a goodbye contact?'

Cheryl answered: 'I have already mentioned it to Rihanna, and the department will make a formal offer – through her solicitor – nearer the time, but we are not expecting Rihanna to attend a goodbye contact. She would find it too upsetting.'

Tom nodded and made another note on his pad. Then, there being no other business, he said: 'The next review is due in six months. But from what Viera has told us Harrison will almost certainly be with his adoptive family by then. I therefore suggest we set a date for the next review and confirm or cancel it nearer the time. Is the second of May all right for everyone?'

Viera, Cheryl and Jill checked in their diaries for next year and confirmed it was, while I made a note of the date on a piece of paper which I tucked into my fostering folder, to transfer to my diary when I bought one for next year.

Tom thanked us all for coming, thanked me for the coffee and then left with Cheryl and Viera. After I'd seen them out I returned to the sitting room, where Jill was bouncing Harrison gently on her lap.

'It sounds as though Viera is very close to finalizing the adoption plans,' Jill said positively, as I sat on the sofa.

'Yes,' I agreed thoughtfully.

Jill glanced at me. 'In the New Year you'll have to start preparing the kids and yourself for Harrison leaving.' Jill wasn't being unkind, but part of her role was to make sure the foster family was prepared when they had to say goodbye to a foster child; otherwise it could have a negative impact, not only on the carer and her family but also on the child who was leaving, who would sense their negativity.

'I know,' I said. 'But we'll have a lovely Christmas all together first before I think about Harrison going. I'm looking forward to Harrison's first Christmas.'

Jill glanced at me again. 'So what's wrong?'

I shrugged. 'I like Christmas but I feel very sad for Rihanna. I began Christmas shopping yesterday and bought some little presents for Harrison – a feeding beaker and plate, and a little jumper. They all have *Baby's First Christmas* printed on them. I can't help thinking how sad Rihanna must be in the build-up to Christmas. She won't be part of Harrison's first Christmas – or any of his Christmases, come to that. Christmas is such a family time and I can't begin to imagine how awful it must be for those separated from their families. I take it Cheryl hasn't heard any more from Rihanna since that meeting in October?'

'No, or she would have said.'

I was silent for a moment, and then added lamely: 'I'll obviously take plenty of photographs of Harrison's first Christmas, so at least Rihanna will have those to remember it by.'

Jill paused from bouncing Harrison and looked at me carefully. I felt a lecture coming on. 'Cathy, in an ideal world no child would ever be abused, neglected or separated from their parents. No parent would ever lose their child. In an ideal world every child would wake on Christmas morning in a nice warm bed, surrounded by sacks of presents, with two loving parents asleep in the room next door. But sadly this is not an ideal world and is never going to be. All we can do is to try to make the best of our little bit of the world. Giving Harrison a lovely Christmas and taking photographs is the best you can do for him and his mother.'

I met her gaze. 'I know, Jill. And we will have a lovely Christmas. I just hope Rihanna finds some peace too.'

The build-up to Christmas, having begun at the beginning of November, gathered momentum throughout the month so that by the start of December, Christmas was everywhere. Adrian and Paula were busy rehearsing their school Christmas play as well as letting me know what presents they hoped Father Christmas would bring them. The advertisements on television were dominated by Christmas, and the question on most people's lips was: *What are you doing for Christmas?* I was now shopping and wrapping presents at every opportunity, as well as planning what we would eat over the festive season. My parents and my brother and his wife would be coming for Christmas Day, and Adrian and Paula would be seeing their father on Boxing Day, as they had the year before. Harrison was now eating solid food (which I pulped in the food processor), and I planned to do the same with his Christmas dinner so that he could experience all the new tastes.

On Sunday 4 December, I bowed to pressure from Adrian and Paula and agreed to put up the Christmas decorations early, rather than waiting until the following weekend as I'd planned. So while Harrison had his morning nap I braved the loft again and, keeping a watchful eye for any spiders, I brought down the boxes of decorations which we'd carefully packed away the year before. I returned to the loft for the Christmas tree which, while artificial, was very realistic and difficult to tell from a real tree, except that it didn't drop pine needles everywhere. Adrian and Paula were very excited, to put it mildly, and helped me carry the boxes downstairs, where we opened them in the sitting room. It was magical discovering all the glittery decorations again – the tinsel, garlands, a model of Father Christmas on his sleigh, glass baubles and so on – and I was soon in the Christmas spirit. I went up the ladder and began hanging the ceiling decorations while Adrian and Paula assembled and then decorated the Christmas tree. When Harrison woke from his nap I carried him into the sitting room and sat him on the floor so that he could watch.

He was now able to sit unaided without toppling over and he soon became enthralled by the activity, as the brightly coloured decorations appeared around him. At five months old he had a wide range of sounds and his gurgling had developed into babbling, which would eventually lead to words. Each time Adrian and Paula took a Christmas decoration from the box and before they hung it on the tree they showed it to him and said the word a couple of times: *Star, star; angel, angel; holly, holly; bauble, bauble* and so on. With each new word Harrison grinned, pursed his lips and then made a noise as he tried to repeat the word, at which we all clapped.

A Baby's Cry

By three o'clock the house was looking very festive. I returned the empty boxes to the loft and then made dinner. After we'd eaten we grouped around the television and watched a Christmas film, which had become a little family tradition. Although we were now in the Christmas spirit I was aware that the children had school the following day, so at seven o'clock, despite protests and requests to stay up later, I began the bath and bedtime routine. Adrian and Paula were still very excited – counting the days to Christmas Eve and reminiscing about last Christmas. Eventually the children were in bed; by eight o'clock Paula and Harrison were sound asleep, and Adrian was finishing a chapter in his book before switching off his light. I went downstairs and made a cup of tea, which I took into the sitting room. I sat on the sofa and admired the decorated room; it looked very pretty. I knew I was tired, but I hadn't realized how tired I was, or that I was nodding off to sleep, until I came to with a start, woken by a noise.

My eyes shot to the clock on the mantelpiece. It was 9.10. I was immediately on my feet, going out of the sitting room and down the hall, assuming one of the children had woken and called out and I'd subconsciously heard them. But at the foot of the stairs I jumped as the front doorbell rang – one short sharp press. I realized then it must have been the doorbell that had woken me, for it was still all quiet upstairs. I wondered who could be calling at this time. I wasn't expecting a visitor and it seemed too late for a door-to-door salesperson or charity collector; possibly it was carol singers but I couldn't hear any singing. As a woman living alone I was cautious about answering the door late at night and always checked the security spyhole first. If it was someone I didn't know I didn't open the door.

Still slightly light-headed from having woken with a start and then rushing down the hall, I was also a little anxious, for like many people I worried that a late phone call or a visitor could bring bad news – of a road accident or even a death in the family. All manner of thoughts flashed through my mind as I took the few steps to the front door. Although it was pitch dark outside, the porch light, which I left on all night, would allow me to see the caller through the spyhole. I slid the circular flap to one side and peered through. It took a moment for me to focus and to see the woman at my door. She was wearing a headscarf and looking down, so I couldn't see her face. It wasn't until a second later when she looked up that I saw it was Rihanna.

Chapter Twenty-One

Honour

My heart thudded and all manner of anxious thoughts rushed through my mind as I looked into the security spyhole and at Rihanna. She couldn't see me – the front door was solid wood – but she could see the hall light shining through the small window above the door. As I watched she moved her gaze from the door and looked down again so that I couldn't see her face. But there was no mistake: it was certainly her. I watched her for a second longer and then took a step back.

What did she want? What should I do? Not answer the door and hope she would go away? Call the police or open the door and tell her she had to go? Although Harrison was on a Section 20 I had the right to refuse Rihanna entry to my house – she couldn't just come in. I didn't know what to do. Had she been an abusive violent parent whose child was in care under a Full Care Order I would have called the police. But Rihanna had been cooperating with the social services, so they hadn't seen the need to apply for a Full Care Order, which would have given Harrison greater security and meant she couldn't remove him without a court order. And while I knew that if Rihanna tried to snatch Harrison, the social services would apply for such an order, that didn't help me now.

With my heart still thumping loudly and my thoughts whirling I went up to the door again and peered through the spyhole.

Rihanna hadn't pressed the bell again but she was still there, now looking at the door. I could see her face illuminated by the porch lamp and it showed no signs of anger (I'd never seen her angry), just a blank, expressionless gaze. She waited a little longer and then turned from the door and began to walk away – down the path and towards the front gate. In that moment I made a decision, based not on rational thought but on instinct and empathy.

Placing my hand on the doorknob I turned it and quietly opened the front door. Rihanna stopped at the end of the path and turned to look at me. In a heavy coat to protect herself from the cold and a dark headscarf, she was silhouetted against the street lamp. I held the door open with one hand, and she stood looking at me from the end of the path with the same expressionless gaze. Then I said quietly: 'Rihanna, what do you want, love?'

I was expecting her to say she wanted to see Harrison, in which case I would gently tell her that she needed to speak to Cheryl to arrange contact and hope she accepted this and left. I waited by the door, but when she spoke she didn't ask to see Harrison. Taking one step up the path she said quietly: 'I need to talk. Will you hear what I have to say?' It was said rationally, but with a sadness that came from the very depths of her soul.

Taken aback, I looked at her for a moment without replying. I had three children asleep upstairs whose safety was paramount. Had Rihanna appeared irrational and distraught, I would have sent her away without hesitation and closed the door. But she didn't; she seemed calm and in control, and not angry or upset.

'Please, Cathy,' she said. 'I won't ask to see Harrison or wake your children. I just need to talk.' She spoke quietly and slowly but with the same dreadful sadness. I had to make a decision.

I knew I was taking a chance, but the same instinct that had made me open the door in the first place told me Rihanna didn't pose a threat to the children or me, and I said: 'You'd better come in.'

'Thank you,' she said; then with her head lowered and concentrating on the ground she came slowly down the path.

I opened the door wider, stood aside to let her in and then quietly closed the door again after her. She stood in the hall, her head slightly bent, and avoided my gaze.

'We can go through to the sitting room,' I said quietly, pointing down the hall. It was still quiet upstairs, so I guessed the children hadn't heard the doorbell ring or the front door open and close.

I led the way down the hall and into the sitting room, where she stood nervously in the centre of the room. 'Sit down,' I said gently.

With her head still slightly lowered as though she was ashamed to meet my gaze, Rihanna took off her headscarf and then sat on the edge of the sofa. I didn't offer to take her coat, as it might have created the impression she was staying longer than I anticipated. I would hear what she had to say but that was all. I sat in the armchair, at a right angle to the sofa, looked at her and waited. Her expression was downcast and she kept her eyes trained on the floor. The gaily coloured Christmas decorations we'd hung that morning seemed a cruel contrast to her sadness.

'Harrison is asleep,' I said awkwardly, after some moments.

Rihanna raised her head and gave a small nod; then her gaze went to the photographs of Harrison on the mantelpiece.

'Thank you for looking after him,' she said quietly, so that I wondered if she'd come here to ask me to adopt him again, although Cheryl had already made it clear to her that wasn't possible.

'He's a very good baby,' I said.

Rihanna nodded again and then met my gaze. 'Cathy, I'm sorry to arrive here like this. I would never normally behave so badly. But I've carried the burden of what I've done around with me for so long, and I can't do it any longer. I need to tell you why I can't keep Harrison. I need you to understand. But you must promise me you won't tell anyone. My life could be in danger if you did.'

I was taken aback, both by her directness and that she now wanted to tell me what had been a closely guarded secret. It was a moment before I replied. 'Rihanna,' I said carefully, 'as a foster carer I can't promise I won't tell anyone. If you tell me something that could affect Harrison then I will need to tell my support social worker, who will pass it to Cheryl. I'm sorry.'

She hesitated and I wondered if she was going to stand and leave, which in some ways would have been easier and was what part of me hoped she'd do. Yes, I was intrigued to know what Rihanna wanted to tell me, and yes, I felt dreadfully sorry for her, but I certainly didn't want to place my children, Harrison and myself in danger by learning something I should not have known.

Rihanna didn't stand and leave; she stayed on the sofa, sitting stiffly upright with her coat buttoned up and her headscarf in her lap. She concentrated on the floor as she began to speak. 'I will tell you and then you can decide what you should do.' She paused, as though gathering her thoughts. For some time all that could be heard was the ticking of the clock and the faint movement of the Christmas decorations on the ceiling as they stirred slightly in the warm air.

'My family and my work colleagues believe I am a respectable single woman,' Rihanna began. 'A woman who has chosen a career over marriage. They did not know I was pregnant or that I now have a baby. I hid my pregnancy from everyone. Only the social services knew. Towards the end of my pregnancy, when I could no longer hide it, I took extended holiday from work and away from my parents. I told my work colleagues and my family I was going to India, in search of my roots, which they accepted. I didn't attend the antenatal appointments, although I did have a scan. I monitored my pregnancy myself. I knew everything was progressing as it should because of my medical knowledge. I am a doctor, though not in paediatrics. Then, at the end of my pregnancy, Cheryl arranged for me to be admitted to hospital, maintaining the strictest confidentiality. I live and work in a neighbouring county, which is why I came here to have my baby – in secret.'

Rihanna paused and I waited, my mouth dry and my senses alert. She took a moment, as though composing herself, and then looked at me in earnest. 'Harrison is not the product of a casual relationship,' she said firmly. 'I've never had a casual relationship in my life. I have known Harrison's father for twelve years. We met at university. He is also a doctor, but does not live or work near here. We loved each other dearly, but we can never marry, Cathy. If Harrison's existence became known one of my cousins would kill him and very likely me too. You see, Harrison's grandfather is Jamaican. He settled here and married an Englishwoman. Harrison's father is mixed race.'

She fell quiet, looked away and wrung her headscarf in her lap, while I stared at her and tried to make sense of what she was telling me. I consider myself reasonably well educated and not usually slow to grasp a point, and I live in a culturally diverse community, so I'm aware of different customs and beliefs, but I sat there, looking at Rihanna, without any idea of the problem she was trying to describe.

'Yes?' I said eventually, expecting more. 'Harrison's father has dual heritage?'

'And my family is traditionally Asian,' Rihanna added.

Slowly the light began to dawn. 'And your family would be opposed to you marrying Harrison's father because of his culture?'

'More than that!' Rihanna cried, becoming agitated for the first time. 'If my parents found out they would never speak to me again. I would be ostracized from them for life. I would have no family. My name would be banned from the house and all the photographs of me, my clothes and my belongings would be burnt. It would be as though I didn't exist. I have cousins who are stricter and more narrow-minded than my parents and would see killing Harrison's father and me necessary to save our family's pride and honour. You've heard of honour killings?'

'Yes, I have,' I said, shocked to the core. And as I began to grasp the horrendous implications of what Rihanna was telling me my next thought was: 'Does Harrison's father know he has a baby?'

Rihanna shook her head. 'No. How could I tell him and put his life at risk? He is a good, kind man who loved me dearly; maybe he still does. I love him. If I'd told him he would have wanted to marry me, and my family would never have approved. My cousins would have tracked us down. We would never have been safe, ever. That's the truth, Cathy. The police can only do so much. I knew I couldn't go through with a termination, so when I was four months pregnant I told Harrison's father I didn't want to see him any more. I told him I had met someone else. I hadn't, but I thought it was the kindest way to let him go. He cried. I felt dreadful, but what else could I do? It was for his own good, for his own protection. We kept our relationship secret for twelve years and I will always love him. But now he is safe and free to find someone new to love.' Rihanna fell silent and her face was creased in pain.

While I'd heard of honour killings – from the newspaper and on television – those cases had seemed distant; so far removed from my life that the implications hadn't really touched me. Now, in my living room, sat a decent, intelligent, kind and hard-working woman whose life had been ruined and put in danger simply because she loved the wrong man. I was shocked, not only by the culture that allowed this but by Rihanna's family, who were upholding this dreadful attitude.

'Would you like a glass of water?' I asked quietly after a moment, seeing her discomposure.

'No thank you,' Rihanna said. 'I will tell you my story and then go. I want you to know.' She gave a small sniff before continuing. 'I was living with my parents when I found out I was pregnant; it is not unusual for a single Asian woman to live at home and contribute to the household budget. When I discovered I was pregnant I began looking for a flat to rent. I couldn't risk my family finding out. My sister is engaged to be married to a man from a highly respectable family and if it came out – even if the father wasn't known – he would view my pregnancy as bringing shame and dishonour on his family as well, and break off the engagement. My sister would never find another suitor and her life would be ruined too because of my actions. So I moved into a flat, and when I visited my parents I wore a sari, which hid my bulging stomach. I never normally wore a sari and my parents were pleased I was now doing so. Ironic, isn't it?' Rihanna said with a small sad smile. 'The only reason I wore the sari was to hide the child they would never have accepted.'

I nodded, sad and serious.

'Right from the beginning I knew I would have to give up my child,' Rihanna continued. 'I contacted the social services and Cheryl agreed to meet me. She has been very good to me; I couldn't have managed without her. She told me she had come across a case like mine before – an Asian teenage girl who wanted to marry an English boy. It's more common than you think. Although I knew I wouldn't be able to keep my baby I took much pleasure in choosing clothes for him.' Rihanna gave a small wistful smile. 'When my bump became too big to hide I told my family and my work colleagues that I was going to India. I stayed in my flat and only went out in the evening to buy food. I watched a lot of television and read many books – anything to pass the time. It was lovely feeling my baby grow and move inside me. Yet the bigger my baby grew the closer I came to losing him. I knew I would have to part with him at birth. Cheryl found me a solicitor and also arranged my admission to hospital, so that when I went into labour the hospital was expecting me. As you know I had my baby and then came away.'

I nodded again.

'A week later I returned to work and continued visiting my family as though nothing had happened. No one noticed anything different about me or if they did they didn't say. Inside I was destroyed and weeping. I was hurting so badly but I couldn't tell anyone. I was a mother who would never see her baby again.' Rihanna stopped as her face finally crumpled and tears fell – quiet, stifled tears that made my heart ache for her.

I stood and went to sit beside her on the sofa and took her hand.

'Losing my baby hurts so much,' she said through her tears. 'I thought the pain would ease and eventually go. I thought if I got on with my life and didn't see Harrison I would forget him. But I can't forget him and the pain of losing him grows worse each day. I thought if I saw him with you it might help reassure me, so I stood in your street and caught a glimpse of him, but it didn't help. I accepted Cheryl's offer of the photographs but those didn't help either. I thought maybe if I met you it might help, so I asked for that meeting. I was also hoping that perhaps you could keep Harrison; I had this idea that if you kept him I could visit him at weekends.' Rihanna turned to look at me, her eyes and cheeks wet. 'In some countries if your baby is adopted and someone else brings them up you can still see them when you want,' she said, 'but you can't here.'

'No,' I said gently. 'I'm afraid the system here doesn't allow that.' Although I'd often thought it should.

'I'm so unhappy,' Rihanna said. 'The pain grows. I feel I'm being punished for loving a man I knew my parents would not have approved of. It's a punishment that will continue forever.' Rihanna stopped but her tears continued to fall silently. She took a tissue from her pocket and pressed it to her cheek.

What could I possibly say that would help? While I now understood the reason for Harrison coming into care and the high level of security surrounding him, it didn't provide any answers. In some ways I'd have been better off not knowing; then I could have continued believing that Harrison was the product of an illicit affair between two famous people whose reputations would have been ruined if their baby's existence had become known. Instead, the reality was that Harrison was the result of a loving partnership of twelve years; a baby who should have been brought up, and loved and cared for, by his own parents had it not been for a family misinterpreting the word honour.

'And you're sure your parents wouldn't change their minds if they knew they had a grandson?' I asked, aware that some mothers of pregnant teenage girls reject their daughters to begin with and then go on to support them and their grandchild.

Rihanna shook her head and wiped her eyes. 'No. We are a close family and I have cousins whose families are far stricter than my parents. They would put pressure on my parents and make their lives unbearable.'

We fell silent again as Rihanna dabbed her eyes. I had never felt more impotent to offer help in my life. I could see that Rihanna's situation was impossible; there was no way out other than to have Harrison adopted, as Rihanna had decided, and lose him for good. 'I'll have to tell Jill, my support social worker, what you have told me,' I said presently. 'But it will be kept confidential and won't go any further.'

Rihanna nodded. 'I understand. Thank you for listening, and thank you for looking after Harrison. I won't keep you any longer. I'll go now.' Clutching her tissue and headscarf Rihanna stood to leave. I stood too.

'What will you do now?' I asked, concerned for her safety.

'Continue as best I can,' Rihanna said dejectedly. 'And hope the pain goes away. I'll go to my flat now; then tomorrow I'll go to work as usual and pretend nothing is wrong, as I have been doing since I first found out I was pregnant.' With her head down Rihanna crossed to the sitting-room door and I followed her down the hall. At the foot of the stairs she paused and glanced upstairs. 'Will you say goodbye to Harrison for me, please? Tell him I love him?' Her eyes immediately filled again with tears.

'Yes, I will,' I said. 'Or you could.'

She looked at me with a start.

'Do you want to go up and see Harrison in his cot?' I asked. 'He's asleep. He won't know you're there.' I'd said it instinctively, feeling it was the right thing to do. I now trusted Rihanna and believed she didn't pose a threat to Harrison, my children or me; otherwise I wouldn't have suggested it.

Rihanna hesitated and looked anxiously up the stairs. 'Do you think I should?' she asked, child-like and vulnerable.

'Yes, I do,' I said. 'But it has to be your decision.'

She hesitated again, then said, 'Yes please, Cathy. I'd like to say goodbye to Harrison.' And just at that moment, Harrison did something he hadn't done in the evening for a long while: he woke with a small cry.

Chapter Twenty-Two
A Baby's Cry

'He's awake,' Rihanna whispered with a mixture of surprise and concern. 'I heard my baby's cry.'

'So did I,' I said. 'But he's not normally awake at this time. He sleeps very well.' It was almost as if Harrison had sensed his mother's presence, for we'd been very quiet and I was sure our whispered voices hadn't woken him.

I saw Rihanna's anxiety and uncertainty increase; perhaps she was wondering if now Harrison was awake she should leave without seeing him, or possibly that I might withdraw my offer.

'This way,' I said decisively, so there was no room for doubt, and began to go upstairs.

Rihanna followed, her footsteps treading lightly behind me on the carpeted stairs. The landing light was on as usual in the evening, and she followed me silently round the landing, past Adrian's and Paula's bedrooms, and to Harrison's room. I always left his bedroom door ajar so that I could hear him if he woke, but of course he hadn't woken in the evening since the second night he'd slept in his own room – over two months ago.

I eased his bedroom door further open. The glow from the landing fell softly into the room, allowing enough light for us to see without switching on the main light, which would have startled him. Rihanna paused at the door and I gestured for her to follow me in. She joined me beside his cot. Harrison was lying on his back and was wide awake. When he saw us he grinned, first at me and then, turning his head slightly so that he could see, at Rihanna. Her hand shot to her mouth to stop her cry from escaping.

Had Harrison woken any other night – without Rihanna present – I would have checked that he was dry and comfortable, given him a hug, then resettled him and left him to go back to sleep. However, tonight wasn't 'any other night' – far from it. This was likely to be the one and only time Rihanna would have a chance to see and hold her baby before he was adopted.

Lowering the side of the cot I reached in and as I did Harrison smiled and stretched out his arms, ready to be picked up. I lifted him out of the cot and his little arms closed around my neck. Supporting him in the crook of my arm I turned him to face Rihanna so that he could see her and she him. The light from the landing softly illuminated the three of us by the cot. Rihanna still had her hand pressed to her lips and hardly dared look at her son; while Harrison, unaware of the enormity of the situation, grinned at her and then let out a large burp.

I laughed. 'So that's what woke you, young man,' I said quietly, nuzzling his ear.

He gurgled and grinned and I smelt that gorgeous warm baby smell, so sweet and pure, and I knew Rihanna could smell it too.

She was still standing a little way in front of us, her hand covering her mouth and watching him in awe, not daring to touch him; while Harrison, now relieved of indigestion, clearly felt much better and was ready to play. Always a sociable baby, he wasn't upset by a stranger suddenly appearing in his bedroom; or perhaps he suspected this lady wasn't a stranger and was significant to him. He grinned at Rihanna, looked around the room, made a few endearing babbling sounds and then reached out a hand towards her. For a moment Rihanna just looked at his hand without making any attempt to touch or hold it, as though she was scared to make contact. Then slowly, very slowly, she lowered her hand from her mouth and, reaching out, encircled Harrison's hand in her own. They looked at each other for a moment and then Harrison began wriggling and leaning towards her, which I recognized as a sign he wanted to be held by her.

'Would you like to hold him?' I asked gently.

Rihanna hesitated and then gave a small nod. Letting go of Harrison's hand she tucked the headscarf she'd been clutching into her coat pocket and held out her arms, ready to receive him. I gently eased Harrison into her arms, where he rested comfortably against her chest. With his head on her shoulder he snuggled his face into her neck, and I smiled. Then after a few moments Rihanna slowly allowed her head to relax on to Harrison's, so that her cheek was resting lightly on his forehead. Her eyes closed and the room grew quiet and still.

I continued to look at mother and child, bathed in the soft warm glow of the landing light, and my heart ached for them. It was a portrait of true serenity, love and peace: a picture of the perfect union between a mother and her baby, albeit temporary. What thoughts were going through Rihanna's mind as she finally held her son I couldn't begin to guess, but Harrison had stopped his previous wriggling and hardly stirred. He lay contentedly against Rihanna as though knowing this felt right and making the most of every moment.

It was after ten o'clock and I was hoping Adrian and Paula wouldn't wake, for if they discovered Harrison's mother here it would be difficult for me to explain and they could have found it unsettling. They had accepted that Harrison was a baby whose mother couldn't look after him and who was being found new parents and would be adopted. If they didn't wake I wouldn't tell them of Rihanna's visit; there was no need for them to know. But I was already aware that tomorrow I would have to tell Jill that Rihanna had called and I'd invited her in and then suggested she saw Harrison, and she would pass the information on to Cheryl.

Harrison was still lying contentedly against Rihanna, his head resting on her shoulder and his face snuggled into her neck. With her eyes lightly closed, she was breathing in and appreciating every moment of their limited time together. Every so often she turned her head towards him and lovingly kissed his forehead. Harrison responded with a little sigh of contentment and snuggled closer to his mother, soaking up her love. After a few minutes his breathing began to deepen and I saw his legs and arms go limp as he started drifting into sleep. Rihanna held him close and swayed slightly, gently rocking him; then she looked at me and whispered, 'I think he's asleep.'

I nodded.

'Shall I put him in his cot?' she asked quietly.

'Yes please.'

'Can you help me?' she said, uncertain.

I moved closer to the cot and lightly supported Harrison's back as Rihanna changed the position of her hands so that she could lower him easily and gently into the cot. As she did and his body uncurled on to the mattress, he snuffled but didn't wake. Rihanna pulled the covers up to his chin and then leant over and kissed his forehead.

'Goodnight, my love,' she whispered. 'Try to forgive me. I'll always love you, wherever you are. Goodbye, my son.'

Straightening, she stepped away from the cot and immediately crossed to the bedroom door. I raised the side of the cot and followed Rihanna out of the bedroom, pulling the door slightly to behind me. I wondered if she would want to stay and talk, but she hurried down the stairs and to the front door.

'Are you all right?' I asked, joining her in the hall.

She nodded and took her headscarf from her coat pocket. Her face was expressionless, as it had been when she'd arrived, as though she was trying to blot out emotion and struggling to keep control.

'Thank you, Cathy,' she said quietly, her voice trembling. 'Thank you for everything.'

Quickly looping her headscarf over her head she tied it loosely under her chin and I opened the front door. 'Look after yourself, Rihanna,' I said, as she stepped out and into the cold night air, but there was no reply.

I watched her go down the path and then on to the pavement, where she disappeared from view. Mother and child were now separated again after the briefest of reunions.

I closed the front door and then locked and bolted it for the night. It was quiet upstairs; the children hadn't woken and Harrison had returned to sleep. As I went thoughtfully down the hall towards the sitting room, I wondered if Harrison would remember his mother's visit in the morning. I knew that at his age babies could remember significant events for up to a week, although of course Harrison wouldn't know the significance of what had happened tonight – that he had met his mother and she had said goodbye.

In the sitting room I took my fostering folder from the bookshelf, picked up a pen and sat on the sofa, where I opened the folder and selected a new sheet of paper. I thought that if I wrote up my log notes now rather than leaving it until the morning, it might help exorcize the thoughts and emotions that were chasing through my mind, and which I knew would keep me awake.

I filled in the date at the top of the sheet and then wrote: *Rihanna came to the house at 9.10 p.m. and said she wanted to talk to me. I invited her in and ...* I paused and looked up, my thoughts consumed by the image of Rihanna on my doorstep, not arriving but leaving my house. Dignified as always but obviously badly hurting inside, she was now on her way home to a flat where presumably the only evidence or reminder she had a son were the photographs I'd given to her. Then the following day she would have to put her sorrow on hold so that she could go to work and tend to the needs of her patients, all the while aching for the child she had lost. I thought of Harrison's father – a good, kind man, Rihanna had said – who would continue to live his life believing his partner of twelve years had left him for another man, and unaware he had a son. I also thought of Rihanna's family, who were doubtless also good, kind people but who, if they discovered Harrison's existence, had been conditioned to believe they needed to reject their daughter and even put her life in danger to maintain their family's honour.

Then I thought of Rihanna again and the poignant image of her in the bedroom holding her son. It touched me now, as it had then, and I felt my eyes mist. Whether or not I'd made the right decision in inviting Rihanna into the house and then suggesting she saw Harrison I didn't know, but in the morning I would find out. Once Adrian and Paula were at school I'd have to telephone Jill and tell her everything. What she and then Cheryl did with that information was out of my control.

I looked down again at the sheet of paper and continued writing: *Rihanna said she needed to tell me the reason she could not look after her son ...* I wrote until I'd finished the evening's events; then I went to bed exhausted, emotionally drained but able to sleep.

The following morning Harrison was awake first, as usual, and when I went into his room he looked around as though expecting to see someone else with me. I picked him up, kissed and hugged him, and then went about the morning's routine, while wondering how Rihanna must be feeling as she made her way to the hospital where she worked as a doctor.

A Baby's Cry

Once Adrian and Paula were at school – it was the last week of term before school broke up for the Christmas holiday – I phoned Homefinders but Jill was in a meeting. I left a message with her colleague asking if she would phone me as soon as she came out of the meeting and then busied myself – with housework and playing with Harrison – while waiting for Jill to return my call. At 11.15 Jill phoned and straightaway asked me if everything was all right.

'Rihanna came here last night and told me all about Harrison's background and the reason for the secrecy,' I said.

'She told you?' Jill exclaimed in astonishment. 'She told you everything?'

'Yes – well, I assume it was everything. I'm certain it was all true.' I was kneeling on the floor in the sitting room, keeping Harrison amused.

'So who is Harrison's father?' Jill asked, unable to hide her intrigue.

'No one famous,' I said. 'Not that it helps. It's all so sad, Jill.' And I began telling Jill what Rihanna had told me. I said that Harrison was a result of a loving but forbidden partnership which had lasted twelve years and which Rihanna had ended when she'd found out she was pregnant. I explained why the secrecy was necessary to protect Rihanna and Harrison's father; and I ended with where Rihanna was now – alone in a rented flat, going to work each day while aching for her son. Jill listened in silence as I spoke, just occasionally sighing – with sadness, at the hopelessness of Rihanna's situation and also, I suspected, with frustration that such an attitude as Rihanna's family's still existed today and wrecked lives. I got to the point where Rihanna was about to leave the house (without seeing Harrison) when Jill interrupted and exclaimed: 'So Rihanna didn't ask to see Harrison? She just came to talk to you?'

I paused. 'She didn't *ask* to see Harrison, no. But I suggested she did.'

Jill fell quiet again as I told her what had happened then: that I'd invited Rihanna in with the offer that she could go upstairs and see Harrison, which she had accepted. I told Jill, Harrison had been awake but Adrian and Paula had stayed asleep and therefore didn't know Rihanna had been. I then described the scene in Harrison's bedroom as Rihanna held her son and finally kissed him goodnight and said goodbye. I finished by saying that Rihanna had thanked me and then left, not in tears but obviously very upset.

'I'm not surprised she was upset, poor woman,' Jill said. 'You're right, it is so sad. And unnecessary!' she tutted, but when she spoke again it was with professional detachment. 'Harrison is in care under a Section 20, so from that point of view no court orders were broken when you allowed Rihanna into your home. I'll obviously have to update Cheryl and she may feel it's necessary to apply for a care order until Harrison is adopted. If she does, you know you won't be allowed to let Rihanna into your house again? Any contact will need to be arranged in advance and supervised at the family centre.'

'Yes, I know, Jill,' I said.

'And the other issue is – and I'm sure you thought about this before you invited Rihanna in – now you've done it once, Rihanna arriving on your doorstep might become a regular occurrence. In which case the social services would certainly apply for a care order – to protect Harrison. They'll be starting introductions to the adoptive parents in February, so it isn't in Harrison's interests to begin building a relationship with his birth mother now, only to say goodbye in a couple of months. I'm afraid Rihanna has left it too late.'

'I know,' I said. 'I'm sure she does too. She won't come back again.'

'Did she tell you she wouldn't?'

'No, but she said goodbye to Harrison. It was final. While she couldn't bring herself to attend a goodbye contact at the family centre, this just happened naturally. But I'm sure it was goodbye for Rihanna.'

'All right. Let's hope so. And Rihanna seems to be coping? She wasn't overtly distraught?'

I hesitated. 'She goes to work each day, so I suppose she must be coping.'

'Well, let's hope she'll accept the counselling that Cheryl has offered. I'll ring Cheryl now and update her. Make sure you write everything you've told me in your log notes in case there are any repercussions. And Cathy?'

'Yes?'

'I'd have done the same in your position and let Rihanna in. So don't beat yourself up about it.'

'Thanks, Jill.'

Chapter Twenty-Three

Late-Night Caller

In the days that followed Rihanna's visit it occurred to me that while Rihanna had mentioned Harrison's father a number of times when she'd been telling me her story, she hadn't ever referred to him by name – just as 'Harrison's father'. I assumed she had purposely avoided saying his name to maintain confidentiality and protect him. I wondered if his surname was really Smith. When I'd collected Harrison from the hospital the nurse had told me that Harrison had his father's surname, Smith, and Cheryl had told Jill that Rihanna had checked in and out of the hospital using the name Smith. But Smith is the most common surname in the UK and is sometimes used as an alias, if someone wants to hide their true identity. However, whether Smith was the family name or not was of little consequence really, for once Harrison was adopted he would be given his adoptive parents' surname. I also wondered why Rihanna had chosen the first name Harrison, a name that is uncommon in the UK (and which Harrison would keep after the adoption), but it hadn't seemed appropriate to ask her when she'd visited.

With Christmas fast approaching the week beginning 12 December was a busy one socially. On Tuesday it was the Homefinders Christmas lunch for its foster carers and, as in previous years, they'd booked (and paid for) a nice meal for all the carers at a local pub restaurant. We had a room to ourselves over the main pub, and the carers with pre-school children could bring them rather than finding babysitters. The agency provided two nannies to keep the babies and children amused while the carers ate. It was a lovely meal in a relaxed and festive atmosphere and gave the carers a chance to chat to each other and catch up on news. On Wednesday morning I went into school to watch Adrian's and Paula's Christmas play, which was performed in the main assembly hall. As I'd done when watching the school's summer play, I purposely chose a seat at the end of a row and near a door so that if Harrison became restless I could easily slip out. But he was as enthralled as I was by the children's nativity play and sat on my lap watching and listening attentively to the children on stage. Adrian was one of a large group of shepherds and Paula was an angel. I wasn't the only parent who was misty-eyed at the closing scene when the children, grouped around baby Jesus and with the angel's costumes sparkling in the light, sang 'Away In A Manger' in their sweet little voices. I looked at Adrian and Paula and felt incredibly proud. I knew how lucky I was, not only to be blessed with two wonderful children of my own but also to be allowed to foster more.

On Thursday, Adrian and Paula had their Christmas parties at school and took in lemonade and party food to share. As I was in the PTA (Parent Teacher Association) I helped at the party, which was in the main hall. I took Harrison with me, and the parents organized games for the children and then set out the party food on long tables. The children made such a fuss of Harrison that when the party had finished he didn't want to leave; Adrian and Paula looked proud that Harrison was their foster sibling.

Friday was the last day of term and school was due to finish early – at 1.15 p.m. That morning Jill visited me for her four-weekly supervisory meeting. The meeting followed the format of the previous supervisory meetings and after we'd discussed Harrison's development, she checked and signed my log notes and then brought me up to date.

'Cheryl phoned yesterday,' she said. 'She's spoken to her manager about Rihanna coming here, and she's also spoken to Rihanna on the phone. Cheryl and her manager are satisfied that Rihanna won't try to see Harrison again, so they won't be applying for a Full Care Order now.'

'Good,' I said.

'However,' Jill added, 'Cheryl said that having spoken to Rihanna she doesn't think that seeing Harrison has helped her. Rihanna is still grieving badly for her son.' Although this sounded like a criticism of me – for suggesting Rihanna saw Harrison – I didn't think Jill intended one. Jill is always plainly spoken and had admitted on the phone she'd have done the same in my position.

Jill continued with an update on the progress of the adoption: 'The choice of couple has been finalized,' she said. 'The couple have been notified they've been successful. The other four couples who were shortlisted will have also been notified that they have been unsuccessful,' she added.

I nodded but I felt sorry for those other couples who for six months had been preparing themselves for the possibility of adopting, and had now been rejected and would have to start the process all over again – searching the registers for another child to adopt. Often couples (who have already been approved as suitable adopters) spend years applying to adopt specific children, having their hopes continually raised and then dashed. I think the whole system needs a radical overhaul, so that children who are in care are matched with suitable adoptive parents much sooner.

Jill then said a planning meeting had been arranged in the New Year – for Wednesday 18 January, when Harrison's adoptive parents would meet me and learn about Harrison first hand. The couple already had basic details about Harrison and the photographs I'd given Viera, but on the 18th they would learn more from me about Harrison's routine, likes and dislikes, etc. and could ask me questions. At this point the couple still had the option of pulling out and not proceeding with the adoption, but of course very few do. Couples who reach this point know how lucky they are to have the chance to adopt a child and are fully committed. Jill, Viera, Cheryl, possibly Cheryl's manager and the couple's social worker would also be present at this meeting. I made a note of the date of the meeting in my diary and then Jill asked me, almost suspiciously: 'You haven't heard any more from Rihanna?'

'No,' I said. 'I'd tell you if I did.' Which she accepted.

That afternoon, the last day of school, I met Adrian and Paula at 1.15 and they came out very excited and carrying Christmas decorations they'd made in class, Christmas cards from their friends and a gift each from their teachers which was very generous. The playground was alive with the sound of excited children – all happily breaking up from school and looking forward to Christmas, as well as parents calling 'Happy Christmas' to each other. Once home and out of the school routine we could relax and enjoy the final build-up to Christmas. I love Christmas – the magic never wears off for me – but I had to admit there was a cloud hanging over this year's festive season, and that was my thoughts and worries about Rihanna and how she would be coping. I didn't know Rihanna's religion and quite possibly she didn't celebrate Christmas, but in England you can't avoid the festive atmosphere of Christmas whatever your religion. And being surrounded with images of happy families with their children would be a cruel reminder to Rihanna of what she had lost. But I knew I had to let go of her pain and be positive, for in two months Harrison would be settling in with his adoptive parents, who would love and care for him as Rihanna would have done.

By 23 December I was more or less prepared for Christmas. I just needed to collect the turkey, fresh fruit and vegetables the following day – Christmas Eve – and then there would be no more shopping until well after Christmas. I'd wrapped the presents to go in the children's pillowcases on Christmas night, and they were hidden in my wardrobe. The pile of presents – from friends, and relatives we wouldn't see over Christmas – had grown under the tree, and the children were also looking forward to seeing their father on Boxing Day, when they would exchange presents with him.

It had taken some time to get the children into bed and asleep that night as they were very excited; even Harrison had taken longer than usual to settle, wanting to play peek-a-boo through the side of the cot rather than lie down and sleep. It was after 9.30 by the time all three children were asleep and I was downstairs tidying up. Then at ten o'clock I went through to the sitting room and switched on the television to watch the news.

Just as I sat down I heard a tapping sound, so I was on my feet again, going into the kitchen. Sometimes the cat flap on the back door sticks and Toscha taps on it with her paw, asking to be let in. However, when I went into the kitchen I saw that she was already asleep in her basket. I went to the cat flap and checked there wasn't another cat trying to get in, as had happened once before. But there wasn't another cat and the cat flap appeared to be working normally. I glanced around the kitchen; then I switched off the light and returned to the sitting room. But before I'd sat down I heard the tapping again. Silencing the television I crossed to the French windows, where I gingerly lifted back one curtain and peered into the darkness, wondering if there was something on the patio making the noise. The tapping sounded again and it was then I realized it wasn't coming from the patio or the kitchen, but from behind me: from down the hall. Someone was tapping quietly on the front door. Carol singers? Kids messing around? I wondered. But it was too quiet for that. The hall light was on and I went down the hall and to the front door, where I slid the cover on the security spy hole.

'Oh no!' I gasped out loud, as I saw who was on the doorstep.

Illuminated by the porch light, facing the door and with tears streaming down her face, stood Rihanna. My heart sank as anxiety gripped me. Jill had been right when she'd said that allowing Rihanna to come in once could encourage her to return, and Cheryl, her manager and I had been wrong. Badly wrong. What was I supposed to do now? The social services hadn't applied for a Full Care Order; Harrison was still in care on a Section 20, so technically I could let Rihanna in to see Harrison, although as before I could refuse her entry as it was my house. But unlike before she was now obviously very upset and I doubted it was in either her or Harrison's best interests to allow her to come in and see him. I considered opening the door on the safety chain and telling her through the crack that she should go home and phone Cheryl first thing in the morning, but I felt that as Harrison's mother she deserved more than that – being dispatched through a crack in the door.

She tapped lightly on the door again and slowly, reluctantly and not knowing what to do, I turned the doorknob and opened the door, my heart pounding. Rihanna looked at me from her tear-stained face; she wasn't wearing a headscarf and her hair was dishevelled. More of Jill's words came back: ... *coping?* ... *overtly distraught?* Clearly she wasn't coping now and was obviously distraught.

'I'm sorry,' she began, her face creasing with more tears. 'I know it's late. I hope I didn't wake the children. I tapped rather than using the bell.'

I gave a small nod and tried to think of what to say – gentle words that would send her away and, I hoped, encourage her to accept Cheryl's offer of counselling.

'Cathy,' she said, delving into her coat pocket for a tissue and barely able to speak, 'you won't believe what's happened tonight. I had to come straight here.'

I was about to say that I was sorry, but that whatever had happened, I couldn't let her in, and she needed to go home and phone Cheryl in the morning, but she suddenly reached out and grabbed my arm. I started and took a step back.

'Cathy, I have to see you,' she said. 'I told my parents this evening. I told them all about Harrison and his father.' I stared at her, aghast, as her hand tightened on my arm. 'You won't believe what's happened,' she said again.

I was sure she was going to say that she was now on the run and in fear of her life and needed a safe place to hide, or even that she was running away and wanted to take Harrison with her. I felt my legs tremble and a cold shiver run down my spine. But what Rihanna said was not as I'd imagined, although it was no less shocking: 'Cathy,' she said, wiping her eyes as more tears fell, 'I've told my parents everything about Harrison. They are very, very upset, but they are going to help me.'

It took me a moment to realize what Rihanna was saying and that her tears were not of sadness but of joy.

'Oh Cathy,' she said, finally releasing my arm, 'can I come in? I have to see you. So much has happened.'

Foster carers often have to make snap decisions – weigh up a person's sincerity, motive and intentions, and decide if that person is telling the truth and can be trusted. I now had to decide if Rihanna *was* telling me the truth, in which case I would let her in; or if, unbalanced by grief, she'd concocted this story to get into my house and possibly snatch Harrison or do us harm. Her eyes hadn't left mine as she'd been speaking and I decided what I saw was sincerity. I opened the door wider and stood aside to let her in.

'Thank you,' she said quietly, stepping past me and into the hall.

I closed the front door and then showed her through to the sitting room, where I also closed the sitting room door so that we wouldn't disturb the children sleeping upstairs. Picking up the remote control I switched off the television, as Rihanna perched on the sofa. I sat in the armchair and looked at her. The Christmas decorations stirred silently overhead and the lights on the Christmas tree glowed.

'I don't know where to begin,' she said after a moment, tears springing to her eyes again. 'So much has happened tonight. It's like a miracle. I went to my parents straight from work. I never thought this could be happening.'

I waited while she composed herself as conflicting thoughts dashed through my mind. I didn't share Rihanna's euphoria for if, as she said, the impossible had happened and her parents were going to help her, I could already see all sorts of problems, which I doubted Rihanna had considered.

'Only my mother was at home when I arrived,' Rihanna began. 'My father and sister were still at work. I told my mother I had something to tell her: something that would make her upset and angry, but which I had to share. Cathy, I knew I couldn't live a lie any longer and it would be better if my family never spoke to me again than I continued as I had been. It was unbearable. So I took my mother through to the lounge and made her sit down. She kept offering me something to eat, which is what she always does when I visit. I then told her about the relationship I'd been having with Harrison's father; that it had begun at university and had developed and continued for twelve years, until I found out I was pregnant. I said that although I loved Harrison's father I knew we couldn't be together, so I ended the relationship before I had the baby. When I started to tell my mother about Harrison she didn't believe me and laughed. She asked where I'd been hiding a baby, thinking I was joking. I explained about foster care and I told her about you; then I showed her the photographs of Harrison, which I carry in my handbag.' Rihanna maintained eye contact as she spoke.

'My mother started to believe me then and was very angry and upset. She called me lots of bad names and said I had brought shame on the whole family. I left the house in tears, knowing I would never see my family again. I went back to my flat and sat and cried for ages; I felt so alone. Then at about eight o'clock my father telephoned. I was surprised to hear him as I knew my mother would have told him what I'd said to her when he got home from work. His voice sounded flat and disapproving, but not angry; he said he wanted to come to my flat to talk.'

Rihanna paused and took a deep breath before continuing. 'I was scared, Cathy. I didn't think my father would hurt me but I knew my cousins could. I guessed my mother would have phoned her sister and told her. When I heard the doorbell ring I was nearly sick with worry. My father was alone and he looked dreadful – tired and ill – and I knew I was responsible. I said I was sorry for bringing shame on our family. He didn't say anything; he just walked past me and went into the living room and sat down. It was only the second time he'd been to my flat and I saw him look around at all the photographs of Harrison I have propped along my bookshelves. I offered him a drink but he refused. I sat down and there was this awful silence when he couldn't look at me; then he said: "I am very disappointed with you, Rihanna. You went behind our backs and saw a man who you knew we would not have approved of. You deceived us for a long, long time. That was wrong of you. Now there is a child whose existence you have kept hidden with more lies. I understand from your mother that the child is being looked after by the state. I am embarrassed. He is our responsibility and I will not have him living on charity and brought up by strangers. The child is innocent. He is also our grandchild."'

As Rihanna said the word 'grandchild' she stopped, overcome by emotion and delved into her pocket for a tissue. Wiping her eyes she took a moment before continuing. 'My father said that although he was disappointed in the way I'd behaved he recognized we lived in England in the twenty-first century and that times were different. He said he didn't condone what I'd done, but that the baby should not be an orphan and abandoned on the state. He said our family had a duty to the child and that he would stand by me so that I could fulfil my duty.' Rihanna paused again and looked at me intently. As I met her gaze anxiety gripped me. 'Cathy, I know this seems incredible but my father is waiting outside in the car. He wants me to take Harrison home with me now.'

Chapter Twenty-Four

Harrison

Hearing that Rihanna now wanted the baby she'd abandoned into foster care should have been good news. It should have sent me hugging and kissing Rihanna, crying with joy. The perfect end to her story and so wonderful that it was happening just before Christmas. But as I sat in the armchair and gazed at Rihanna, as astonished and overcome as she was by her father's unexpected change of attitude, I desperately sought the right words to deal with what could be a very ugly scene.

'Rihanna, I'm very pleased your father is taking a supportive role,' I began carefully. 'And I appreciate he is a proud man who is having to come to terms with an awful lot. But have you thought through the implications if you were to take Harrison now? I mean—'

'Oh yes!' Rihanna cried, interrupting and child-like in her enthusiasm. 'I want Harrison more than anything in the world. I always have done.'

'I know,' I said slowly. 'And I've always thought you'd make an excellent mother. But on a practical level have you thought about how you'd look after Harrison if you took him tonight? Do you have a cot, bedding, food, nappies? There's been no transition period for Harrison to get used to you; he's going to be very upset and cry a lot. And who will look after him tomorrow when you go to work?' These were not my only concerns but, aware that Rihanna could take Harrison if she wished, I was being very diplomatic and careful in what I said.

'We'll manage,' Rihanna said. 'My mother's still very upset but Father says she'll recover; then she'll help me, as this has Father's backing.'

'And what about your cousins?' I asked. 'I thought you feared their reaction if they found out?'

'Father says he'll speak to his brother-in-law. He says they need only know I have a baby; they don't need to see Harrison or know about Harrison's father.'

'And what about your sister?' I persisted. 'You said if her fiancé found out about Harrison it could jeopardize her marriage or marriage prospects?'

'I don't know,' Rihanna said, sighing. 'So much has happened tonight. Father says he needs time to think about what to tell my sister.' Which didn't lessen my concerns that Rihanna and her father had acted impulsively – without thinking through the many and far-reaching implications.

'Rihanna,' I said seriously, 'can I tell you what I think you should do – from my experience of being a foster carer?' She gave a small, unconvincing nod and I knew she was only half-listening to me. 'I think you should see Harrison tonight but leave him here. This will give you and your father a chance to think—'

'No,' she said, interrupting and shaking her head. 'I've been apart from my son for too long. I don't want to spend another night lying awake in bed and thinking of him. I want him with me tonight.'

'Please listen,' I said more forcefully, overriding her excitement. 'Apart from the practical aspects of looking after Harrison – where he will sleep and what he will eat, etc. – and the confusion it would cause him if you took him tonight, what do you think the social services will do when they find out?' I finally had her attention.

'I don't know,' she said, looking at me, concerned.

'I do. If you take Harrison now I will have to phone the emergency duty social worker and tell him you've taken Harrison. I can't do anything else. Because you put Harrison in care voluntarily – under a Section 20 – you won't have broken the law, but suddenly removing Harrison from care will raise concerns with the social services. They will almost certainly apply for an Interim Care Order, or even an Emergency Protection Order if the police are involved. This means Harrison will be brought straight back here by a social worker with the police. Then, in the weeks that follow, your solicitor will have to hire a barrister and you will spend months going to court trying to build a case to show why you should have Harrison returned to your care. During that period you will probably have supervised contact for a few hours a week. If the social services are concerned about your mental health, which they are likely to be if you just snatch Harrison, then they will ask for a psychiatrist's report, which will take even more time. Your family's history will be examined and only when all the reports have been written will the judge make his or her decision. And make no mistake, it will be the judge's decision if Harrison lives with you or goes for adoption, not yours or your father's. Do you understand?'

I had spoken plainly, bluntly, but Rihanna needed to be aware of the likely consequences if she took Harrison now. The euphoria had gone from her face and she stared at me anxiously. I felt sorry that I was responsible, but I'd been a foster carer for long enough to know that what I'd said was true.

'But he's my baby and I love him,' she said plaintively. 'I put him in foster care because I couldn't see any other way. Now there is another way and I want to look after him. I love Harrison and I want him back.'

'Yes, I understand that,' I said more gently. 'But taking Harrison tonight is not the way forward. What you should do is this: see Harrison now and then leave him here and go home. Tomorrow, phone your solicitor first thing in the morning and tell her everything you've told me. Your solicitor will then advise you on how best to proceed. She will inform the social services and apply for contact for you so that you can see Harrison. Contact can usually be set up straightaway under a Section 20 if the social services feel it is appropriate, but as the offices are closed over Christmas it might take a few days.'

Rihanna sighed.

'There will be a lot going on behind the scenes,' I continued. 'Meetings, reports – and there's the adoption plans to put on hold. But all that will take less time than if you take Harrison now and the social services apply for a care order. Also, if you are seen to be doing the right thing and acting rationally then the social services are more likely to support your application to have Harrison returned to you.'

'And the social services will definitely let me have Harrison if I do as you say?' Rihanna asked anxiously.

'I can't promise,' I said. 'But there is a much better chance if you do this in a planned and controlled manner than if you take him tonight, believe me.'

She fell silent.

'Do you want to talk about this with your father, as he's in the car?' I suggested a moment later.

'Yes, I should.' She nodded. 'I hadn't really thought about all the things you've said. I don't think my father had either.'

'No,' I agreed.

Rihanna stood; I stood too, and then I went with her to the front door. I watched her go down the path; then I heard a car door open and close behind the hedge followed by silence, so I guessed Rihanna had got into the car to talk to her father. The night air was freezing; a frost had already settled on the roof-tops and pavement, glistening in the light from the street lamp. It was a beautiful night befitting Christmas in England, which I would have appreciated had it not been for the events now unfolding.

I closed the front door and then stood for a moment, deep in thought, before going down the hall and into the sitting room. I hovered anxiously in the middle of the room, surrounded by the decorations but with all thoughts of Christmas now gone. It was nearly eleven o'clock and I would normally be on my way to bed now, but I knew there was little chance of that, whatever Rihanna decided. If she went against my advice and took Harrison I'd have to telephone the duty social worker and then spend most of the night on standby, receiving calls updating me until Harrison was returned, and even if Rihanna didn't take Harrison I doubted I would sleep after all this.

As I waited in the sitting room for Rihanna to finish talking to her father I fretted over the image of Harrison crying if he was woken in the night and then taken from the house by a virtual stranger. I dearly hoped Rihanna and her father made the right decision, for all their sakes.

A few minutes later I heard a tapping on the front door, and I returned down the hall and lifted the flap on the security spyhole. Rihanna stood alone on the doorstep and I opened the door.

'Sorry, Cathy,' she said awkwardly. 'My father is asking if he can meet you. Can he come in just for a few minutes?' She looked tired and strained and I thought she had been crying again.

I hesitated. 'Why does he want to meet me?' I asked uneasily.

'To talk to you about Harrison, just for a moment.'

'All right,' I agreed.

A Baby's Cry

Rihanna disappeared back down the path as I held open the door. I glanced upstairs. It was still quiet; thankfully the children hadn't woken. It would be bad enough if Adrian and Paula had to wake on Christmas Eve morning to find Harrison gone, but even worse if they woke and saw him being taken. I heard a car door open and close, and then Rihanna appeared at the end of the path with her father just behind her. About five foot ten inches tall, he was smartly dressed in a three-quarter-length grey coat over a suit and tie. Rihanna came in and then her father paused on the doorstep and offered his hand.

'Thank you for agreeing to see me,' he said tightly but politely.

I gave a little smile and shook his hand, and he stepped in. Rihanna, now familiar with the layout of my house, was walking down the hall towards the sitting room while her father hovered uncertainly in the hall.

'We'll go into the sitting room to talk,' I said, closing the front door, and I nodded for him to follow his daughter. I guessed Rihanna's father was in his late sixties. He was clearly a proud man, and I could also see he felt uncomfortable coming into my house.

I followed them down the hall and into the sitting room, where I quietly closed the door. Rihanna was already sitting on the sofa, while her father hesitated in the centre of the room.

'Do sit down,' I said to him.

He sat on the sofa next to his daughter and I saw his gaze flicker around the Christmas decorations before settling on the photographs of Harrison propped on the mantelpiece. I sat in the armchair and looked at them. Seated side by side on the sofa I could see a strong family likeness between Rihanna and her father – similar to the likeness I'd seen between Rihanna and Harrison. I wondered if her father could see the likeness too from Harrison's photographs. He moved his gaze to me.

'Thank you for looking after my daughter's child,' he said stiffly. 'I should give you some money towards the costs you have incurred.' He began reaching inside his jacket for his wallet.

'There's no need,' I said quickly. 'I'm given an allowance by the state, to which you have contributed through your taxes.'

Rihanna touched his arm and he took his hand from his jacket pocket and returned it to his lap. I wondered if his visit and his wish to support Rihanna were more about repairing family pride than a real desire to play a part in the lives of his daughter and grandchild. There was a small silence before he said: 'As a parent you will appreciate how difficult this is for me. I've had a dreadful shock this evening. Not only have I learnt that my daughter has been seeing a man she knew her mother and I would not have approved of, but I have also learnt I have a grandson who has been kept secret from us.'

I glanced at Rihanna, who was sitting slightly hunched forward and concentrating on the floor. She was a child again in her father's presence, a naughty child who had done wrong, and I had difficulty equating this woman with the competent doctor she was in her working life.

'You will appreciate just what a shock this has been,' her father said again. 'I have another daughter who is due to marry next year. I also have a large extended family, who will need to be told something. Rihanna's actions have made things very difficult for all of us, but that is for me to deal with.' He paused. 'Now I know I have a grandchild he is my responsibility. It is my wish we should take him home with us tonight. However, I understand you have objections to this.'

'Not objections,' I said, meeting his gaze. 'But I have concerns, which I have discussed with Rihanna.'

'Would you explain your concerns to me, please?' he asked tightly.

'If Rihanna gives her permission, yes,' I said. He looked taken aback, presuming, I suppose, that I, like Rihanna, would concede to his wishes. I felt a small satisfaction in empowering Rihanna. 'Confidentiality forbids me from discussing Rihanna's case without her permission, even with her father,' I added.

'It is all right to tell my father,' Rihanna said quietly.

I now told Rihanna's father what I had told Rihanna: that I believed taking Harrison would be very upsetting for him and would also upset the social services. I explained what I thought Rihanna should do: leave Harrison here and then contact her solicitor first thing in the morning.

Her father nodded non-committally as I spoke and when I'd finished he asked: 'Have you had a lot of experience in dealing with the social services?'

'Yes. I have been fostering for ten years.'

He nodded again. 'Then we must take your advice and do as you say.' Which surprised me as, given his previous authoritative attitude, I had expected him to argue. 'We will leave the child here and I will contact my solicitor first thing in the morning and see what he has to say.'

'Father, I've told you I have a solicitor already,' Rihanna said quietly, without looking at her father.

Her father glanced at me, apparently embarrassed, and then addressed his daughter. 'Rihanna, which solicitor we use is for us to decide outside this house. It is no concern of this lady.'

'Agreed,' I put in, not appreciating being sidelined. 'But you will need a solicitor who is well practised in family law. Rihanna's solicitor is experienced in this type of law and also knows Rihanna's case well. She has been involved right from the beginning. I would think very carefully before you change solicitor now, at such a delicate stage in the proceedings.' Rihanna glanced at me gratefully, and I threw her a small smile.

Her father gave another non-committal nod and then, fastening one button on his coat, stood, ready to leave. Rihanna was immediately on her feet too. 'We have kept you long enough,' he said formally. 'Thank you for your time.'

Again I was surprised – by his sudden departure. I wasn't completely clear why he'd asked to see me, unless it was to confirm what Rihanna had told him or to offer me money. 'Wouldn't you like to see Harrison before you go?' I asked them both.

He looked at me and then at Rihanna, confused.

'My baby is called Harrison,' Rihanna clarified, so I guessed he hadn't had a chance to familiarize himself with the name yet, which was understandable.

He hesitated, and his eyes flickered again to the photographs of Harrison on the mantelpiece and he looked almost scared.

'We'll go up quietly so that we don't wake him or my children,' I said, crossing to the sitting-room door. It seemed appropriate he saw Harrison and I'd already told Rihanna she could see him.

Rihanna followed me, and her father followed her as we went down the hall and up the stairs. I heard the stairs creek behind me and hoped again we wouldn't wake Adrian and Paula, who would be very unsettled if they found strangers in the house in the middle of the night. We arrived outside Harrison's bedroom door, which as usual I'd left slightly ajar so that I could hear him if he woke. Easing the door open, I stepped in; the light from the landing fell gently into the room, giving enough light for us to see without waking him. Rihanna and her father joined me beside the cot and the three of us gazed down at Harrison. He was flat on his back, arms spread wide apart with his mouth relaxed, open in sleep. The soft toy panda and teddy bear Rihanna had bought for him sat on guard at the foot of the cot. All that could be heard for some moments was the faint creak of the radiator as the central heating hummed, and Harrison's light breathing. The three of us gazed down on him and he lay innocent of the attention.

Presently Rihanna leant forward and lightly adjusted the covers around his chin. I looked past her to her father, and in that moment any doubts I'd had as to his sincerity vanished. His eyes brimmed with tears and his bottom lip trembled as he tried to contain his emotion. A minute later he took a white cotton handkerchief from his jacket pocket and, pressing it to his eyes, walked from the bedroom. Rihanna quickly kissed Harrison's forehead; he snuffled but didn't wake, and she went out after her father. I also left the room, easing the door to behind me.

Downstairs I joined Rihanna and her father in the hall. 'We'll do as you say,' her father said, going to the front door, clearly embarrassed by his show of emotion and wanting to be away.

'Thank you,' Rihanna said gratefully to me and kissed my cheek. 'I'll be in touch.'

I nodded. 'Take care and good luck.'

Once they'd gone I closed and bolted the front door with utter relief, and then switched off the porch light. I went through to the sitting room, where I took my fostering folder from the shelf and, opening it, began writing up my log notes. I knew I needed to do this before I went to bed if there was to be any chance of sleep. There was a lot to write; I finished one page and went on to the next. The clock on the mantelpiece ticked past midnight; it was now officially Christmas Eve.

I knew the path ahead was not going to be as easy or straightforward as Rihanna and her father believed. The social services would need to be absolutely certain that if they returned Harrison to Rihanna it was best for him. There were many outstanding issues that were worrying me, as I knew they would worry the social services. How would Rihanna's extended family react when they were told of Harrison? If Harrison was thought to be in any danger from threats from Rihanna's cousins the social services would not return Harrison to Rihanna. Then there was Rihanna's mother, who had yet to come to terms with the news she had a grandchild, and if she didn't, the social services would view her rejection in a very negative light. I also knew the racist attitude of Rihanna's father towards Harrison's father (which was presumably upheld by the rest of the family) would count against Harrison being returned to Rihanna.

And what about Harrison's father? I wondered now as I had before. Didn't he have a right to know he had a child now that the fact was out in the open? And didn't Harrison have a right to know who his father was and even have him in his life? The social services might think so. And, on a purely practical level, how would Rihanna look after a baby when she had a demanding job with very long hours? There were many issues to which the social services would want answers and I knew it could take months before a decision was reached. In the end the decision could be that Harrison should be adopted. That Rihanna had had a change of heart didn't mean the social services would too.

I eventually finished writing up my log notes and, closing the folder, returned it to the shelf. What tomorrow would bring or where Harrison would be next Christmas Eve I'd no idea.

Chapter Twenty-Five
Best Christmas

'And I thought you were phoning to wish me a Merry Christmas!' Jill joked, as I finally finished telling her all about Rihanna's and her father's visit of the night before. It was 9.45 on Christmas Eve morning and I'd been talking to Jill on the phone for nearly half an hour. 'I'll phone Cheryl straight-away,' Jill now said more seriously. 'She'll probably want to speak to you. Are you at home today?'

'I'm going shopping this morning but I'll have my mobile with me. I'll be in this afternoon and obviously this evening – it's Christmas Eve.'

'All right. I'll phone Cheryl now. And Cathy?'

'Yes?'

'You handled the situation well. If you hadn't been able to persuade Rihanna and her father out of taking Harrison, the police would certainly have been involved, resulting in court action. The social services might yet apply for a care order but it's not so likely. So well done.'

'Thank you,' I said, relieved I'd done the right thing.

Having said goodbye to Jill I changed Harrison's nappy and dressed him in his outdoor clothes, ready for our shopping trip. At the same time I called Adrian and Paula to come and put on their shoes and coats, but they were too excited with thoughts of Christmas to want to bother with food shopping. However, when I pointed out that there wouldn't be a Christmas dinner if we didn't go to the high street they were ready in five minutes. 'We won't be long,' I said, for I had no more desire to shop on Christmas Eve than they had.

But once we were in the high street there was such a festive atmosphere that our shopping trip became quite enjoyable. Decorations and lights festooned the shops and hung across the street; a small choir from our local church sang carols in the square; and a man dressed as Father Christmas sat in a large model sleigh, handing out sweets to the children as he collected money for charity. While shopping we met people we knew, all of whom stopped to wish us a Merry Christmas and a Happy New Year, as we did them, so our quick trip to the shops became extended, but pleasantly so. My mobile phone didn't ring, which was something of a relief as it would have been difficult to maintain confidentiality in the busy high street. I sometimes have to creep down an alleyway to take a call about a child I am fostering or find a quiet corner if I'm in a shop. Sometimes I simply have to tell the social worker I'm in a public place and that I will return their call as soon as I can. But Cheryl didn't phone until we were home again and I'd unpacked the shopping, and then her call was brief.

'Thanks for all you did last night,' she said. 'Jill has phoned, and also Rihanna and her father phoned me first thing this morning. I've spoken to them at some length. I've explained to them the process we have to follow in considering Rihanna's application to have Harrison returned to her. I've made it clear that a lot of work has to be done before a decision can be reached. I've also told Rihanna and her father that there is little the department can do over the Christmas week, as we have only a skeletal emergency staff. Rihanna would like contact and I've spoken to my manager. Cathy, this is what I would like to suggest to Rihanna, if you agree.'

'Yes?' I asked tentatively, wondering what I was being asked to commit to.

'Rihanna is entitled to some contact with Harrison at this point, whatever the eventual outcome. I can't set up supervised contact until we have a full staff – after Christmas – so I'd like to suggest that Rihanna sees Harrison at your house, with you present, if you agree. It would only be for one hour, and on a day to suit you and your family.'

'I see,' I said hesitantly.

'You can say no if you wish,' Cheryl added.

'I'm just concerned about the impact this will have on my children,' I said. 'They are at home from school all over Christmas and the New Year. What can I tell them? They're prepared for Harrison being adopted.'

'Which he might be yet,' Cheryl said. 'It's up to you, Cathy. If necessary Rihanna will have to wait until the New Year, when we can arrange supervised contact at the family centre.'

Then I had a thought. 'Could Rihanna come on Boxing Day?' I asked. 'Adrian and Paula will be out with their father then.'

'I'll phone her now and ask. What time on Boxing Day?'

'Is twelve o'clock all right?'

'I don't see why not. I'll get back to you.'

We said goodbye and fifteen minutes later Cheryl phoned to confirm that twelve o'clock on Boxing Day was fine with Rihanna, and also thanked me on Rihanna's behalf. 'Rihanna has given permission for me to give you her mobile number,' Cheryl said, 'in case you have to change arrangements.'

I reached for a pen and paper and wrote down Rihanna's mobile number as Cheryl gave it to me. 'It would make sense for Rihanna to have my mobile number too,' I said. 'Shall I text it to her?'

'Yes, if you're happy doing that. Thank you.'

Best Christmas

Cheryl and I wished each other a Merry Christmas and we said goodbye.

Once I'd hung up, so that I didn't forget, I immediately entered Rihanna's telephone number in my mobile and then texted her so that she had my number: *See you on 26th Dec at 12. Cathy Glass.* A minute later my phone bleeped with an incoming text: *Thank u. I'm so excited!*

I hoped Rihanna's excitement wouldn't be short-lived, for as Cheryl had explained to her she was having contact because she was entitled to it; it didn't mean Harrison would be returned to her. As a foster carer I'd seen many cases where regular contact between a child and the parents had been maintained even though there was no chance of the child being returned to live with the parents. While foster carers, social workers and other professionals working in social care would question if it was really in the best interests of the child (or parents) to encourage a bond that would eventually have to be broken, it was what the court had directed so it had to be followed. I feel there are many areas in social care where a more holistic, realistic and long-term appraisal of the situation would avoid further heartache for children and their parents.

Putting aside my thoughts and worries about Rihanna I concentrated on Christmas. While Adrian and Paula played and kept Harrison amused in the sitting room I went into the kitchen to prepare as much as I could for the following day. There would be eight of us including my parents and my brother and his wife for Christmas dinner, and they would be arriving at about eleven o'clock on Christmas morning. I made the stuffing for the turkey and put it in the fridge; then I carefully took our best crockery and cutlery (reserved for guests and special occasions) from the cupboard. I put these to one side with the decorative Christmas tablecloth, napkins and Harrison's *First Christmas* beaker, plate and bib. Although at nearly six months Harrison would be too young to remember Christmas I'd take lots of photographs; these, together with the Christmas memorabilia, would go with him when he left and form part of his history, which he would appreciate when he was older.

As bedtime approached Adrian and Paula grew more and more excited until it was time for bed and they could hang their pillowcases on the end of their beds, ready for Father Christmas. We'd already hung a pillowcase on the end of Harrison's cot, for while Harrison was too young to understand Father Christmas would call and fill his pillowcase with presents, it was important for Adrian, Paula and me that Harrison was fully included in our family's Christmas.

'What time does Father Christmas come?' Paula asked me for the third time that evening as I kissed her goodnight.

'When you're asleep!' Adrian called excitedly from his bedroom.

I smiled at her. 'He's right.'

While Paula, aged five, believed in Father Christmas, Adrian, aged nine, had big doubts. He questioned the existence of Father Christmas, while not wanting to completely disbelieve. So when he'd asked me outright if Father Christmas existed, rather than spoiling the magic by harsh reality and saying no, or lying and saying yes, I'd said: 'Father Christmas is part of the magic of Christmas and it's nice to believe,' which Adrian had accepted.

Not understanding what all the excitement was about Harrison was fast asleep at his usual bedtime, while Adrian and Paula lay in their beds, too excited to sleep. They'd left their bedroom doors open and every so often called excitedly to each other across the landing; I could hear them from downstairs and smiled. Children who are too excited to go to sleep on Christmas Eve are part of the joy of Christmas. Eventually Adrian and Paula would fall asleep, safe in the knowledge that when they woke they would find their pillowcases brimming with presents and that Christmas Day would be one of the best days of their lives.

Sadly many children never experience the joy of Christmas and wake to another day of abuse and neglect, where the most they can hope for is to escape another beating, and party games are as unlikely as finding their parents sober or not suffering the effects of drug withdrawal. Christmas dinner for those children is likely to be whatever they can find in the bottom of the fridge; sometimes there is nothing and they make do with dry cereal – there always seems to be a packet of cereal in the home of neglected children but rarely fresh milk. The gap between well-looked-after children and those who are neglected and abused is never wider than at Christmas. That night as I went to bed I thought of little Ellie who, now in care, would be experiencing her first proper Christmas, and the thousands of children for whom tomorrow would be no more than another day of suffering.

'He's been!'

'Father Christmas has been!'

I heard Adrian's and Paula's voices calling from their bedrooms the following morning. I turned over and, opening my eyes, looked at the bedside clock: 6.30. Not too bad, I thought, as last year they'd woken at 5.15 on Christmas morning.

'Merry Christmas!' I called back.

Traditionally in our house on Christmas morning we all group in one bedroom and I watch Adrian and Paula unwrap their presents. Pushing my feet into my slippers, I slipped into my dressing gown and, picking up the camera from on top of the chest of drawers where I'd left it ready the night before, I padded round the landing. I quickly checked on Harrison, who was still asleep, and then went into Paula's bedroom. Adrian was sitting on the foot of Paula's bed, having brought in his pillowcase full of presents, and Paula was propped up in bed with her pillowcase bulging beside her. They grinned as I entered and I gave them both a kiss.

'Merry Christmas,' I said again.

'Merry Christmas, Mum,' they chorused.

Delving into their pillowcases they began unwrapping their presents, while I stood to one side, smiling happily and taking photographs.

The look on children's faces as they tear off wrapping paper to reveal a gift they've wanted for some time is priceless and makes all the work that goes into Christmas completely worthwhile. I stood beside Paula's bed, caught up in their joy as she and Adrian repeatedly dipped their hands into their pillowcases, held up another present and then unwrapped it.

'How did Father Christmas know it's just what I wanted?' Paula exclaimed over and over again.

While Adrian smiled and said, 'Thanks, Mum,' each time he unwrapped a present.

Apart from their main gifts – toys they'd previously mentioned they'd like for Christmas – there were 'stocking fillers' of chocolate novelties, fancy socks, a mug each emblazoned with their favourite Walt Disney cartoon, and an art and craft activity set. They were so pleased and grateful it touched me deeply and again I appreciated how lucky I was to have my children. Just as Adrian and Paula finished unwrapping their presents we heard Harrison call out as he woke. Leaving their opened presents on Paula's bed, they came with me to Harrison's room.

'Happy Christmas,' we chimed. Harrison greeted us with a big smile and then pursing his lips blew a raspberry, which was a new trick of his and always made us laugh.

Best Christmas

'Look, Harry!' Paula exclaimed, pointing to the pillowcase of presents on the end of his cot. 'Father Christmas has been!'

Harrison grinned and blew another raspberry. I lowered the side of the cot, lifted him out and quickly put a dry nappy on him, while Adrian unhooked the pillowcase and propped it on the floor. Having fastened the last of the press-studs on his sleep-suit I sat Harrison on the floor beside his pillowcase and took the first photograph. He looked slightly startled as the flash went off and then he grinned and clapped his hands in appreciation. Adrian and Paula knelt either side of him and began taking the presents from the pillowcase and helped him unwrap them. Indeed they unwrapped the presents for him, as to begin with Harrison was more interested in the brightly coloured wrapping paper that crinkled and crackled rather than the present inside. But as the presents emerged – a play centre with buttons to push that made various sounds; two first books; a push-along car; a soft toy in the shape of a fire engine – he began to take more interest. The final photograph I took was of Harrison nestled like a hamster in the middle of his presents and wrapping paper and grinning at the camera. 'Perfect,' I said, and it was.

I returned Harrison to his cot with a couple of his new toys while I showered and dressed. Adrian and Paula returned to Paula's room and played with their presents, and also kept an eye on Harrison. Once I was ready I dressed Harrison and took him downstairs, where I gave him a breakfast of porridge. Presently Adrian and Paula appeared in their dressing gowns but didn't want any breakfast, just a drink, as they'd eaten a large chocolate bar each from their selection boxes. 'No more chocolate until later,' I said, and they agreed.

By eleven o'clock we were all ready, and excitedly awaiting the arrival of my parents and my brother and his wife. The Christmas tree lights glowed, Christmas music played in the background, the vegetables for dinner were prepared and the turkey was cooking in the oven. My parents arrived first, laden with presents. We all kissed and exchanged Christmas greetings; then once they'd taken off their coats we went through to the sitting room, where we put the presents they'd brought under the tree to be opened later. I made them coffee and warmed mince pies; then my brother and his wife arrived, also with a bag of gifts. From then on our Christmas really got under way, with games, lots of fun and laughter and a huge Christmas dinner; then in the afternoon we settled around the Christmas tree and opened our presents.

My brother and his wife as usual made a great fuss of Adrian, Paula and Harrison. I knew they were trying for a baby and I hoped they didn't have to wait long, for it was obvious how much love they had to give a child and what great parents they'd make. I took lots of photographs, as did my parents and my brother and his wife. Our Christmases are always well photographed and afterwards I choose the best family group photograph, which I have enlarged and then frame and display on the wall in the sitting room; my parents and brother do the same at their houses. Each Christmas seems even better than the last, and I knew how lucky I was to have such a wonderful family and to be able to enjoy Christmas with them.

I didn't say anything to my parents (or my brother and his wife) about Rihanna's visits or that she'd changed her mind and now wanted to parent Harrison. It wasn't the place or time and I knew my parents, in particular, would be very worried if they knew of the uncertainty now surrounding Harrison's future. As it was, they believed Harrison would be adopted and if that changed – nothing was certain yet – I would tell them.

It was after ten o'clock when all our guests finally made a move to go, and Adrian, Paula and I saw them off at the door. 'Thanks for a lovely day, and for all our presents,' Mum said again, while Dad said, 'Best Christmas ever,' and we all agreed.

Best Christmas

I'd put Harrison to bed an hour before, as he'd started to fall asleep on my mother's lap, and, having closed the front door on another clear but cold night, I steered two tired but very happy children up the stairs and into the bathroom for a quick wash before they climbed into their beds. As I kissed first Paula and then Adrian goodnight their smiling faces said it all: their hopes, dreams and wishes for a magical Christmas had come true and I knew they would sleep well tonight.

Having looked in on Harrison – he was fast asleep – I went downstairs to make a cup of tea before going to bed, for I too was exhausted. It then occurred to me that I hadn't checked my mobile phone since that morning; I'd been too busy having fun. Returning downstairs I took my phone from my handbag and opened the messages. I had four texts – three from friends wishing me a Merry Christmas, and one from Rihanna: *Hi Cathy, is it OK if I bring my mother tomorrow?* Sent at 2.15 p.m.

I paused for a moment with my phone in my hand. Clearly Rihanna's mother must be over the shock of learning she had a grandchild and now wanted to see him. I wasn't sure this was a good idea at this point, for if Harrison was adopted she wouldn't see him again. Wouldn't it be better to wait until the social services had made their decision, and if Rihanna was to be allowed to keep Harrison for her to see him then, rather than start to bond with him now and then have to say goodbye in a couple of months? However, as Harrison was still in care on a Section 20 Rihanna could make this decision and it wasn't my place to object, so I texted back: *Yes. See you at 12.*

Chapter Twenty-Six
Little Brother

The house seemed morbidly quiet after all the fun and laughter of the day before, as though it has been abandoned, which in a way it had. Adrian and Paula were out with their father; Toscha had finished off some turkey leftovers and was now in the garden; which left Harrison and me in the sitting room, awaiting the arrival of his mother and grandmother. Rihanna hadn't said if her father was coming but I had assumed he would be.

Harrison and I were on the floor in the sitting room. Harrison was sitting in the middle of the playmat my parents had bought him as a Christmas present and I was kneeling beside him, showing him all the different activities that were incorporated into the mat. He was completely enthralled by the various colours, sounds and textures that the mat offered as he touched it. It was a lovely present and I knew it would keep him amused for hours

At exactly twelve o'clock the front doorbell rang and Harrison looked up towards the sound. 'I'll be back in a minute,' I said. Standing, I went down the hall to answer the door.

Rihanna stood in the porch, holding a shopping bag containing gaily wrapped Christmas presents and smiling. Her mother and father stood just behind her, looking sombre and uneasy.

'Hello. Do come in.' I smiled warmly.

Little Brother

'This is my mother,' Rihanna said, as they stepped in.

'Hello,' her mother said quietly to me.

'Pleased to meet you,' I said and shook her hand, and then Rihanna's father's hand. 'Can I take your coats?' I asked.

Rihanna and her mother took off their headscarves and gloves and tucked them into their coat pockets and I hung their coats on the hall stand as her father hung up his own coat. Rihanna's mother, much shorter than her husband and daughter, was dressed smartly in a blue two-piece woollen suit with matching accessories. All three of them took off their outdoor shoes, which was considerate, and paired them with ours in the hall.

'Harrison is in the sitting room,' I said.

Rihanna led the way down the hall, followed by her parents and then me.

'Hello Harrison!' Rihanna cried as she entered the sitting room. 'Have you had a nice Christmas?' She knelt down beside Harrison. 'What have you got there?' she said, pressing the furry picture of the cow on the playmat. The picture mooed, Harrison grinned, and Rihanna pressed it again while her parents stood by awkwardly.

'Do sit down,' I said to them. 'Can I get you a tea or coffee?'

'No thank you,' her father said on behalf of all three of them.

Her parents sat on the sofa and I sat in the armchair as Rihanna continued to play with Harrison on the mat. Rihanna seemed to be reasonably relaxed with him, instinctively knowing what to do, despite the little time she'd spent with him. 'Was this a Christmas present?' Rihanna asked Harrison, referring to the mat.

Harrison grinned and gurgled and pulled the tail on the woolly monkey, which made another sound.

'It was a present from my parents,' I said.

'That was kind of them,' Rihanna said, looking up at me. 'Please thank them from me.' Then to Harrison: 'Look. I've brought you some presents too.' Delving into the shopping bag Rihanna had brought with her she began taking out the brightly wrapped presents and setting them next to Harrison. Soon he was surrounded by parcels of various shapes and sizes.

'He'll need some help unwrapping them,' I said.

Rihanna took one of the presents and, holding it just in front of Harrison, began picking off the sticky tape, 'Like this,' she said to him, gradually removing the paper to reveal the present, which was a push-along truck. He grinned and Rihanna began to unwrap the next present.

Having seen many presents opened the day before Harrison now had a better idea of what was required and was soon grabbing the paper and helping Rihanna unwrap the parcels, which made her very happy. 'What a clever boy you are!' she said, delighted. Then she looked at me again. 'Do you think you could take some photographs of us? I've brought my camera.'

'Yes, of course,' I said, standing and going over.

Rihanna took her camera from her bag and, opening the lens, showed me which button to press. I knelt on the floor a little way from them and as Rihanna and Harrison began unwrapping the next present together I took a photograph and then another. Harrison, used to having his photograph taken, seemed to pose, and Rihanna and I laughed. I glanced at her parents, who were sitting stiffly upright on the sofa; her father was expressionless, while her mother was stony-faced. It was obviously very difficult for them; not only were they having to come to terms with having a grandchild but also that this could be one of the few times they would see Harrison if he was adopted, for Cheryl would have explained that nothing was definite yet.

'Would you like a photograph of you all together?' I asked, glancing at her parents.

'That would be nice,' Rihanna replied eagerly. 'I'll sit on the sofa between my parents with Harrison on my lap.'

Rihanna stood and then carefully lifted Harrison from the playmat and carried him to the sofa, where her parents moved apart so that she could sit between them. I cleared away the wrapping paper from the floor so that it wouldn't be in the photograph and then stood a little way in front of the sofa and looked through the lens of the camera. It could have been the perfect family photograph – with grandparents sitting either side of their daughter and her baby – except their tension was visible on their faces. Rihanna was smiling but her parents weren't and looked very sombre; then Harrison turned away from the camera and playfully tried to grab his mother's hair.

'Harrison, over here!' I called lightly, to attract his attention. He turned and looked at me and therefore at the camera. 'On the count of three, smile,' I said, which is what we always say in my family when taking a group photograph so that everyone is posed and ready and smiling at the camera. 'One ... two ... three,' I said, and took the photograph.

I knew as I pressed the button on the camera that while Harrison and Rihanna had been smiling, and that her father had made a brave attempt to smile, her mother had remained expressionless. I handed the camera back to Rihanna.

She checked the photograph on the viewer and then said: 'Mum, you're not smiling.'

'What is there to smile about?' her mother said quietly.

'My child. Your grandson,' Rihanna returned. Her father looked embarrassed.

I wasn't sure if I should offer to take another photograph for which perhaps her mother could be persuaded to smile, but Rihanna stood and, moving away from the sofa, returned the camera to her bag. 'Thank you, Cathy,' she said pointedly to me, and I felt the atmosphere grow even more strained.

A Baby's Cry

'Are you sure you wouldn't like a coffee?' I offered.

'I would like one,' Rihanna said. 'Thank you.' Her parents shook their heads.

'Milk and sugar?' I asked her.

'Just milk, please.'

I went into the kitchen, where I could hear Rihanna's hushed but firm voice as she talked to her parents. Presumably she was remonstrating with them, for when I returned to the sitting room with Rihanna's coffee, her father said: 'I should apologize. My wife and I are still finding this all very difficult.'

'It's understandable,' I said and smiled. Rihanna's mother nodded stiffly but didn't say anything.

Usually when a baby or child is present the most formal or difficult of situations or gatherings becomes easier, simply because a baby or child is uninhibited and provides a focal point for the adults in the room and they relax. However, as Rihanna returned to sit on the floor and play with Harrison, occasionally reaching for her cup to take a sip of coffee, her parents stayed on the sofa, watching but not saying anything, and the atmosphere grew more and more strained. It was hardly surprising, therefore, that Harrison eventually grew fractious; children and babies are far more sensitive to atmosphere than many adults appreciate. He grumbled and moaned and lost interest in the toys, and then began looking around for me. I went over and checked his nappy but he was dry; then I fetched his beaker of water, wondering if he was thirsty. I passed the beaker to Rihanna so that she could give it to him, but he rejected it and kept pushing it away and grumbling.

'He's usually a very happy baby,' I said. Then I realized it wasn't the best thing to say, as it could have implied it was Rihanna's presence that was upsetting him. 'I expect it's all the excitement,' I added.

Rihanna tried again to distract him from his grumpiness by playing with the mat and the toys she'd given him, but Harrison wasn't having any of it and he niggled and whined. Then he pulled a face as though he was going to cry.

'What's the matter with him?' Rihanna asked me, clearly worried at not being able to placate him.

'He's probably tired,' I said. 'We were late last night.' Which was true, although Harrison had slept in and hadn't appeared to be tired previously. 'Try rocking him,' I suggested. 'He likes a cuddle.'

Still kneeling Rihanna carefully lifted Harrison off the mat and, laying him against her chest, began gently swaying. It seemed to work for a moment and he was quiet and still, but then a minute later he began agitating again and struggled to be put down. I didn't want to intervene and take Harrison from Rihanna, as it could have undermined her confidence by emphasizing her failure to settle him. I felt sorry for Rihanna; she clearly wanted this visit to be a great success and Harrison seemed to be working against her.

'He's tired,' her mother said tightly after a moment. 'We should leave.'

'Yes,' her father agreed, and stood.

I glanced at the clock; there was still ten minutes to the end of their planned hour's visit, but her parents were obviously ready to go. Rihanna, still holding Harrison, didn't say anything, but picked up her shopping bag, stood and went out of the sitting room. Her parents followed in silence. In the hall they unhooked their coats from the hallstand, as Rihanna passed Harrison to me so that she could put on her coat. Harrison immediately stopped grumbling and sat happily in my arms, watching the adults put on their coats and shoes.

'He just needed a change of scenery,' I said. Her parents nodded.

'Goodbye,' her father said, one hand on the doorknob, as her mother tied her headscarf.

'Goodbye,' I said to them both with a small smile.

Her father opened the front door and he went out with his wife as Rihanna hung back and turned to Harrison and me. I could see the look of determination on her face even before she spoke.

'With or without their support I will look after Harrison,' she said. 'How long do you think it will be before I can start seeing him regularly?'

I knew I had to be careful in what I said. Rihanna was in a fragile state and I didn't want anything I said now being later misinterpreted. 'I understand Cheryl will be looking into setting up regular contact when all the staff are back after the Christmas break,' I said.

'In a week, then?' Rihanna said.

'I don't know, but I should think so.'

'Good. I'll tell my solicitor. I'm using the same one. My father's solicitor wasn't a specialist in family law.'

I nodded. Rihanna kissed Harrison goodbye. 'See you soon,' she said to us both. Taking her headscarf from her pocket she looped it over her head and tied it as she went down the path, determination in her footsteps.

I closed the front door against the cold and breathed a sigh of relief. While it hadn't been the most difficult contact I'd ever supervised, it certainly hadn't been the easiest. Rihanna's parents clearly had a long way to go before they could provide Rihanna and Harrison with the support her father had originally offered, and part of me wondered if they ever could. Rihanna seemed determined to go ahead and parent Harrison without them if necessary, but I wondered if she fully appreciated all the practical implications of that. As a single parent and with no family support network Harrison would be wholly reliant on her for all his needs for many years to come.

Little Brother

With another small sigh I carried Harrison through to the kitchen, where I sat him in his high chair and gave him lunch. After lunch I took him upstairs and put him in his cot for his usual afternoon sleep. Downstairs again I went into the sitting room and, opening my fostering folder, I began writing up my log notes. I knew Cheryl would want a detailed report of Rihanna's and her parents' visit when she returned to the office, so I wrote a dispassionate and objective account of the contact, which I would later type up and send to Cheryl and Jill.

Harrison woke after his usual one-hour's sleep and played happily for the rest of the afternoon. Adrian and Paula returned at six o'clock from their day out with their father, carrying their opened Christmas presents from him. They waved him off at the door and then excitedly told me all about their great day out and the pantomime they'd seen that afternoon.

Harrison was very pleased to see Adrian and Paula too, and wouldn't let them out of his sight. I thought how unsettling it must have been for him to see Adrian and Paula disappear from his life for the day and Rihanna and her parents, who were in effect strangers, appear in their place. Harrison was too young to understand that the change was only temporary and that by the end of the day his life would return to normal. When Harrison eventually left us to move to his permanent family – whether it was to adoptive parents or his mother – there would be a carefully planned timetable of introduction, allowing him to gradually spend more time with his permanent family and less with us. This is true for all children who leave a foster family to be adopted or return home and reduces the trauma, but it is crucial for babies and young children, who have not acquired the necessary language skills to have the move explained to them.

We had a late supper that evening, seated around the table finishing off Christmas Day leftovers, and Adrian and Paula were still talking about the day out with their father. I wondered if Harrison would ever experience a day out with his father. I hoped so, for all children benefit from having a father figure in their lives even if their parents don't live together.

The following day Jill phoned and once we'd asked each other if we'd had a nice Christmas I told her about Rihanna's and her parents' visit. Jill wasn't pleased that Rihanna's mother had come and then made no effort to interact with her grandchild, although that wasn't how I'd phrased it. 'It was difficult for them,' I said again.

'Well, the grandparents will need to get their act together before the assessments start or it will count against them,' Jill said, in her usual straight-talking manner.

'Yes. Rihanna asked me when I thought contact would begin and I said about a week.'

'At least. There's only a skeleton staff in until New Year.'

We wished each other a Happy New Year and Jill thanked me for facilitating contact in my home on Boxing Day.

The children and I made the most of the winter break from school and, wrapped up warmly, went to the park when the sun shone or stayed indoors and played with Christmas toys and games when it rained. We also had some friends to visit who had similar-aged children to Adrian and Paula. I didn't hear anything further from Jill or Rihanna until after the New Year – Tuesday 3 January, which was the first day most offices were back at work with a full staff.

Jill phoned at two o'clock and, having quickly asked if we'd had a nice New Year, apologized for the short notice and then said: 'Cheryl's just phoned. It's been decided that supervised contact between Rihanna and Harrison will take place on Tuesdays and Thursdays, four o'clock to five-thirty. They want it to begin straightaway. Sorry, Cathy, but can you take Harrison to the family centre at four o'clock this afternoon?'

I glanced at my watch. 'Yes, I can.'

'And you can collect him again at five-thirty.'

It was a statement not a question. Foster carers are expected to take children to and collect them from contact, often driving miles across the county and rearranging or cancelling their own family's plans to do so. 'Yes,' I said again.

'Will he need feeding?' Jill asked.

'Yes, he usually has his dinner during that time.'

'Can you take it with you, all prepared, so that Rihanna can feed him?'

'Yes, although it will have to be a jar of baby food tonight as I won't have time to prepare and cook dinner before we leave.' I briefly wondered when Adrian, Paula and I would find time to eat. 'I'll also take a change of nappy and baby wipes, in case he needs changing,' I said.

'Thanks, Cathy. I'll confirm the contact with Cheryl now.'

'Jill,' I said concerned, 'Harrison has only seen Rihanna three times, and very briefly. And it was at home with me. To go from that to one and a half hours in a strange setting could be very unsettling for him. Shall I stay to help Rihanna if necessary?'

'I'll mention it to Cheryl but part of the purpose of the contact will be to assess how Rihanna copes with looking after Harrison.' Which did nothing to ease my concerns for Harrison and seemed unfair to Rihanna. Surely it would have been better for them both to have had a couple of short contacts at the family centre first while I was present or waiting out of sight to help if necessary. As it was they were both being 'thrown in at the deep end', but other than making the offer to help there was nothing I could do. It wasn't my decision.

Once Jill and I had said goodbye I went straight into the kitchen, where I took two jars of baby food (which I kept for emergency use) from the cupboard: a chicken and vegetable casserole and a jar of rice pudding. I also took a clean bib from the drawer and a plastic spoon from the sterilizer and put these, together with the jars of food, into Harrison's baby bag. The bag already contained clean nappies, wipes, a change of clothes and other essentials, and was taken with us whenever we were away from the house. I would leave the bag with Rihanna at contact.

Now came the difficult part, I thought: I had to tell Adrian and Paula where we were going and why. They were still unaware that Rihanna had seen Harrison or that she had applied to have him returned to her. With contact now starting I needed to bring them up to date, although I'd have to be careful what I said about Harrison's future, as where he would live permanently was as yet undecided. Leaving Harrison on his playmat for a few minutes I went upstairs and into Adrian's room, where he was trying to teach Paula Monopoly – a present he'd had from my brother for Christmas.

'No, Paula,' Adrian was saying, slightly exasperated. 'I've told you before you can't build a hotel unless you own four houses first.'

Paula sighed, returned the hotel to the box and took out a house, which she placed on Old Kent Road.

'Sorry to interrupt,' I began, 'but just to let you know we will have to go out later – at three-thirty. Harrison has contact with his birth mother at the family centre.' I used the term birth mother to distinguish Rihanna from the adoptive mother Adrian and Paula were expecting to meet at some point during the introductory period if the adoption went ahead.

'That's nice,' Paula said, more interested in how she could build a hotel on Old Kent Road.

'I'll miss *Teenage Mutant Ninja Turtles,*' Adrian said, which was his favourite television progamme.

'I'll record it,' I said.

Adrian threw the dice and they both continued playing. I returned downstairs, aware that the children had been too absorbed in their game to appreciate the implications of what I'd said. I'd explain it to them later. I took Harrison into the kitchen and sat him in his high chair so that I could keep an eye on him while I prepared dinner for us, which I would cook on our return from contact.

Later, when we were in the car and on our way to the family centre, Adrian asked: 'Mum, who did you say Harrison was seeing tonight?'

'His birth mother,' I said, glancing at him in the interior mirror.

'I didn't think Harry had a mother,' Paula said.

'All children have mothers, silly,' Adrian said. 'It's just that some kids don't see their mothers.' Which is what I'd said to Adrian and Paula a number of times before, only without the 'silly'.

'So why's Harry suddenly seeing his mother?' Adrian now asked. 'I thought he was going to be adopted.'

'He might still be adopted,' I said, with another glance in the interior mirror. 'But his birth mother has asked to see him and the social worker has agreed.'

'So Harry will have two mummies and daddies?' Paula asked, understandably confused.

'No. One,' I said. 'The judge will have to decide if Harrison will live with his birth mother or the couple who want to adopt him.'

Paula thought about this for a moment and then said: 'So one mummy and daddy won't have a baby. That's very sad.'

'Yes,' I agreed. And not for the first time my heart went out to the adoptive couple who'd spent Christmas and New Year believing that very soon they'd have their longed-for baby and would now have learnt that they might not.

A Baby's Cry

Then Paula's little voice came again from the back seat, plaintive and upset. 'Mum, I don't want Harry to see his mother, and I don't want him to be adopted. He can't leave us, he's our little brother.'

Chapter Twenty-Seven

Contact

By the time I'd found a place to pull over and stop Paula was crying openly. Adrian, sitting on one side of her, had his arm around her and was trying to comfort her, while Harrison in his car seat on the other side of Paula was looking at her, very concerned. I cut the engine and released my seatbelt, aware that I had to comfort Paula, but also aware that we were going to be late for contact. I turned and, kneeling, reached over to the back seat and took Paula's hand.

'Harrison is only going to see his mother for an hour and a half,' I said. 'Then we'll collect him and he'll come home with us.' For I wondered if Paula had misunderstood and thought that Harrison was staying with his mother for good.

Paula shook her head and more tears fell. 'I don't want Harry to go ever. Not to his birth mother or the other mummy. He's my baby brother and I love him.'

'Oh, darling, I know you love Harry,' I said, stroking her hand. 'We all do. But like the other children we've looked after, at some point the judge will decide that Harrison will have to go to a forever family. The judge made the right decision for the other children, didn't he? They're happy. So I know he'll make the right decision for Harrison.' It was the best I could offer, for I couldn't lie to Paula.

'I'll tell the judge Harry will be happy if he stays with us.' Paula said, giving a small sniff.

I glanced at Adrian, who was sitting very still and quiet, internalizing his feelings as he so often did. 'You know, Harrison is lucky because he has two mummies the judge can choose from,' I said to them both.

'Will we still see Harry when he leaves?' Paula asked, her tears stemming a little.

'I hope so. I'll ask the social worker if we can keep in touch.' Although whether we stayed in contact with Harrison would ultimately be the decision of his forever family.

I gave Paula's hand a little reassuring squeeze and then let go so that I could find a tissue in my bag. As I did, Harrison did something he hadn't done before: pursing his lips he pressed them to Paula's cheek, giving her a kiss. It was the first kiss he'd ever given, a developmental milestone, and how wonderful that he'd chosen this moment to do it!

Paula smiled and wiped her eyes dry. 'Harry kissed me.'

'I know. Are you all right now, love?' I asked.

She nodded.

'Good girl.'

I'd known from when I'd first seen Harrison that we'd all love him and would find saying goodbye very difficult. But I had to believe – as I'd just told Paula and Adrian – that the judge would make the right decision and Harrison would be happy with his forever family, whether it was his mother or the adoptive parents.

I glanced again at Adrian, who was still sitting very quiet, and I smiled reassuringly. I would talk to them both again later but for now I needed to get Harrison to contact. 'All right?' I said to them both and they nodded.

I turned in my seat to face the front, started the car and pulled away. In the interior mirror I saw that Adrian was holding one of Paula's hands again and Harrison was now holding the other. It was the image of perfect sibling love and I felt very sad, for whatever the outcome – whoever Harrison eventually went to live with – the end result would be the same for us. Harrison would no longer be part of our family and I knew we would feel his loss for a long time to come.

It was 4.10 by the time I arrived at the family centre, and I parked on the forecourt. As my car was immediately in front of the main entrance and visible from reception, to save time I decided to leave Adrian and Paula in the car rather than take them in. 'I'll be as quick as I can,' I said. 'Stay put.'

Grabbing the baby bag from the front seat, I got out, went round to the rear of the car and lifted Harrison from his seat. With the baby bag over my shoulder and Harrison in my arms I hurried up the short path and to the door, where I pressed the security buzzer. The door released and I went into reception; a contact supervisor, whom I hadn't met before, was already waiting for me.

'Are you here for the Smith contact?' she asked, using Harrison's surname.

'Yes. Sorry I'm late.'

'The mother is in the contact room waiting. Do you want me to take the baby or will you?'

'I'll take Harrison to Rihanna,' I said, not appreciating the use of 'mother' and 'baby', instead of their names, which sounded disrespectful.

The contact supervisor turned and I followed her down a corridor towards the rear of the building, where the contact rooms were grouped. Contact supervisors vary in their professionalism: some are excellent, while others, in my view, shouldn't be in post. No formal training is necessary to be a contact supervisor and the only qualification required is some experience of working with children and a driving licence. Yet the contact supervisor's role is important and their reports contribute to the decisions made by social workers and ultimately the judge. Contact used to be supervised by the social worker involved with the family, which was a lot better, as they already knew the family well.

At the end of the corridor we turned right into the Blue Room. There were six contact rooms in the centre, named after colours; each was furnished like a sitting room with carpet, curtains, sofa, table and chairs, highchair, cot and plenty of games and puzzles for the children. Rihanna was sitting on the sofa but stood as soon as she saw Harrison. Her face lit up.

'Hello, Cathy. Hello, Harrison. How are you?' she said, coming over.

'He's been fine,' I said, placing Harrison in her outstretched arms. 'How are you?'

'Good now today has finally arrived. It's been a long time coming.' She hugged Harrison hard and smothered him in kisses. Harrison looked around, bemused.

'I've brought a bag with everything you'll need,' I said, taking the baby bag from my shoulder and unzipping it. 'I'll quickly run through it with you.'

'Thanks,' Rihanna said, not looking at the bag and more interested in petting Harrison.

'These two jars are for his dinner,' I began, taking out the jars of baby food. 'He usually has his dinner at five o'clock. I've put a bib in the bag. You can give him his dinner in the high chair, but you'll have to feed him. He can feed himself with finger food, but he is too young to use a spoon yet.'

'Will you remember all this?' the contact supervisor said to Rihanna, noticing she wasn't looking. Rihanna stopped kissing Harrison and, turning her attention to me, looked at the baby bag I was holding open.

Contact

'These two jars,' I continued, 'are his main course and pudding. If he doesn't want all his pudding don't worry. I still give him a bottle of milk at bedtime. I've packed a spoon. It's sterilized, so you don't need to wash it first. He'll want a drink with his dinner and I still boil his water, so in this beaker is his water. It's sealed: you just turn the lid like this,' I said, showing her.

Rihanna was now concentrating hard and looking serious, and I could tell she was struggling to take all this in. Baby feeding and baby routines are easy once you know how, but as every new parent knows they can appear very daunting to begin with. Although Rihanna was an intelligent woman this was a new world to her, as it is for most first-time parents. 'And if he needs a change of nappy,' I finished, 'the nappies are in the bag, with baby wipes, and disposable nappy bags.'

'I see,' Rihanna said slowly. 'Do I need safety pins for the nappies?'

'No, they're disposable.' I quickly took one of the nappies from the bag and showed her the sticky fastener on either side. 'Is there a changing mat here?' I asked the supervisor.

'There should be,' she said, glancing around the room. 'I'll find it later if we need it.'

'If you use the changing mat,' I said to Rihanna, 'wipe it down first with one of these anti-bacterial wipes.' I showed her the pot of wipes in the bag. 'If there isn't a mat you'll have to change him on the floor. There's a small blanket at the bottom of this bag; put that on the floor – it's clean.' Rihanna nodded but continued to look daunted. 'Don't worry,' I said. 'You'll be fine once you've done it. You've got my mobile number; if you're not sure about anything give me a ring.'

'All right, Cathy,' she said, appearing slightly reassured that I was on the end of the phone if needed. 'It's a pity you couldn't have stayed for the first few contacts. I'd have felt happier.'

And not for the first time I wondered why the social services didn't always listen to the intuitive voice of good sense instead of relying on procedure.

'You'll be fine,' I said again to Rihanna. 'Phone if you need me. Have a good time and I'll see you at five-thirty.' Leaving the baby bag on the sofa I smiled at them both, came out and then hurried to the car.

There was just enough time to drive home, cook dinner but not eat it, before we had to return to the family centre to collect Harrison at 5.30. I knew I needed to be better organized for the next contact on Thursday because Adrian and Paula would be at school and I'd have to collect them and go straight to the family centre. Tonight, however, we settled for a quick snack until we could eat dinner after contact.

Rihanna hadn't phoned, so I was optimistic that the contact had gone well and I'd been worrying unnecessarily. I parked on the forecourt and took Adrian and Paula into the centre. It was now dark and cold, so I wasn't going to leave them in the car. They'd been into the family centre before and knew they had to wait in reception and look at the children's books there while I went into the contact room to collect the child we were foster-ing. There was always someone in the office to keep an eye on children waiting in reception.

When I arrived outside the Blue Room the door was closed, so I knocked and went in. I knew as soon as I entered and heard Harrison grizzling that he'd been fretful and had given Rihanna a hard time. That was before I saw the mess! The room looked as though a tornado had swept through it, picking up and depositing at random anything that came into its path. Apart from the toys (belonging to the centre), which had presumably been used to try to placate Harrison and were now dotted around the room, the contents of the baby bag were strewn liberally on every available surface. The blanket was in a heap on the floor, surrounded by nappy bags, baby wipes and three clean but unusable nappies with their sticky fasteners torn off. The two jars of baby food, now empty, were on the tray of the high chair with the spoon, all of which was caked in an unhealthy-looking mixture of chicken casserole and rice pudding, as were the bib and some of the floor. And when I looked at Rihanna, who was pacing the room with Harrison in her arms, I saw that her clothes also bore the stains of what must have been a very interesting meal! I was about to quip something light-hearted about them having had quite a party but I could see from Rihanna's face that this had been no party. She looked hot, flustered and close to tears.

'Oh, Cathy,' she said, coming over. 'I've made such a mess.'

Understatement, I thought. 'Don't worry,' I said. 'We'll soon clear it up.'

'Nothing went right,' Rihanna lamented. 'Harrison wouldn't open his mouth when I tried to feed him. Then when I got some food into his mouth he spat it out. I tried to change his nappy but he kept wriggling and turning over. I nearly phoned you but I knew I should do it myself.' Rihanna glanced in the direction of the supervisor, who sat at the table and was still busy writing.

'Don't worry,' I said again. 'It was strange for both of you. It will be easier the next time.' But obviously Rihanna was worried – not only by her inability to perform what had probably appeared to her to be simple parenting tasks, but also that the contact supervisor had recorded her failure, and indeed was still doing so. Contact supervisors have to make notes during contact as aide memoires for when they write up their reports later, but I'd seen it done far more subtly. Writing so conspicuously must have made Rihanna feel very self-conscious and nervous.

A Baby's Cry

With my arrival Harrison had begun grinning and babbling happily, and struggling to be out of Rihanna's arms and into mine. I ignored him, not to be unkind, but because to have taken him now would have undermined Rihanna's confidence further. 'You play with Harrison while I tidy up,' I said to her. I turned to the surrounding mayhem.

As well as having to gather together the contents of the baby bag, which I would need to take with me, I had to make sure the contact room was left clean and tidy, as it was supposed to be at the end of each session. I began with the high chair, removing the jars and spoon, wiping it down and then collapsing it and stowing it in the cupboard. I then tidied away the toys that belonged to the centre, returning them to the toy boxes. Then I threw the torn nappies away, folded the blanket and put that together with the other items that were mine into the baby bag. It only took five minutes and the contact supervisor could have helped but she didn't, preferring to continue writing her notes, although goodness knows what she was writing – details of my tidying-up? Rihanna was now more relaxed and was cuddling and talking to Harrison, who was his usual sociable self and was smiling at her and no longer struggling to be put down. Finishing the tidying, I zipped up the baby bag, threw it over my shoulder and went over to take Harrison and say goodbye to Rihanna.

'Thank you, Cathy,' Rihanna said with a smile, as she passed Harrison to me. 'What would they say at work if they knew I couldn't feed or change a baby?!'

'All new parents are the same,' I reassured her. 'I'll let you into a secret.' I saw the contact supervisor look over, as secrets aren't allowed at contact, but I ignored her and continued anyway. 'When I was first asked to look after Harrison, I was very worried I wouldn't know what to do. Although I've had two children of my own the youngest, Paula, is five, so it was a long time since I'd made up formula or changed a nappy. I hadn't fostered a baby, so I was convinced I wouldn't know what to do. And to begin with everything took ages, but we got by, and Harrison didn't know any different.'

'Really?' Rihanna exclaimed, surprised and relieved. 'But you seem so experienced and confident.'

'And soon you will be too. It's just practice. Another couple of contact sessions and you'll be fine, I promise you.'

If only that had been true.

Chapter Twenty-Eight
The Decision

I was better organized on Thursday. Adrian and Paula had returned to school for the spring term, and having seen them in I returned home, took down the Christmas decorations and then in the afternoon cooked dinner. I plated up ours and mashed Harrison's, which I put in a sealed container for Rihanna to reheat in the microwave at the family centre. I collected Adrian and Paula from school in the afternoon and drove straight to the family centre, where they waited in reception as they had before. Harrison must have remembered being upset at his previous visit, for as soon as we entered the Blue Room he began crying. Not loud sobs but grizzling – enough to unsettle Rihanna, who was standing in the centre of the room, nervously awaiting our arrival.

'Oh dear,' she said, concerned, as she came over. 'He doesn't want to stay with me.'

'Of course he does,' I said.

Rather than pass Harrison to Rihanna and leave her to settle him I decided to try to placate him before I left. I began walking around the room, pointing out all the colourful pictures on the friezes, hoping he would feel more comfortable if he was used to the room before I left him.

Rihanna was soon joining in: 'Look at this big yellow sun and these pretty little birds,' she said, making a big effort, while trying to hide her anxiety.

The Decision

We did a tour of the room and Harrison, while not crying, was not smiling either. Time for plan B, I thought. I slipped the bulging baby bag from my shoulder and passed it to Rihanna. 'There are some of his favourite toys in there,' I said. 'Take them out and show them to him. They'll make him feel more secure.'

'Good idea,' Rihanna said, unzipping the bag.

She began taking out the small toys one at a time and, holding them up to Harrison, pressed them, for they all made an appealing noise of some kind: the small toy dog barked, the bird tweeted and the clown laughed. Seeing the familiar toys and hearing their welcome sounds in an unfamiliar place reassured Harrison. He soon forgot his disquiet and began smiling at the toys and then at Rihanna. 'There we go,' I said, transferring Harrison from my arms into her arms. 'A happy baby. His dinner, nappies and everything else you might need are in the bag.'

'Thank you so much, Cathy,' Rihanna said gratefully. 'See you later.'

And I left Harrison happily in his mother's arms.

But when I returned at 5.30 it was a very different matter. I heard Harrison sobbing as soon as I walked into reception. So did Adrian and Paula.

'Isn't that Harrison crying?' Adrian asked, concerned.

'It could be,' I said. 'You two wait here and look at the books while I go through.'

Once again, leaving Adrian and Paula in reception, I went down the corridor and towards the Blue Room. Harrison's cries grew louder the closer I got. The door to the Blue Room was closed and I knocked, but I doubted they could hear over the noise Harrison was making. I knocked again and went in. Rihanna was standing in the centre of the room with Harrison in her arms, pacing up and down and trying to pacify him. And while the room wasn't in the chaos it had been on Tuesday, I took no comfort from this, for clearly Harrison was very upset and had been crying for some time. His cheeks were hot and wet and his eyes red. As soon as Rihanna saw me she came over.

'He wants you,' she said, 'not me. He won't stop crying.' She placed him in my arms.

'Why didn't you phone me?' I asked, concerned that Harrison had been crying for so long.

'I have to do this myself if there's any chance of me having Harrison back,' Rihanna said, close to tears, and glancing at the supervisor. 'You won't be there if he's living with me. I have to learn to look after him myself.'

'But this is only the second session here,' I said. 'He's not used to you yet. It will take time.' Harrison had stopped crying now and was smiling at his mother and me.

'How long do you think it will take for him to get used to me?' Rihanna asked mournfully.

I didn't know, but I was sure this wasn't the way to go about mother and baby establishing a relationship. 'I think we need to do this more gradually,' I said. 'So Harrison has time to get used to you here before I leave. Shall I ask Cheryl if I can stay for a while at the beginning of the next few sessions?'

'Oh, yes please, will you?' Rihanna asked gratefully, while the supervisor continued to write.

So that is what I did. Once Adrian and Paula were at school the following morning, I telephoned Jill and put forward my suggestion, strongly: 'It's ridiculous to leave Harrison with his mother in a strange room and expect her to just get on with it. The supervisor doesn't help; she just sits there writing. Harrison was so upset yesterday his eyes were red and puffy. It's cruel, and it's undermining Rihanna's confidence. I think it should be a gradual introduction, with me staying at the beginning – say for half an hour. Then when Harrison is used to the room and Rihanna I can gradually withdraw. There will still be time for the social services to do their assessment once he's more settled with his mother.'

'Absolutely,' Jill said, with no objection. 'It's a wonder this wasn't a planned introduction from the start. It would have been if it was adoptive parents Harrison was seeing. And given that Harrison doesn't really know Rihanna the same should have applied. I'll speak to Cheryl and get back to you.'

'Thank you, Jill. It wasn't only upsetting for Rihanna and Harrison, but Adrian, Paula and I found it very upsetting too. We hate seeing Harrison cry – he's usually so happy.'

'I understand,' Jill said.

Jill phoned back later in the afternoon, having spoken to Cheryl, who'd spoken to the contact supervisor, who'd confirmed Harrison had been upset at contact and wouldn't settle. Cheryl also said Rihanna had phoned her that morning and had asked if I could stay at the start of some of the sessions. Cheryl now agreed this was the best way forward.

'Cheryl said she'll leave the exact details of the timescale to you and Rihanna to decide,' Jill added. 'Can you phone Rihanna this evening?'

'Yes, of course.'

'What will you do with Adrian and Paula while you're with Rihanna and Harrison?' Jill asked.

'I'm not sure yet. I'll sort something out.'

'Let me know if you need the agency to provide a sitter.'

'Thanks, Jill. I will.'

Once the children were in bed that evening I telephoned Rihanna, who was expecting my call. She already sounded more relaxed now that she knew we would be doing a gradual introduction, and was again looking forward to seeing Harrison, although she remained concerned that Harrison would remember their 'bad start', as she called it, and it could affect their relationship.

'Forget all that,' I said. 'This is a new start and Harrison will soon forget he was upset. I won't leave the two of you alone until he is happily settled, OK?'

'OK,' Rihanna said, slightly reassured.

'This is what I suggest we do,' I continued, 'but we can adjust it as necessary – depending on how quickly Harrison settles. I thought I'd stay in the contact room for half an hour at the next session. That should give Harrison enough time to feel reasonably secure and settled. Assuming he's happy, I'll slip out of the room, but I'll stay in the building. If he becomes fractious or cries and you can't settle him, phone or text me, and I'll reappear in the room. I won't rush in and take him from you; I'll just wander in and look at some pictures or a magazine. Having me present – a familiar person – will reassure him. Then once he's happy again, I'll slip out, but I'll stay in the building in case I'm needed again. We'll do this for as long as is necessary, all the while gradually reducing the time I spend in the room. My guess is that in a couple of weeks you two won't need me there at all. What do you think, Rihanna?'

There was silence for a moment. I thought she was going to object to my suggestion, perhaps feeling it was too intrusive, or perhaps having decided she needed to do it all alone. But when she spoke I realized it was emotion that had stopped her from speaking and that she was probably crying on the other end of the phone.

'Oh, Cathy,' she said, her voice faint and uneven. 'Thank you so much. I don't know what I'd do without you. I love Harrison and I want him desperately, but I feel under so much pressure to prove myself. You've given me confidence. I'm sure I can do this with your help.'

The Decision

I too swallowed hard. 'You'll be fine,' I said. And I desperately hoped she would be.

We began the new arrangement at the next contact – on Tuesday the following week. I stayed in the contact room for about half an hour and once Harrison was ignoring me and playing happily with Rihanna I quietly slipped out. I went to the waiting room, where Adrian and Paula were amusing themselves with games and puzzles provided by the centre. When I'd explained to them what I planned to do to help Harrison see Rihanna I'd given them the choice of going to a friend's house while I was at contact, going home where Jill would provide a sitter or coming with me. They'd opted to come with me, so they waited at the family centre for the whole one and a half hours, although with all the games and puzzles the time passed quickly and they quite enjoyed themselves.

During the first contact Rihanna texted me three times to ask me to return to the room. Each time I slipped in quietly and stayed in the background, wandering around the room and looking at the pictures until Harrison settled. During the second contact she texted me twice; on the third occasion it was only once, when Harrison appeared to be running a temperature (we later discovered his first tooth was coming through). From then on Rihanna didn't need me at all, although I stayed in the building for two more sessions just to make sure.

Although Adrian and Paula didn't complain about being in the family centre rather than at home watching their favourite television programmes, I was aware how disruptive the month had been for them. I was also aware that we would be doing something similar with adoptive parents if Harrison wasn't returned to Rihanna but went instead for adoption; nothing had been decided yet. I knew there was a lot going on 'behind the scenes' during this time that would allow the social services to make their decision; Rihanna had mentioned at the start of one contact that her parents had been visited by a social worker, but she didn't elaborate. I knew Jill would tell me anything I needed to know and that as soon as a decision on Harrison's future had been made she would inform me. In the meantime I continued with the routine of school and contact, and I was still visiting the clinic every week to have Harrison weighed. I told Rihanna at contact of Harrison's progress as well as entering his weight gain in the red book.

At one contact I introduced Adrian and Paula to Rihanna, for she had never met them. At the end of February, Rihanna agreed there was no need for me to stay in the family centre and that I should go home and she would phone if she needed to. She didn't phone for she had now established a relationship with Harrison and had gained the confidence to look after him and to allow him to put his trust in her.

Harrison grew a second tooth at the front at the bottom, and at the beginning of March he began to crawl. He'd been getting into the crawling position for some weeks but had kept collapsing when he'd tried to move forward. Then one Sunday he suddenly mastered the skill and took off, scampering crab-like across the floor and laughing, very pleased with himself, as we were. Crawling is a wonderful developmental milestone and opens up a whole new world for a small child, but it also meant that at home we had to be even more watchful. Now he was no longer content to sit on the playmat or in his bouncing cradle: he wanted to explore everything, and I mean everything! I fixed the stairgate into position, covered the plug sockets and moved the potted plants out of reach. I texted Rihanna that Sunday and told her Harrison was crawling, so at the next contact she was waiting excitedly to see him doing it for herself. As I set him on the floor he was off, and I saw Rihanna's eyes mist. She was so proud of him; it was just a pity she hadn't been there to see him on Sunday when it had happened for the first time.

Now eight months old, Harrison understood a lot of what was said to him and had begun forming his first words, one of which was *Mama*, which he used for Rihanna and me. He also said *car, cat* and *bye bye* so sweetly it made you want to cry. During this time I saw the bond between Rihanna and Harrison develop to the point where Harrison was reluctant to leave at the end of contact. This was good progress as long as the social services decided that he should live with his mother; otherwise it would have all been for nothing, and Rihanna and Harrison would both suffer dreadfully if they never saw each other again.

I kept my log notes up to date, and halfway through March Cheryl phoned and asked if I could send in a brief report on Harrison's recent progress, and how he was after contact, so that she could include this information in her final report. That evening, referring to my log notes, I typed the update on Harrison's progress and then wrote that Harrison was always pleased to see his mother, enjoyed the time he spent with her and had recently become reluctant to leave her. I knew that as Cheryl was writing her final report the decision on Harrison's future wasn't far away, and I sincerely hoped it was the right one, which in my opinion was that Harrison should be returned to his mother.

A week passed and then when I answered the phone one day Jill said, 'Cheryl has just phoned. The social services have made their decision.' My heart started thumping wildly in my chest before Jill said: 'I think you'll be pleased to know that Harrison is to be returned to Rihanna to live.'

'Thank goodness,' I said, finally allowing myself to breathe.

'Cheryl still has some concerns about the extended family,' Jill added. 'But not enough to stop Harrison from going to live with his mother. Cheryl is going to phone you later with the proposed timetable for the move. She wants Harrison to spend time at Rihanna's flat first, starting with an hour and then rising to an overnight, with a move in two weeks' time.'

'Two weeks,' I repeated. 'That's not far ahead.'

'No, but Rihanna has already established a relationship with Harrison over the last three months at the family centre. Cheryl doesn't want to drag the introduction on any longer than is necessary.'

'I understand,' I said.

'You'll have to start preparing Adrian and Paula for Harrison leaving,' Jill said pointedly.

'Yes, I know.'

'Well, thanks, Cathy. I'll be in touch,' Jill wound up the conversation, aware I needed time to adjust. For while I was very pleased Harrison would be going to his mother, Adrian, Paula and I would miss him dreadfully, and so too would my parents.

I'd taken Jill's telephone call in the sitting room. I was on the sofa and Harrison had been crawling on the floor. He was now at my feet, holding on to my leg and trying to pull himself up to a standing position, which he'd recently started doing. He was grinning, feeling very pleased with himself. I picked him up and balanced him in a standing position on my lap. I wrapped my arms around his little body and held him close. His soft cheek pressed against mine and his chubby little arms slipped round my neck. I rested my head lightly against his and closed my eyes. I could smell the warm scent of his body, hear his faint regular breath and feel the soft caress of his skin as it touched mine. There wouldn't be many more times when I could hold and cuddle him. Soon he would be in his mother's arms. And while Adrian, Paula and I had known right from the beginning that at some point Harrison would leave us, it didn't help. We loved Harrison and that wouldn't stop even after he'd gone.

A short while later Rihanna texted: *Have you heard the good news?* I texted back: *Yes! Fantastic! Well done.* I was grateful she couldn't see my tears. When Cheryl phoned an hour later I'd recovered sufficiently to tell her I was pleased to hear the decision, and then I wrote down the proposed timetable of the move Cheryl now read out to me, a copy of which she said she'd put in the post.

It was Tuesday and contact at the family centre was to go ahead that night as usual, but that would be the last contact at the centre. On Wednesday I had to take Harrison to Rihanna's flat for 10.30 a.m., the address of which Cheryl now gave me and I wrote down. Harrison and I would stay at the flat for an hour and then come home. Cheryl suggested I took some of Harrison's favourite toys for him to play with, ones that could be left there. On Thursday we were to go again, this time for two hours; I was to stay for the first hour and then leave Harrison with Rihanna for the second hour. On Friday I was to leave him for the whole two hours. Cheryl said these two visits should coincide with lunchtime so that Harrison could get used to eating in his new home.

'Do you want me to take his lunch with me?' I asked.

'No, Rihanna will be responsible for that now. She already has a good idea of what he likes from contact at the family centre, and she can ask you if she's not sure.'

The arrangements were to continue over the weekend: on Saturday and Sunday I was to leave Harrison at Rihanna's for three hours each day. Then if everything was going well, on Monday, Tuesday and Wednesday (of the following week) I was to take Harrison to Rihanna's as soon as I'd dropped Adrian and Paula at school, and then collect him at four o'clock, after I'd collected the children. 'It will be reassuring for Harrison to see your children in his new home,' Cheryl said. 'And it will be nice for them too.'

'Yes,' I said, not convinced, and wondering how Adrian and Paula would feel about this.

Cheryl finished detailing the timetable of the move by saying that on Thursday (of the following week) Harrison would sleep in his new home, and then Rihanna would bring him to me in her car on Friday to collect his belongings and say goodbye. 'I've suggested Rihanna be with you at ten o'clock on the Friday. Can you pack Harrison's belongings on the Thursday evening so he's ready?'

'Yes. Adrian and Paula will have to say goodbye on Thursday morning,' I said, thinking aloud. 'That will be the last time they see him if he's sleeping at Rihanna's on Thursday and moving while they're at school on Friday.'

'Yes,' Cheryl said absently, preoccupied with checking the arrangements and making sure she hadn't forgotten anything.

'And Rihanna has a car seat, cot and high chair?' I asked.

'She will have by then,' Cheryl said. 'I'll check she has everything she needs when I visit. I'm planning on visiting them at least twice during this introductory two-week period. I'd also like you and the children to visit a week after Harrison has left you. It will be reassuring for Harrison to see you, and for you and your children.'

'Yes,' I said, not sure how Adrian and Paula would cope with this.

'Well, thanks for all you've done, Cathy,' Cheryl said. 'Who'd have thought when I first placed Harrison with you that he'd be returning to his mother? A truly happy ending, eh?'

'Yes,' I said. But my thoughts were with Adrian and Paula, whom I would have to tell that Harrison would be leaving us for good very soon.

Chapter Twenty-Nine
Letting Go

'This will be the last time we have to go to the family centre,' I said to Adrian and Paula, once we were in the car and on the way there. 'After tonight Harrison will be seeing his mother at her flat, to prepare him for going home.'

'So he is definitely going to his mother?' Adrian said.

'Yes. I heard today.'

'When?' Adrian asked sombrely.

'In two weeks, and before then he'll be seeing his mother every day. You'll be able to come with me when you're not at school and see where he's going to live.' I was trying to focus on the positive.

'Can Harry still come and see us after he's gone?' Paula asked.

'I'm not sure, love,' I lied to soften the blow. 'We'll have to wait and see.' For I knew that once we'd visited Harrison to say our last goodbye (a week after the move) whether or not Rihanna kept in touch was up to her, and something told me she might not – that she might want to forget this difficult and painful time in her life and move on.

'I hope Harry does come and play,' Paula said. 'I like playing with him now he can crawl. I'm going to miss him.'

'Yes, I know, love. We'll all miss Harrison,' I said. I glanced in the rear-view mirror at Adrian, who was looking out of the side window, deep in thought, and as usual internalizing his feelings. 'We'll all take time to adjust,' I said. 'But it will be nice for Harrison to live with his mother.' I saw Adrian give a small nod.

The children sat very quietly in the car for the remainder of the journey; even Harrison was quieter than usual and seemed to sense that he was approaching a turning point in his life. When we arrived at the family centre Rihanna must have been looking out for us from reception, for as I carried Harrison up the path with Adrian and Paula walking either side of me she came rushing out. With a large smile on her face she threw her arms around Harrison and me and hugged us hard; then did the same to Adrian and Paula, who looked quite bemused.

'Congratulations,' I said to Rihanna, as I passed Harrison to her. 'You've done very well.'

'Thanks, Cathy,' she said, smothering Harrison in kisses. 'And thanks for all your helpful advice.'

'You're welcome.'

We went into the centre and then into the Blue Room, where I put the baby bag on the sofa, as I'd done at previous contacts. But unlike at the contacts before there was no supervisor present and there wouldn't be one tonight. Now all the reports were written and the decision had been made on Harrison's future there was no need for Rihanna and Harrison to be supervised or monitored. This contact was really to give Rihanna and Harrison a chance to finish off their visits at the centre, collect any of their belongings they'd left there and say goodbye to the supervisors who'd become part of their lives for the last three months. Goodbyes are always considered important for families with children in care, as change can occur frequently and some-times at very short notice.

Having seen Rihanna and Harrison into the Blue Room I told her I'd see her at 5.30, and the children and I came away and returned to the car.

'No more rushed dinners after tonight,' I said, as we got into the car. For every Tuesday and Thursday for the last three months we'd been dashing home with just enough time to gobble down dinner before returning to collect Harrison. 'And you'll be able to watch your favourite television programmes again,' I added positively.

'When's Harry going?' Paula asked in a plaintive voice from the back seat.

'In two weeks' time,' I said. 'But he'll be seeing his mummy every day before then, and also staying the night before he moves.'

'I wish you were Harry's mummy,' Paula said. 'Then he could stay with us, and be *our* baby forever.'

'I know, love, but I'm afraid that's not possible. And it's right that Harrison should be with his own mummy.'

There was a pause before Paula asked, 'Mum, can you make a baby for us? Like my friend Selina's mummy has?'

I smiled and glanced in the rear-view mirror. I saw Adrian, who unlike Paula knew where babies came from, look away, embarrassed. 'No, love,' I said. 'Selina's mummy and daddy live together, so they were able to make the baby together. Unfortunately, I don't live with your father any more, do I? So it's not possible. But we'll foster again, and then you'll have another foster brother or sister.'

There was another pause before Paula asked: 'Why do you have to live with a daddy to make a baby?'

Adrian sighed. 'Mum will tell you when you're older,' he said to Paula.

'Oh, I know,' Paula said. 'It's like those rabbits on the farm we saw last year.'

'Yes, just like the rabbits,' Adrian and I agreed.

* * *

When we returned to the family centre to collect Harrison at 5.30 it was obvious Rihanna couldn't wait to leave, and who could blame her? Her future with Harrison had largely depended on what had happened in the Blue Room and the pressure must have been enormous. Now all that was behind her: she knew Harrison was being returned to her and their future was secure.

'I'm ready!' she called, as soon as we entered the Blue Room. 'Let's go!'

Handing me the baby bag Rihanna scooped Harrison into her arms. 'Goodbye, Blue Room,' she said, turning him to face the room for one last time.

Harrison said a perfect 'Bye bye' to the room and gave a little wave, which made us all laugh.

The children and I returned to the corridor and Rihanna followed, pointedly closing the door behind her as though shutting it on that part of her life forever. 'Never again,' she breathed, cuddling Harrison close and smiling at me.

I returned her smile. 'Finished. You've done very well,' I said again.

We went down the corridor as a group, with Rihanna walking beside me and holding Harrison, and Adrian and Paula just in front. We paused outside reception for Rihanna to say goodbye. Two contact supervisors were inside the office, chatting to the receptionist. 'Goodbye, everyone,' Rihanna called lightly.

They paused from talking and looked over. 'Goodbye and good luck.'

'Thanks,' Rihanna said, and pulling open the outer door stepped outside. 'Thank goodness,' she sighed, hugging Harrison and breathing in the fresh spring air. 'How could I have been so stupid? I nearly lost my son for good.'

We followed Rihanna down the path and to my car, where I opened the rear door. Adrian and Paula scrambled in and then I stood aside to let Rihanna strap Harrison into his car seat.

Letting Go

'I'm going shopping tomorrow after I've seen you,' she told Harrison as she fastened his seatbelt, 'to buy you everything you need. A car seat, cot, high chair, pushchair, nappies, and lots and lots of toys.'

Harrison giggled.

Leaning in, she kissed him goodbye and then closed the car door. Straightening, she looked at me. 'I didn't dare buy the baby equipment before I knew, in case he didn't come to me ...' Her voice fell away and I knew she was close to tears. 'I'll see you tomorrow,' she said quickly and, turning, walked towards her car. I knew then that Rihanna recognized, as I did, just how close she had come to losing her son for good.

That evening I explained the timetable of Harrison's move to Adrian and Paula. They obviously had conflicting feelings: on the one hand they were pleased Harrison was able to live with his 'real mummy', as they called her, but they also knew how different life was going to be for us without him.

'At least Harry's mummy is nice,' Paula said, as I tucked her into bed that night. 'It would be worse if Harry had a horrid mummy like Ellie's.'

I was slightly surprised Paula still thought of Ellie – the six-year-old girl we'd fostered for a week on respite the year before. But I suppose the fact that Ellie's suffering had been so great, and that Ellie's mother had failed to protect her daughter, was something Paula would remember for a long time, possibly forever.

'The social services wouldn't have let Harrison go to his mummy if they didn't think she was nice and knew she could look after him,' I said. 'One of the reasons Harrison saw his mummy at the family centre was so that they could do what's called an assessment – to make sure his mummy was nice and could look after him.'

'Did you have to have an assessment when you had Adrian and me?' Paula asked.

I smiled and touched her forehead. 'No, love. You weren't in foster care.'

Paula looked at me thoughtfully. 'I think Harry's mummy loves Harry. I think she knows she did the wrong thing when she put Harry in foster care.'

'Yes, I think so too, love. Sometimes we make decisions because we can't see any other way. Then something happens that allows us to see things differently. Fortunately Rihanna had time to put things right.'

'Do you think Ellie's mummy will put things right so Ellie can go home?' Paula now asked me doubtfully.

'I don't know,' I said. 'But the judge will make the decision.' I doubted Ellie would be returned home; the level of abuse had been horrific and as far as I knew Ellie's mother was still living with the abuser, which would prohibit any chance of Ellie returning.

The following morning after I'd taken Adrian and Paula to school I popped home briefly for the baby bag and the bag of toys I was taking with us, and then I drove to Rihanna's flat, which was about a thirty-minute drive away. I parked outside the small development of privately owned flats and, with the bag over my shoulder and Harrison in my arms, I went up the short path, which was flanked by neatly tended gardens. We had arrived slightly early but Rihanna was ready. As soon as I pressed the security buzzer beside the door to the flats Rihanna's voice came through the grid: 'Hi, Cathy. Come on in.'

The door clicked open and as Harrison and I went in Rihanna appeared from a ground-floor flat. 'Great to see you!' she cried, and opened her arms wide ready to receive Harrison: 'Come to Mummy.'

Letting Go

I placed Harrison in her arms. He was looking around, aware this was a new setting. 'Welcome home,' Rihanna said to him, covering him in hugs and kisses. She looked very well – vibrant and full of life. And a very different person to the one who'd loitered outside my house and then knocked on the door late one night, distraught and needing to talk. Now she looked like any young mother.

'Come on in,' she said again, leading the way across the hall to her flat.

I followed her in, closed the front door and then followed her into the lounge-cum-dining room. 'This is lovely,' I said. The room was spacious, light, neutrally decorated and tastefully furnished.

'Thank you,' she said. 'I'm renting the flat at present but I'm going to buy it. The landlord wants to sell, so it makes sense for me to stay here now I'm settled. It doesn't need much decorating and it's got two good-size bedrooms, so it's ideal.'

'Fantastic,' I said. 'And being on the ground floor is useful. You won't have to struggle with the pushchair up and down stairs.'

'Exactly,' Rihanna said, still hugging and kissing Harrison. 'It's worked out very well. Do sit down. Can I get you something to drink?'

'No thank you, I'm fine, but Harrison will be ready for his mid-morning snack. He usually has it about now.' Rihanna nodded. 'I wasn't sure what you had here,' I said, 'so I've packed his beaker, milk and a banana.' I passed Rihanna the baby bag, put the bag of toys on the floor, and then sat in one of the armchairs. Having used the baby bag at contact for the last three months Rihanna was familiar with its contents. Sitting on the sofa with Harrison on her lap, she unzipped the bag and took out the beaker and carton of milk, which she successfully opened with Harrison bouncing up and down, impatient for his snack.

'I'm buying a high chair and everything else I need this after-noon,' Rihanna said, concentrating on helping Harrison guide the beaker to his lips. 'I'll be better prepared when you come tomorrow.'

'You're doing fine,' I said. 'I'll leave the bag of toys here with you,' I said, pointing. 'They're all familiar to him, so it will help him to settle tomorrow when I leave for the second hour.'

'Thanks,' Rihanna said. 'Harrison seems quite happy with me, I guess from all that contact.'

'Yes,' I agreed.

Rihanna helped Harrison with his beaker of milk and then peeled the banana for him while I described his routine, which I'd also written down for her. 'It would be a good idea to keep his present routine going to begin with,' I said, taking the folded sheet of paper from my bag and placing it on the coffee table. 'Then once he's settled you can change the routine to suit you. Who will be looking after him when you go to work?'

Rihanna looked at me, surprised. 'Didn't Cheryl tell you?' I shook my head. 'I'm taking a year off work to look after Harri-son full time.'

'That's a good idea,' I said. 'It'll give you both time to adjust and also enjoy each other's company. Babies grow up so quickly it's nice if you can make the most of it while they're young.'

'Absolutely,' Rihanna said. 'I've missed enough of Harrison's life already. I don't want to miss any more. I might take longer than a year if I can afford to. Work are being very understand-ing now they know about Harrison.'

Having finished his snack, Harrison was eager to get down from Rihanna's lap and play. She wiped his mouth on a tissue and then put him on the floor with toys she took from the bag. His face lit up when he saw the familiar toys in this as yet un-familiar setting. While he played we continued to talk. I had a few questions of my own I wanted to ask Rihanna, but I didn't want to appear rude or intrusive. I thought Rihanna and I had formed a good relationship during the last three months of contact so I took a chance.

'Will Harrison be seeing his father?' I asked after a moment. 'I was wondering if you'd told him about Harrison now it's all out in the open.'

Rihanna hesitated, then keeping her gaze on Harrison said: 'I haven't told him yet. I feel Jacob has a right to know but I'll wait until Harrison is settled in with me first. Once I get over these two weeks I can think about telling Jacob.'

It was the first time Rihanna had referred to Harrison's father by his first name. 'He's going to have quite a shock if you tell him,' I said.

Rihanna nodded. 'And I'll need to be very careful how I do it. I understand he has a new girlfriend now.'

'Oh,' I said.

'I don't blame him,' Rihanna said quickly, glancing at me. 'It's been over a year since I finished our relationship. Jacob's a good man. He deserves a proper relationship after all the years we spent hiding ours. I hope he's happy.' Her selfless attitude touched me and I so wished things could have been different.

'And there's no chance the two of you could have a proper relationship now?' I asked, ever hopeful.

'No. Never,' Rihanna said bluntly, and I knew not to press her further.

The rest of the hour went very quickly and soon it was time for Harrison and me to leave. Rihanna put Harrison into his coat and then carried him to the front door of the flats, where she passed him to me.

'See you tomorrow,' she said, kissing him.

'See you tomorrow,' I said. 'Bye.'

'Bye bye,' Harrison chuckled.

* * *

275

That evening, over dinner, I told Adrian and Paula that Harrison had seen his mother at her flat during the day, and that it had gone very well. It was important that during this two-week introductory period Adrian and Paula adjusted to Harrison leaving, just as Harrison was adjusting to being with his mother in his new home. As most of the visits were scheduled to take place when Adrian and Paula were at school, there was a chance they could miss out on this valuable transition period and then suddenly find the day had arrived when Harrison was leaving for good.

'You'll be able to see Harrison's new home on Saturday, when we take him for his three-hour visit,' I said.

They nodded but didn't say anything, and I knew they were finding it very difficult.

The following day, Friday, when I arrived at Rihanna's flat, having taken Adrian and Paula to school, she couldn't wait to show me all the baby equipment she'd bought the previous afternoon. I gasped when I entered the lounge which, with all the purchases, had been transformed from a single lady's apartment into a family home. A new high chair was standing at the far end of the room next to the dining table and chairs, and there was a playpen containing new activity toys to the right of the room. Three large soft toys – a zebra, elephant and rabbit – sat proudly in one armchair, and on the floor beside the sofa was a small child's chair, ready for when Harrison was a little older.

'He's a very lucky boy,' I said.

Rihanna smiled, pleased, and with Harrison in her arms led the way into the kitchen, where she began opening various cupboards and drawers to show Harrison and me more of her purchases: a toddler's plate, bowl, beaker and cutlery set; bibs; a new food blender for mashing his meals; a selection of tinned puddings and other packet food I'd told Rihanna Harrison liked, including porridge and teething rusks.

'I've made Harrison chicken, mashed potato and peas for his dinner today,' Rihanna said excitedly. 'I've cooked and mashed it, and it's in the fridge ready for later.'

'Lovely,' I said, impressed by how well organized she was. 'He'll like that.'

'It's your favourite, isn't it?' Rihanna said to Harrison, kissing his cheek.

Harrison chuckled and snuggled his face into his mother's hair, which he seemed to like the feel of.

'I'll show you his bedroom,' Rihanna said, leading the way out of the kitchen.

I followed her through the lounge and into the hall, where we turned left. I gasped again as we entered Harrison's bedroom, which was now a nursery. 'You have been busy!' I said.

Rihanna smiled. 'Yes, I was up most of the night assembling the furniture and getting everything ready. I'm pleased with the result. It looks good, doesn't it?'

'Yes,' I agreed. 'It certainly does.' Harrison chuckled.

A new white cot stood against one wall, complete with a decorated bumper, bedding and entertainment mobile. Against another wall was a 'changing station' with nappies, lotions and baby wipes laid out ready. Next to that was a small white wardrobe with a matching chest of drawers. Brightly coloured nursery curtains with pictures of animals and alphabet shapes hung at the windows, and matched the circular rug in the centre of the floor.

'I'll paint the walls when I have a chance,' Rihanna said. 'But the yellow is fine for now, isn't it?'

I nodded. 'Harrison won't worry about wallpaper until he goes to school,' I said. 'Then once the children get talking suddenly Batman wallpaper becomes a "must have", or at least it did for Adrian.'

Rihanna laughed. 'Then we'll go shopping and choose some, won't we?' she said, bringing Harrison into the conversation. Harrison agreed by burying his face in her hair again and giving it a little tug.

As detailed in Cheryl's timetable of introduction I stayed with Harrison and Rihanna for an hour and then left them for the second hour. There wasn't time for me to go home, so I left my car outside Rihanna's flat and walked to the local shops, where I bought a newspaper. I took it to a café nearby and spent an unusually relaxing forty-five minutes catching up on the news over a leisurely coffee until it was time to walk back.

Rihanna opened the door with Harrison in her arms and looked anxious. Oh dear, I thought, whatever has happened now? 'He hasn't eaten any of his dinner,' she said, worried. 'I don't know what's the matter with him.' Harrison grinned while Rihanna was clearly upset.

'Don't worry,' I said, going in. 'It's his first meal here; it's bound to be strange. That's why Cheryl included lunch in his visits – to get him used to eating here. I'm sure he will be fine tomorrow.'

And he was.

On Friday, as timetabled, I left Harrison with Rihanna for the whole two hours and when I returned they were both grinning happily. 'He loved the macaroni cheese I made him!' Rihanna exclaimed as soon as she opened the front door. 'He ate the lot, and then had rice pudding.'

'Fantastic!' I said, and Harrison clapped his hands in appreciation.

Chapter Thirty

Upset

'Is this it?' Paula asked as we drew up outside the flats where Rihanna lived at eleven o'clock on Saturday morning.

'Yes,' I said, parking the car and switching off the engine.

'It's very big,' Paula said.

'They're flats,' I explained. 'Rihanna lives in one of them, not the whole building.'

'Oh, I see,' Paula said, while predictably Adrian had fallen silent on our arrival and said nothing.

Rihanna knew I would have Adrian and Paula with me as it was Saturday, and just as we were getting out of the car she appeared through the outer door. 'Hi, everyone,' she called brightly, coming down the path. 'How are you all?' She took Harrison from me and gave him a big kiss.

'We're good,' I said. 'And you?'

'All the better for seeing you,' Rihanna said to Harrison, giving him another kiss. He laughed and jumped up and down in her arms.

I saw Adrian and Paula looking carefully at Rihanna and I could guess what they were thinking. She was so happy now, and had much greater confidence with Harrison than the last time they'd seen her at the family centre. I also knew that seeing Rihanna and Harrison in what would soon be his new home would be good for Adrian and Paula and help them adjust to him going, although we wouldn't be staying for long. The three-hour visit was for Harrison to spend more time alone with his mother, to continue the bonding process. As it was a nice day I was thinking of taking Adrian and Paula to a local park and then having some lunch out.

'Come on in,' Rihanna said, leading the way into the flats.

Once inside Rihanna's flat Adrian and Paula stood awkwardly in the lounge-cum-dining room while Harrison, now on his third visit and used to the flat, was eager to be on the floor playing with his toys. Rihanna put him on the carpet and, taking a few toys from the playpen, set them next to him.

'So this is my living room,' Rihanna said with a smile to Adrian and Paula. 'I think Harrison will be happy here, don't you?'

They each gave a small shy nod.

'I'll show you the kitchen,' Rihanna said to them. 'It's through here.'

I stayed with Harrison in the lounge while Rihanna took Adrian and Paula into the kitchen. They didn't make any comment but then children of their age wouldn't – for them a kitchen, however neat and well stocked, wasn't something particularly interesting that they would comment on. 'Would you like to see Harrison's bedroom?' I heard Rihanna ask, and they both said yes.

The three of them reappeared and crossed the lounge but Harrison wasn't going to be left behind this time and scuttled after them on all fours. Rihanna picked him up.

'Through here,' I heard her say to Adrian and Paula.

'It's nice,' Paula said from Harrison's bedroom.

'Yes,' Adrian agreed.

'You can come and visit Harrison whenever you want,' Rihanna said kindly.

'We will,' I heard Paula say.

Rihanna showed them the bathroom and then they all returned to the lounge. 'I'm going to miss Harry,' Paula said to Rihanna as they came in.

'Harry?' Rihanna smiled. 'Is that what you call him?' It must have been the first time Rihanna had heard Paula use the shortened form of his name.

'Harrison is too long,' Paula explained. 'Why did you give him that name?'

Well done for asking, I thought, for I'd also wondered why Rihanna had chosen what was an unusual name in the UK, but hadn't liked to ask.

'Harrison means "son of",' Rihanna said. 'It was Harrison's father's middle name. I thought it would be nice for Harrison to have it as his first name. In my family we often use our parents' or grandparents' names for our children.'

'Oh, I see,' Paula said, nodding thoughtfully. While it cleared up another little mystery for me.

Now Adrian and Paula had seen the flat and Harrison was settled and playing happily it was time for us to leave. We said goodbye and, to avoid disturbing Harrison, we let ourselves out. As planned I drove to a local park, where we stayed for an hour. Then we walked into the town, had lunch and then looked in a few shops before it was time to return to Rihanna's for two o'clock.

'Do you think Harry has missed us?' Paula asked, as I drew up and parked outside the flats.

'I'm sure he has,' I said. 'We've been part of his life for a long time, although he's gradually getting used to his mother now.'

Adrian and Paula came with me into the flats and as soon as Paula saw Harrison she rushed over and kissed him. Harrison chuckled. Rihanna told me Harrison had been fine apart from when he'd woken after his lunchtime nap, when he'd cried for a minute until she'd distracted him with toys and then he'd recovered.

'I'm not surprised he was a little unsettled,' I said. 'That was the first time he slept in the cot here, so it must have been strange for him.'

'It was strange for me too,' Rihanna admitted. 'He was only asleep for half an hour but I kept checking on him.'

'I know the feeling,' I said, remembering how many times I'd anxiously checked on Harrison during his first weeks with us.

Rihanna dressed Harrison in his coat and then carried him to the car, where she strapped him into his car seat. She stood on the pavement and waved goodbye, and Harrison waved back.

That night Harrison took a while to settle in his cot and, while not crying, grizzled. I was half-expecting some reaction, as the last time he'd slept in a cot that day had been at Rihanna's; it must have been very confusing for him. It was impossible to expect a nine-month-old baby to understand that all the changes involved in this carefully planned transition were to ensure that the move to his mother ran smoothly. I also thought that once Harrison had moved and was living with his mother he was likely to be unsettled for a few weeks. I think Rihanna appreciated that too, for she'd remarked a few times that it must be confusing for Harrison.

Sunday's contact went as planned, with Harrison again spending three hours with his mother, although this time Adrian, Paula and I went home. When we returned Rihanna said everything had gone well and that as it had been a nice day she'd taken Harrison out in the pushchair for a while, which was good. However, that night Harrison again took a long while to settle with me and I spent some time leaning over his cot and soothing him until he finally fell asleep. Once he was asleep I wrote up my log notes and then I decided on an early night in preparation for the busy and emotionally draining week that lay ahead. The following week I would be taking Harrison to his mother's every day, and he would stay the whole day, then sleep overnight on Thursday, before the move on Friday. Although I sincerely believed it was the right decision to return Harrison to his mother, I was dreading him going, and so too were Adrian and Paula.

'It's only five days to Friday,' Paula said the following morning as we prepared to leave for school. 'Four to Thursday when we have to say goodbye to Harry.'

'Yes,' I said, and concentrated on getting everyone out of the door so that we wouldn't be late for school. There was nothing else I could say.

Following Cheryl's timetable of introduction once I'd taken Adrian and Paula to school I drove straight to Rihanna's flat, arriving at about 9.30. I no longer took the baby bag with me, as Rihanna now had everything she needed to look after Harrison; I knew at some point I'd have to dismantle the contents of the bag, as it was now redundant.

As usual Rihanna was ready when we arrived. I passed Harrison to her and then went into her flat just to say goodbye. A few minutes later I let myself out of the flat and drove home, where I set about clearing up after the weekend.

It was very strange being in the house without Harrison and I kept busy. Jill phoned mid-morning for an update on the weekend contact and I told her it had gone well, although Harrison had become a little unsettled at night, which she agreed was to be expected. She asked me how Adrian and Paula were coping with Harrison leaving and I said they were OK. Jill said she would visit us the following week once Harrison had left, and I fetched my diary and wrote in the appointment. We said goodbye, and then ten minutes later Cheryl phoned and asked for an update. I repeated more or less what I'd told Jill: that the rehabilitation of Harrison to his mother was going well. Cheryl thanked me and said she would be visiting Rihanna and Harrison at their flat that afternoon – the social worker makes a number of visits before and after a child returns to live with their natural parents.

That afternoon when I collected Adrian and Paula from school I didn't have the pushchair with me because we would be collecting Harrison after I'd collected Adrian and Paula. It felt very odd going into the playground without Harrison chattering away in his pushchair, as though part of me was missing, and a couple of friends asked me where he was. I said Harrison was spending time with his mother in preparation for him going home. I could see they didn't know what to say. Confidentiality stopped me from explaining further but they looked at me as one looks at the newly bereaved, feeling they should say something but not knowing what. 'It was the right decision for Harrison to go and live with his mother,' I said positively, and moved away.

When Adrian and Paula came out of school they looked surprised for a moment that I didn't have Harrison with me before they remembered we were going to collect him now.

'Hey, where's your brother?' one boy called to Adrian as we crossed the playground.

Adrian looked very uncomfortable and then relied on his humour to get by. 'Mum lost him at the shops!' he called back. 'She keeps doing it!' I hoped the boy didn't believe him.

We drove to Rihanna's flat and arrived just before four o'clock. When Rihanna opened the door with Harrison in her arms she looked 'hot and bothered' and I wondered what had gone wrong.

Upset

'Cheryl's just left,' she said, showing us into her flat. 'She was here for over two hours! I know she has to observe me with Harrison but I felt as if I was at the family centre again and my life depended on what she wrote.'

'Try not to worry,' I said. 'I'm sure you did very well.'

'I hope so. I think it went all right,' Rihanna said tentatively. 'Cheryl is coming again on Wednesday, and then when Harrison has moved in. She said that visit will be unannounced, so she won't be telling me when she's coming.'

'That's normal,' I said. 'She has to make a few unannounced visits for her report.'

Rihanna nodded and then put Harrison into his jacket, while he looked slightly bewildered, presumably realizing he was on the move again but not understanding why. Rihanna carried him out to the car and strapped him into his seat, but as she said goodbye he began to cry. Rihanna looked at me anxiously. 'He doesn't want to leave me.'

'He'll be fine once we're on our way,' I said.

She said goodbye again and closed the rear car door and then waved until we were out of sight. But Harrison continued to cry.

'Harry doesn't like us any more,' Paula said, close to tears herself.

'Of course he does,' I said, glancing in the rear-view mirror. 'He's just a bit confused.'

Which was only partly true, for I also knew that as a result of all the time Harrison had spent with his mother he was gradually transferring his affections to her. Harrison screwed up his face and opened his mouth wide – a sign he was about to wail – but Adrian leant over and blew a raspberry on his cheek, which made him chuckle instead.

'Well done, Adrian.' I said. 'We'll have to remember that trick for next time.' Adrian blew another raspberry on Harrison's cheek and Harrison giggled loudly, which made us all laugh.

That night Harrison settled more easily at bedtime, possibly because he was growing used to sleeping in two different cots. Once he was asleep I spent some time talking to Adrian and Paula, reassuring them that Harrison would be very happy with his mother, and that Cheryl had said we could visit him about a week after he'd moved. I also reminded them that we would be going to Nana and Grandpa's on Sunday for the day, which was something to look forward to.

Tuesday and Wednesday followed the same schedule as Monday: I took Adrian and Paula to school, Harrison to his mother, collected Adrian and Paula from school, and then the three of us collected Harrison from Rihanna. Although all these visits were important for Harrison so that the move to his mother ran smoothly, by Wednesday I think we were all waiting for the end of the week. It felt as if we were in limbo. I was a part-time foster carer for Harrison, Rihanna was his part-time mother, Adrian and Paula had a foster sibling sometimes, while poor Harrison didn't know whether he was coming or going.

However, when Thursday morning arrived – the time Adrian and Paula had to say goodbye – it was a different matter, and I had mixed feelings as to whether this was the best ending. For while Adrian and Paula would be at school on Friday, and therefore spared the upset of actually seeing Harrison go with all his belongings, not being present denied them closure and seemed to marginalize the enormity of the event for them.

'Why can't Harry go on Saturday?' Paula asked. 'Adrian and me are home then.'

'Cheryl said it had to be Friday,' I said. 'Probably because the social services offices are closed on Saturday.' Which I thought was the most likely reason – Cheryl and her colleagues wouldn't be available on Saturday if there was a problem with the move.

We were in the hall, putting on our shoes and coats, ready to leave for school. I wanted Adrian and Paula to say goodbye to

Harrison now, in the privacy of our home, rather than in the school playground, which might be difficult for them. 'Give Harrison a big hug and say goodbye,' I said lightly to Adrian and Paula, staying positive. 'Say "see you in a week".'

They did, with surprising ease, and we got in the car and I drove to school. It wasn't until we were in the playground and the bell sounded for the start of school that reality suddenly hit. Paula, now realizing this was the last time Harrison would be in the playground, grabbed Harrison's hand and burst into tears.

'I'm not going into school today,' she told him. 'I'm going to stay with you.'

Adrian looked embarrassed but was also clearly upset and reluctant to say goodbye. His face was serious and I knew how he hated seeing Paula cry.

'You'll see Harrison again soon,' I said comfortingly.

Neither child moved and Harrison, who had stopped his usual gay chattering, looked as if he was about to cry too.

'Say goodbye and go and join your friends,' I encouraged Adrian. 'Paula will be fine. I'll explain to her teacher.'

Adrian hesitated and then, kissing Harrison's forehead and giving him a big hug, went over to join his class, who were going into school. I moved round to face Paula, who was still holding Harrison's hand, her little cheeks wet.

'Paula, love,' I said, wiping away her tears, 'you need to go into school too. Harrison will be fine, and we'll talk more this evening. Shall I ask your teacher if you can sit in the quiet room for a while?' The quiet room, also known as the medical room, was attended by a welfare lady, who was kindness itself and made children better if they fell over, fell out with friends or just needed some time out.

Paula slowly nodded. I eased her hand from Harrison's and held it as we crossed the playground to where her class teacher was seeing her class into the building. When her teacher saw Paula upset she exclaimed: 'Dear me, Paula, that's not like you. Whatever is the matter?'

Paula gave a little sob and more tears appeared.

'Could I speak to you?' I asked her teacher. She moved slightly away so that the other children couldn't overhear us. 'Paula is upset because we're having to say goodbye to Harrison,' I said. 'He's leaving us and going to live with his mother.'

'Oh dear,' she said, her brow furrowing. 'I can see why she's upset.'

I nodded. 'I was wondering if Paula could spend a few minutes in the quiet room with Mrs Wilson until she feels better? I'll be home again in an hour, so if Paula's still upset then I could come and collect her and take her home.'

'Of course. I'll explain to Mrs Wilson.' She held out her hand to Paula and said: 'Would you like Mrs Wilson to read you a story?'

Paula nodded, dropped my hand and took hold of her teacher's. 'Bye, Harry,' she said as fresh tears welled in her eyes. 'Bye. I'll always love you.'

I swallowed hard. 'Take care.' I watched her walk into school beside her teacher and then I turned and crossed the playground.

It was at times like that that I questioned if fostering was right for my family and if by fostering I was doing Adrian and Paula real emotional damage. That morning I left the playground with a heavy heart, aware my children were very upset because the baby they'd loved as their little brother was leaving us for good, and it was my fault for fostering.

Chapter Thirty-One
Goodbye Harrison

In contrast to how Adrian, Paula and I were feeling that Thursday morning Rihanna was euphoric. She appeared from the door to the flats as soon as I drew up. With a huge smile on her face she ran down the path and greeted us.

'Hi, Harrison, my treasure,' she cried, opening the rear door of the car as soon as I'd parked. 'You're staying with me tonight! And guess who's coming to see you later?' Harrison couldn't guess. 'Your grandmother!'

'Is she?' I asked, surprised, as I got out of the car.

'She telephoned yesterday evening,' Rihanna said, reaching into the car and unfastening Harrison's seatbelt. 'We had a long talk. Now she's finally accepting I'm serious about bringing up Harrison, and I'm not going to be persuaded out of it, she's having to re-think.'

'Good,' I said. 'I am pleased.'

'She's still got a way to go yet,' Rihanna added.

I nodded, for I remembered the woman who'd sat on my sofa, unable to touch or even talk to her grandson, and thought she did have a long way to go before she became a doting grandmother, but at least this was a start.

I locked the car and followed Rihanna up the path and into her flat. 'You'll need these,' I said, passing her the carrier bag I'd brought from home.

She peered into the bag and sighed gratefully. 'Thanks, Cathy. You think of everything!' Rihanna took out the soft toy panda and bear which she'd originally bought for Harrison and had sat at the foot of his cot every night. Harrison beamed, delighted, when he saw them.

'I should put them in the same place in his cot here,' I suggested.

'Yes, of course,' Rihanna said, understanding the importance of this. 'Then if he does wake he'll see them and feel secure.'

'But don't be surprised if he's a bit unsettled tonight,' I added. 'Although he's used to having a short nap in his cot here during the day it will be the first time he's slept in it at night.'

'I won't panic – don't worry.' Rihanna smiled.

I returned her smile. 'I know you won't. You'll be fine. Well, I'll say goodbye, then. I'm going home to pack all his belongings so I'll have everything ready for when you arrive tomorrow.'

Hearing the word 'bye' Harrison cutely pursed his lips and began leaning from his mother's arms towards me, ready to give me a goodbye kiss. Rihanna and I both laughed. I lowered my head so that my cheek was within his reach and felt his warm lips press lightly against my skin.

'Have a good day,' I said to them both. Turning, I left the room and then let myself out of the flat.

Aware I had a lot of packing to do, I'd left the day free for that purpose. Although Harrison had been spending most of each day with his mother that week, he'd returned each evening, so his belongings were all over the house, as any family member's are. As if to prove the point, as soon as I got home and opened the front door I saw Harrison's winter coat hanging on the hall stand. He'd been wearing a lighter jacket recently but I'd left his winter coat out in case the spring days suddenly turned cold. So that I wouldn't forget it I unhooked the coat from the stand and put it at the foot of the stairs, ready to take up when I next went.

I continued through to the kitchen, where the high chair stood beside the table as I'd left it that morning, with the bib Harrison had been wearing at breakfast on the tray. I put the bib into the washing machine, collapsed the high chair and carried it upstairs, together with Harrison's coat. I propped the high chair against the wall on the landing, ready to go in the loft later, and I took Harrison's coat into his bedroom for when I packed his clothes.

Returning downstairs I filled the kettle and made a cup of coffee. I opened the drawer that contained Harrison's clean bibs and, taking them out, I set them to one side to pack. I washed and dried Harrison's plate, beaker, bowl and spoon, which I also set to one side to give to Rihanna. Although Rihanna had bought her own, these were Harrison's as far as I was concerned and I thought she could use them as spares. I sipped my coffee, then emptied the sterilizing unit and took it to the foot of the stairs, ready to go into the loft later. Returning to the kitchen I cleared out the baby bag, variously disposing of its contents into cupboards and drawers or on the pile to give to Rihanna. I returned the bag for general use to the cupboard under the stairs, from which I took out a couple of large laundry-style bags I'd bought for packing. My thoughts went briefly to Ellie and the horror this cupboard had first held for her until I'd exorcized it by leaping in and out and making her laugh. I wondered how Ellie was doing now and I hoped Jill would tell me the outcome when Ellie's case went to court and a decision on her future had been made.

In the kitchen again, I packed the items to give to Rihanna and then cleared the baby food from the cupboard, throwing away the packets that had been opened and packing the unopened ones to give to Rihanna. It was unlikely I'd be fostering a baby again in the near future. Once the kitchen was clear I went into the sitting room, where I folded and packed the play mat. The first bag was full and I began on the second, filling it with Harrison's toys, of which there were many. Not wanting Adrian and Paula to be confronted with the bags when they came in from school, which they might have found upsetting, once they were full I took them upstairs and stowed them in Harrison's bedroom.

Downstairs again, I finished my coffee, took another laundry bag from the cupboard under the stairs and then checked the sitting room for any stray toys. I found a squeaky toy behind one of the cushions and I packed it. I then went through the rest of the downstairs of the house, picking up any stray toys, and once satisfied I'd spotted everything, I went upstairs to begin on Harrison's bedroom.

Concentrating on the task in hand and avoiding any thoughts of Harrison leaving, I first took the bedding from the cot and put that in the laundry basket. Next, I collapsed the cot and put it on the landing with the other items to go into the loft. I then went into the bathroom, where I bagged up Harrison's bathtime playthings, together with his towel, soap, sponge and flannel, which I would give to Rihanna. It was then I realized that Harrison's car seat and pushchair were still in the car. Going downstairs I went to the car, where I took the pushchair from the boot and car seat from the rear and brought them indoors. I wouldn't need them any more. I carried them upstairs and stacked them on the landing, to be returned to the loft later. All that was left to pack now was Harrison's clothes, and I returned to his bedroom. Reaching on top of the wardrobe, I carefully lifted down the trolley case that Rihanna had packed and left at the hospital for when I'd collected Harrison. Who would have thought that ten months later I'd be repacking it so that Harrison could go home to his mother? It was incredible and fantastic, as Jill had said: a truly happy ending.

Setting the case on the ground I unzipped the lid and, opening the wardrobe door, began taking out and packing Harrison's clothes. As I worked my thoughts went to Harrison's first night with us, when, having settled him in his cot in my bedroom, I'd come in here and opened this case. I remembered my surprise when I'd seen it full of brand-new boy's baby clothes – every size from newborn to twelve months. I remembered the letter I'd found that Rihanna had tucked into the case and which had been addressed: *Dear Foster Carer.* My heart went out to her now, as it had then, as I thought of that letter, so full of love, tenderness and concern, explaining that she'd sent enough clothes for Harrison's first year, believing he would then be adopted. I remembered the dreadful sadness and hopelessness that had spilled from her words – the words of a grieving mother who'd desperately sought a way to keep her baby but had been forced to give him up. I was so pleased for Rihanna now, so very glad her story could have a happy ending and that I was now packing to send Harrison home. But if I was so happy, why was I crying?

My vision blurred with silent tears, for as Harrison was returning to his mother so he was leaving us. I continued packing his little clothes just as lovingly as his mother had done all that time ago. The little white cap and pale blue sleepsuit he'd been wearing when I'd collected him from the hospital; the white blanket he'd been wrapped in. His tiny first-size bootees, vests and mittens; it seemed incredible that big as he was now he'd once fitted into these. Little pyjamas with pictures of Paddington Bear; a romper suit with a motif of Thomas the Tank engine and a matching shirt and jumper. These were all clothes Rihanna had bought for him and which, following her wishes, I'd dressed him in every day. They would now be returned to her, together with the clothes he hadn't yet grown into. As I worked I sensed the loss and emptiness Rihanna must have felt as she'd packed this case, believing she was losing her son forever.

Once the wardrobe and drawers were clear I zipped shut the case and wiped my eyes. Feeling as empty as the room was I came out and closed the door. I went downstairs, took the pole for the loft hatch from the cupboard under the stairs and returned to the landing, where I opened the loft. Taking one section at a time, I heaved the cot piecemeal up the ladders and into the loft, stacking it where it had originally come from; then I returned down the ladders for the other items. Once the landing was clear I closed the loft hatch and returned the pole to the cupboard.

With the baby equipment in the loft and Harrison's belongings packed, ready to be collected the following morning, I wandered into the sitting room, where the photographs of Harrison looked at me from the mantelpiece and wall. The photograph on the wall was framed and part of a display that included photographs of Adrian, Paula, my family and other children we'd looked after, though none had been as young as Harrison. I had many more photographs in albums and I now took from the shelf the one I'd begun when Harrison had first arrived. Sitting on the sofa I opened the first page and looked at the photographs. Harrison, only two days old, fast asleep in his pram with his little fist pressed to his chin as though he was deep in thought. Then pictures of him a week old, ten days; I continued to turn the pages. Some of the photographs were copies of those I'd given to Rihanna while others were personal to us: family photographs showing Adrian, Paula, my parents, my brother, his wife and me at family occasions – birthdays, outings, in our homes and gardens – all of which included Harrison, who of course had been one of my family. My vision blurred again. Dear Harrison, or Harry as Paula liked to call him, how dearly he would be missed. While we'd always known that eventually he would leave us, it didn't make it any easier, for the love of a family is unconditional and can't be turned on and off at will.

I cried quietly until my tears were spent and, then feeling a little better and able to give Adrian and Paula the comfort and support they would need, I left for school. As I entered the playground Mrs Wilson, the school's welfare lady, made her way across the playground, clearly wanting to speak to me.

'Just to let you know Paula stayed with me for half an hour this morning and then joined her class,' she said reassuringly.

'Thank you.'

'I've been keeping an eye on her. I can appreciate why she was so upset. I don't know how you do it, keep having to say goodbye to the children you look after.'

'Neither do I,' I said, and swallowed hard.

Adrian and Paula had become used to me arriving in the playground without Harrison, as we'd been collecting him from his mother's after school, so it wasn't until we were in the car heading for home rather than Rihanna's flat that they realized this was different.

'Oh!' Adrian said. 'Harrison's sleeping at his mother's tonight.'

'Yes, he is,' I confirmed.

'Harry's gone now, hasn't he?' Paula said.

'Yes. His mother will collect his belongings tomorrow. I've packed them, and put all the baby equipment in the loft.'

They fell silent and when we arrived home they were quiet, and then went tentatively from room to room peering in to see what had changed.

'Harry's high chair has gone,' Paula called from the kitchen. Then going into the sitting room where Harry's playmat and toys had previously covered most of the floor: 'It's empty without him.'

'Yes,' I agreed. 'It is.'

I then suggested to Adrian and Paula that they watched some television while I made dinner, which is what they often did at this time. They agreed but without much enthusiasm. I switched on the television, passed the remote to Adrian and left them to choose the channel, while I went into the kitchen and began preparing dinner. As I worked I could hear the sound of the television coming from the sitting room but without Harrison's usual chatter which had made Adrian and Paula tell him to 'sshh' so that they could hear. It had been part of normal family life. Now all I could hear was the television and it sounded hollow.

Toscha wandered into the kitchen, miaowed, wandered out again and then reappeared as if looking for someone. I stroked her and she purred.

When dinner was ready we sat at the table, and the gap that had been left by the removal of Harrison's high chair was cripplingly obvious. No one said anything and we ate in silence, but ignoring Harrison's absence was like ignoring an elephant in the room.

Eventually I said: 'I know we're all missing Harrison, but we have to remember he has gone to live with his mother, which is great.' My words sounded flat, even to me.

Adrian and Paula nodded but said nothing.

'And you'll be able to see him in a week,' I added.

'Not sure I want to,' Adrian finally said.

'Nor me,' Paula agreed. 'It'll be too upsetting.'

'You might feel differently nearer the time,' I said, and then returned to the partially eaten food on my plate.

Goodbye Harrison

After dinner I took the card and leaving present I'd previously bought for Harrison from the bag and called to Adrian and Paula to help wrap the present and sign the card. They said they thought Harrison would like the present – a silver money-box in the shape of a cat – and together they wrapped it; then we signed the leaving card. Clearly Harrison couldn't read yet and whether or not Rihanna kept the card to show him when he was older would be up to her. I hoped she would. Harrison was young enough to forget the time he'd spent with us, and if Rihanna decided to get rid of the Life Story book with its photographs of us he might never know his early history. But that would be her decision.

The rest of the evening continued with the three of us feeling Harrison's absence deeply but saying very little. Then Adrian and Paula started bickering – a displacement for their sadness – which resulted in Paula bursting easily into tears and claiming no one loved her. I spent half an hour comforting her, by the end of which Adrian was feeling neglected: 'She only cries to get attention,' he said. I comforted him too, but was pleased when I could start their bath and bedtime routine; I told myself that once we'd got through tomorrow we could all start to move on.

The following morning the children were still subdued at breakfast and didn't mention Harrison at all. I didn't raise the subject, as they'd said their goodbyes the day before; it was just left for me to say goodbye when Rihanna came at ten o'clock to collect Harrison's belongings. I saw Adrian and Paula into school and then returned home, where I brought all Harrison's bags down from the bedroom and stacked them in the hall. It was now 9.30 and I made a quick coffee and then gathered together the other items I needed to give to Rihanna: Harrison's red book; his Life Story book (which I'd updated the evening before); his leaving present and card; and a cheque made payable to Harrison (for his savings account), which was the allowance I'd received for his clothes and hadn't spent.

At exactly ten o'clock the doorbell rang. I steeled myself and went down the hall and opened the door. The first thing I saw was a huge bouquet of flowers tied with a large gold ribbon. Then Harrison, in his mother's arms, peered round from behind the flowers.

'Boo!' he said, and I laughed.

'For you,' Rihanna said, laying the bouquet in my arms and kissing my cheek. 'Thank you for everything.'

Already feeling pretty emotional I felt my eyes fill with tears. 'Thank you,' I said. 'They're beautiful, but you shouldn't have.' I stood aside to let Rihanna and Harrison in.

'Cathy, you don't know how grateful I am. If it wasn't for you I wouldn't be here now.'

'Oh?' I said.

'When I came to see you that night at the beginning of December you suggested I saw Harrison. That was the turning point for me. It was then I realized how much I loved Harrison and always would. I knew then I couldn't live without him and had to do everything in my power to get him back.'

I smiled, pleased. 'You did it, not me.'

Harrison was now looking at me curiously, probably wondering what he was doing here and if he would be staying.

'How did he sleep last night?' I asked. We were still in the hall, surrounded by the bags I'd previously packed.

'Very well,' Rihanna said. 'He woke once but soon settled.' Her gaze shifted to the cases and she suddenly burst into tears. As she delved into her jacket pocket for a tissue I put down the flowers so that I could take Harrison. 'Sorry,' she said, passing Harrison to me and wiping her eyes. 'Seeing that case' – she nodded to the trolley case – 'brought back all the memories. I can remember how wretched I felt as I packed his clothes. I guess even then I knew I shouldn't be giving him up but I couldn't see any other way.'

I touched her arm reassuringly as she wiped her eyes and tucked the tissue into her pocket. 'Would you like to stay for a while and I'll make us a coffee?' I asked.

'Would you mind if we didn't?' she said. 'I'd rather we left now. Then when you visit next week I'll feel stronger. You don't mind, do you?'

'No, of course not,' I said. 'Come on, I'll help you into the car with the bags.'

Still holding Harrison I picked up a bag with my free hand and led the way out of the door. Rihanna followed with the trolley case and another bag. I opened the boot and we loaded her car. We returned to the house and Rihanna made another trip to the car with the other two bags while I waited inside with Harrison. All that was left now was the carrier bag I'd put to one side. As Rihanna returned to the hall I passed her the bag. 'In there is Harrison's red book,' I said. 'A present and card from us, which the two of you can open at home. His Life Story book, which I think Cheryl has mentioned to you. And a cheque to make up for the clothes I didn't have to buy Harrison.'

'No, I'm not taking that,' Rihanna said, delving into the bag to retrieve the cheque. 'I was grateful you did as I asked and dressed him in the clothes. It helped me, it really did.'

'Please keep it,' I said, gently pushing the cheque back towards her. 'It's payable to Harrison, so put it in his savings account. I'd like it if you did.'

Rihanna hesitated. 'Well, if you're sure.'

'I am.'

'Thank you.' I saw her eyes fill again and Harrison was looking at his mother, most concerned.

I kissed him and placed him in her arms. 'Come on, let's go,' I said. 'I'll see you to the car.'

A Baby's Cry

Leaving the door on the latch I followed Rihanna and Harrison down the path and then waited on the pavement while she put the bag I'd just given to her on to the passenger seat, and then opened the rear door and sat Harrison in his new car seat. Leaning in she fastened the belts and then tested they were secure. Satisfied, she stood back so that I could say goodbye.

I leant in. 'Goodbye, love,' I said. I gently eased my arms around his shoulders and drew him close one last time. I felt his little arms encircle my neck and the soft touch of his skin. His lips pressed lightly against my cheek as he gave me a little kiss. 'Goodbye, love,' I said again.

'Bye,' he said.

I felt my bottom lip tremble as I stood back and Rihanna closed the car door.

'Bye, Cathy,' she said, giving me a hug. 'Thanks again for everything.'

'You're welcome,' I managed to say.

I watched as she climbed into the driver's seat and started the engine. Harrison was looking at me through the side window, his little face so innocent, trusting and loving. I felt a tear escape and run down my cheek. The car began to pull away. I waved and Harrison gave a little wave back. I stayed on the pavement and watched until the car was out of sight; then returning up the front path I went inside and closed the door. That's the trouble with babies, I thought: you can't help but love them.

Epilogue

Jill phoned later that Friday morning to ask if the move had gone well and I said it had. She knew that, as when previous foster children had left us, I would be taking a couple of weeks off from fostering so that I could spend time with Adrian and Paula, which would allow the three of us space to come to terms with losing Harrison. When a foster child, who has been part of the family for a long time, leaves it is like a small bereavement from which it takes time to recover. This is true not only for the immediate family but also for grandparents, extended family and close friends, all of whom have welcomed the child as family and then have to adjust to losing them.

The days immediately following Harrison's departure were strange and unsettling. While Adrian, Paula and I obviously knew Harrison was no longer in the house we still had the feeling that if we went into the right room we would see him crawling across the floor, playing with his toys or just sitting, chattering his baby talk. It seemed unnatural that he wasn't somewhere in the house. I often caught Adrian and Paula looking at the photographs of Harrison on the mantelpiece and on the wall in the sitting room, as indeed I did, when we were supposed to be watching television or reading a book. Paula asked many times if I thought Harry was happy and I said I was sure he was, while Adrian predictably went quiet when Harrison was mentioned. I hoped seeing Harrison the following Saturday settled with his mother would help us to let go and move on.

I left the decision as to whether or not Adrian and Paula came with me to see Harrison to them, but I was pleased when they both said they would come, for I was sure it was what they needed. We dressed smartly for our visit, as there was a sense of occasion, although we were also a little apprehensive.

However, when Rihanna answered the front door our reserve immediately vanished.

'Look at Harry!' Paula exclaimed. Instead of being carried to the door as had happened previously Harrison was now holding his mother's hand and standing beside her.

'Wow!' Adrian said. 'He's walking.'

'Yes, he's toddling everywhere now,' Rihanna said excitedly.

'Fantastic,' I said. I was so pleased he'd saved this developmental milestone for his mother.

We followed Harrison and his mother into their flat, where Rihanna made us a drink and set a plate of homemade pastries on the table, which were delicious. Then while Adrian and Paula played with Harrison, Rihanna told me about her week. She said Cheryl had made an unannounced visit on Wednesday but it had gone well and she hadn't been as anxious as she'd thought she would be. Cheryl had told her she was doing well, and that she'd make two more visits and then write her final report, and that would be the end of the social services' involvement. Rihanna also told me that her parents had visited during the week but that her sister was still angry and had refused to come.

'It's up to her,' Rihanna said, with a small shrug. 'I hope she changes her mind but I can't force her.' So I guessed Rihanna had had to come to terms with possibly losing forever the close

Epilogue

relationship she'd previously enjoyed with her sister, which was sad. Rihanna also said she'd telephoned Harrison's father, Jacob, and was meeting him the following week, when she was going to tell him about Harrison. Rihanna said she knew it was going to be a very difficult conversation and that Jacob had the right to be upset and angry. She was going to suggest he saw Harrison now her family no longer posed the threat it had, but it would obviously be Jacob's decision.

An hour passed easily and at the end of the hour I said we should be going. Adrian and Paula would have liked to have stayed longer, and Harrison was appreciating the attention, but Cheryl had stipulated an hour for our visit, which is usually considered an appropriate time for this type of post-move get-together; longer could be unsettling for the child. Rihanna said she would stay in touch with us; then she took Harrison's hand, and they walked with us to the outer door, where they waved us off. In the car going home Paula and Adrian talked easily about Harrison and I could see our visit had reassured them that he was happy and well settled.

Once a child has left a foster carer the child's family decides if they stay in contact with the foster family. Foster carers are not supposed to initiate contact, for example by phoning, much as they'd like to, as it could be seen to be intrusive and unsettling for the child. Two months after Harrison had left us it was his first birthday and, having not heard from Rihanna in the interim, I sent a birthday card in the post. A week after his birthday I received a short but pleasant letter from Rihanna thanking me for the card, saying Harrison was fine, and hoping we were all well and enjoying the summer. She'd enclosed two photographs of Harrison's first birthday, which showed Harrison sitting on her lap and grinning in front of a large birthday cake in the shape of the figure one.

A Baby's Cry

That was in July, and I didn't hear any more from Rihanna until Christmas. I'd sent Rihanna and Harrison a Christmas card, and one of the cards I subsequently opened was from Rihanna. It contained another short but pleasant letter and two more photographs of Harrison. In the letter Rihanna apologized for not writing sooner but said time seemed to have 'slipped away', which I fully appreciated. She said she was looking forward to Harrison's first Christmas with her and they would be spending Christmas Day at her parents'. She didn't mention her sister but did say that Harrison was seeing his father. The photographs showed Harrison, a sturdy and very handsome little chap aged eighteen months, eating dinner at home and also sitting in a swing in a park.

I didn't see Rihanna or Harrison again, although for the next three years Rihanna sent photographs of Harrison with a short letter twice a year: in July, just after Harrison's birthday, and at Christmas. I too sent Christmas and birthday cards, although I didn't know if Rihanna ever showed them to Harrison or indeed if he knew of our existence. In her letters Rihanna told me she'd returned to work, part time to begin with, and then extended her hours when Harrison started school. Then just after Harrison's sixth birthday Rihanna wrote to say she'd accepted a post in a hospital in another city and they would be moving – to rented accommodation at first while she found somewhere to buy. She said she'd let me know her new address and that Harrison was doing well at school and had a good relationship with his father. She enclosed a school photograph of Harrison, in which he looked very smart in his school uniform. I wrote back thanking her for the photograph, and saying I hoped the move went well, but I didn't hear any more.

So, as with other children we've fostered who haven't kept in touch, we rely on the pleasure we gain from looking at the

Epilogue

photographs in our albums, when we remember Harrison fondly and with much love.

For the latest update on Harrison and also Ellie, please visit www.cathyglass.co.uk